1988

NEW FINANCIAL INSTRUMENTS

DISCLOSURE AND ACCOUNTING

ORGANISATION FOR ECONOMIC CO-OPERATION AND DEVELOPMENT

20017208

Pursuant to article 1 of the Convention signed in Paris on 14th December, 1960, and which came into force on 30th September, 1961, the Organisation for Economic Co-operation and Development (OECD) shall promote policies designed:

- to achieve the highest sustainable economic growth and employment and a rising standard of living in Member countries, while maintaining financial stability, and thus to contribute to the development of the world economy;
- to contribute to sound economic expansion in Member as well as non-member countries in the process of economic development; and
- to contribute to the expansion of world trade on a multilateral, non-discriminatory basis in accordance with international obligations.

The original Member countries of the OECD are Austria, Belgium, Canada, Denmark, France, the Federal Republic of Germany, Greece, Iceland, Ireland, Italy, Luxembourg, the Netherlands, Norway, Portugal, Spain, Sweden, Switzerland, Turkey, the United Kingdom and the United States. The following countries acceded subsequently through accession at the dates hereafter: Japan (28th April, 1964), Finland (28th January, 1969), Australia (7th June, 1971) and New Zealand (29th May, 1973).

The Socialist Federal Republic of Yugoslavia takes part in some of the work of the OECD (agreement of 28th October, 1961).

Publié en français sous le titre:

NOUVEAUX INSTRUMENTS FINANCIERS
Publication d'informations et comptabilisation

Photo Credit: Crédit du Nord

PREFACE

by
Jean-Claude Paye
Secretary-General of the OECD

New financial instruments, in particular those linked with exchange rate and interest rate fluctuations and with stock-market indices, offer participants many advantages in that they allow world-wide, round-the-clock handling of transactions and they increase liquidity. They provide lenders and borrowers with new opportunities and diversify financial intermediaries' profit sources. At the same time, however, there are inherent risks in these new instruments: the risk of the counterpart defaulting, liquidity risks and interest and exchange rate risks. Although these risks can have major implications for the performance and financial situation of firms, they are often not shown in financial statements.

The reason for this is that new financial instruments have developed so rapidly that accounting principles have been unable to keep pace. The existing international standards undoubtedly have their merits, but they do not cover all the instruments and they do not cater for all users in our Member countries.

In order to make good these shortcomings, rules for accounting treatment and disclosure need to be developed without delay, and clearly they must be internationally compatible and sufficiently harmonized to meet the requirements of financial markets which have become largely international. They must also be flexible so that markets retain their creative vitality and, lastly, they should give priority to the economic substance of transactions rather than their legal form.

A second objective must be to ensure that users are in a position to act with full knowledge of the new financial instruments.

Among the users, I might mention:

-- Those at the head of financial institutions, because they need to be able to keep precise track of the internal management of the risks incurred;

-- All banking and stock-market supervisory authorities;

-- Financial analysts, shareholders, employees of the firms concerned and auditors.

3

These users all need to be in possession of accounting details concerning each type of instrument used, the accounting methods applied, the purpose of the transactions conducted (hedging, arbitrage, speculation), the amounts committed, the predicted date for the transactions to be unwound and the nature of the risks incurred by an enterprise dealing in a particular type of transaction.

The quantity and degree of detail of the accounting information required can vary, however. Banking supervisory authorities, for example, can obviously have requirements which are quantitatively greater than those of shareholders, since they have to exercise prudential control and ensure that the norms of government monetary policy are correctly applied by the financial intermediaries. However, there are not at present any sufficiently clear rules in this respect, and it would no doubt be useful if closer and more regular contacts could be organised between those in charge of financial institutions, the accounting profession and the different supervisory authorities. In this way, it will be possible in accounting work to take the reality of business life into consideration.

The OECD is particularly well placed both to help Member country governments and enterprises meet the challenge and to boost the efforts already made. On the one hand, the geographical area it covers includes most of the major financial centres; on the other, the multidisciplinary nature of its working methods allows it to adopt a very diversified approach to problems and to combine pure economic analysis with its expertise on financial markets, accounting, taxation, investment and multinational enterprises.

In this connection, the OECD has at its disposal a reference instrument of particular relevance: the Guidelines for Multinational Enterprises which were adopted in 1976 by all Member country governments. The purpose of the chapter of the Guidelines on disclosure of information is to increase the transparency of enterprises' structures and activities in order better to evaluate their performance and financial situation. If this instrument is to remain pertinent, it must accurately reflect the recent changes in financial transactions affecting firms' day-to-day management. Analysis of the results of the Symposium should provide an opportunity to ensure that this is the case.

The present publication draws together the main contributions made at the Symposium. It is intended as an input to the continuing debate on international harmonization in this important area.

TABLE OF CONTENTS

Chapter IV

NATIONAL AND INTERNATIONAL APPROACHES TO ACCOUNTING
AND REPORTING FOR NEW FINANCIAL INSTRUMENTS

Chapter V

NEW FINANCIAL INSTRUMENTS: MAIN ISSUES OF ACCOUNTING AND REPORTING

Also Available

MULTINATIONAL ENTERPRISES AND DISCLOSURE OF INFORMATION: Clarification of the OECD Guidelines (May 1988) bilingual
(21 88 03 3) ISBN 92-64-03080-8   88 pages   £8.50   US$15.50   F70.00   DM31.00

HARMONIZATION OF ACCOUNTING STANDARDS. Achievements and Prospects (December 1986)
(21 86 07 1) ISBN 92-64-12895-6   148 pages   £11.00   US$22.00   F110.00   DM49.00

"ACCOUNTING STANDARDS HARMONIZATION" Series:

No. 5   CONSOLIDATED FINANCIAL STATEMENTS (October 1988) bilingual
(21 88 05 3) ISBN 92-64-03141-3   81 pages   £6.00   US$11.00   F50.00   DM22.00

No. 4   OPERATING RESULTS OF INSURANCE COMPANIES (May 1988) bilingual
(21 88 02 3) ISBN 92-64-03067-0   72 pages   £7.00   US$13.50   F60.00   DM26.00

No. 3   THE RELATIONSHIP BETWEEN TAXATION AND FINANCIAL REPORTING. Income Tax Accounting. Report by the Working Group on Accounting Standards (June 1987) bilingual
(21 87 04 3) ISBN 92-64-02938-9   144 pages   £5.00   US$11.00   F50.00   DM22.00

No. 2   CONSOLIDATION POLICIES IN OECD COUNTRIES. Report by the Working Group on Accounting Standards (February 1987) bilingual
(21 87 01 3) ISBN 92-64-02876-5   124 pages   £6.50   US$13.00   F65.00   DM29.00

No. 1   FOREIGN CURRENCY TRANSLATION. Report by the Working Group on Accounting Standards (February 1986) bilingual
(21 86 01 3) ISBN 92-64-02729-7   64 pages   £4.50   US$9.00   F45.00   DM20.00

"INTERNATIONAL INVESTMENT AND MULTINATIONAL ENTERPRISES"

THE OECD GUIDELINES FOR MULTINATIONAL ENTERPRISES (April 1986)
(21 86 03 1) ISBN 92-64-12812-3   92 pages   £6.00   US$12.00   F60.00   DM27.00

THE 1984 REVIEW OF THE 1976 DECLARATION AND DECISIONS (July 1984)
(21 84 02 1) ISBN 92-64-12585-X   66 pages   £3.20   US$6.50   F32.00   DM16.00

Prices charged at the OECD Bookshop.

THE OECD CATALOGUE OF PUBLICATIONS and supplements will be sent free of charge
on request addressed either to OECD Publications Service,
2, rue André-Pascal, 75775 PARIS CEDEX 16, or to the OECD Distributor in your country.

INTRODUCTION

by
Jacques de Larosière
Governor,
Banque de France
(France)

Pieter Stek
Chairman, OECD Committee on Financial Markets;
Director, Ministry of Finance
(Netherlands)

Adriaan Gautier
Chairman, OECD Committee on International Investment
and Multinational Enterprises;
Deputy Director, Ministry of Economic Affairs
(Netherlands)

Jean Dupont
Chairman of the Symposium;
Chairman, OECD Working Group on Accounting Standards;
Chairman, Conseil national de la comptabilité
(France)

In his opening statement at the Symposium, Mr. de Larosière highlighted the main features of new financial instruments and the accounting and disclosure issues that arise, and underlined the need for international harmonization of practices:

"The expansion in transactions involving new financial instruments has been substantial world-wide, and the movement has gained enormous momentum in the past two years.

Since the 1970s, agents have been striving to hedge first against exchange rate volatility and then against interest rate volatility. Like commodities futures in the United States, the range of financial futures became more diversified and broadened on American markets, and later in Europe, the Far East and Australia.

Initially the preserve of the major international institutions with the capacity to operate transatlantically, the new financial instruments are now accessible to large and medium-sized national non-financial enterprises. As a result of progress in telecommunications and computer technology, the interconnecting nature of markets and the standardization of instruments, major undertakings can trade round the clock in specialised markets across the globe.

The internationalisation of markets has not only grown but become irreversible now that instruments, techniques, rationales and goals are common to all. Moreover, dealing room staff and supervisors have very often received the same training at university or on the job; the obvious corollary is that they should ideally work under the same accounting standards and rules of disclosure.

There is no need in this forum to point out the benefits of international harmonization. Financial analysts, investors, auditors and supervisory bodies must be able to rely on comparable data. In consolidating accounts, aggregation techniques must be consistent in order to give a faithful image of corporate groups and their strategies. Any distortion can lead to lengthy, costly and time-consuming reprocessing and may even entail the preparation of several different consolidated statements in order to meet some countries' special regulatory requirements.

Given the number of transactions, standardization is more necessary than ever. In the case of credit institutions, the Committee chaired by Mr. Cooke is already working in this direction on an international front, since any standard regulations must clearly be based on an inventory of the features common to all.

Many problems remain in the areas of accounting and disclosure.

To take accounting first, new principles such as the rules for assessing assets, liabilities and even off-balance-sheet items at market prices as well as the practice of recording the difference between the buying price and the market price as current profits have not yet been fully accepted by all the standard-setting bodies. Some technical problems persist and will require further consideration, such as defining organised markets, assimilated markets and over-the-counter transactions. The concept of hedging needs to be refined; spreading the profits and costs of hedges over the residual life of the hedged item still raises questions regarding accounting and tax treatment. As regards communicating meaningful information to third parties, the problems are even thornier. At the end of 1986, for instance, no major country had yet laid down disclosure standards, and any mention of transactions involving new financial instruments in company reports to shareholders was purely a matter of voluntary decision on the part of the firms concerned.

Disclosure principles should be looked at with a new eye, since both in the case of commitments given or received, the new financial instruments are posted off-balance-sheet at their nominal amounts. As a result, these amounts are substantial and bear no relation to the actual risk involved. It is thus difficult to establish a meaningful link between these instruments and balance sheet amounts. Since they are sometimes used to hedge against rate risks, they do not represent an additional risk, but on the contrary offset a balance sheet risk or a pre-existing off-balance-sheet one. It is hence essential that all figures be accompanied by notes, since many readers of financial reports do not necessarily fully understand the complex analyses that must be made on the basis of raw data. A 'net positions' approach would probably be preferable, even though the experts have not yet fully investigated how these positions should be calculated.

Last but not least, efforts are also needed to harmonize accounting standards and tax rules.

What we need are innovative solutions that could pave the way for further harmonization. Paradoxically, accounting standards and forms of disclosure are more easily harmonized for new financial instruments than for the more conventional and familiar domain of traditional bank and non-bank activity.

It is indeed easier to break out of old and sometimes overly rigid patterns of thinking when dealing with new instruments. Certainly, innovators will more easily find a way to devise approaches more attuned to constantly evolving techniques -- all the more so since progress in telecommunications is tending to make them universal."

Mr. Stek drew attention to the interest of financial markets and regulators in the development of coherent and internationally harmonized practices for accounting and risk evaluation:

"The OECD Committee on Financial Markets concerns itself with the efficiency and stability of these markets and their interactions at the national and global level. The Committee is made up of those officials from ministries of finance and central banks who are directly confronted with the market effects of technology, innovation, internationalisation, securitisation, disintermediation, and aggressive competition. Many of its participants are involved in policies of deregulation, liberalisation and monetary and prudential supervision as well as analysis of markets so as to understand the economic significance of such happenings and policies. For this purpose, the Committee maintains contacts with market participants, such as bankers and people from the securities industry. Only three weeks before this Symposium a special session of securities markets participants was held at which the general sentiment was expressed that a level playing field calls for common accounting standards to be utilised for supervisory purposes. More basic even than fair competition is the need for prudential figures that provide a true and fair view of the weight of supervising requirements and the assets they are applied to, i.e. the level of the playing field itself.

The new financial instruments that have emerged carry many benefits to the parties that use them: they permit more sophisticated management of positions and related risks, can increase liquidity, and thereby provide new opportunities for lenders and borrowers, and, moreover, diversify the earning sources of financial intermediaries. However, these instruments are themselves a potential source of risk: credit risk, price risk and liquidity risk as well as the risk of losing control over one's operations as a manager.

New financial instruments such as options, futures, forward rate agreements and swaps embody commitments which, to the extent that assets and liabilities are traditionally defined as items resulting from realised transactions, do not appear in the balance sheet and often remain undisclosed. The same is the case for guaranteed contingencies linked to disappointing outcomes of one's clients' businesses or operations.

Inability of regulatory authorities and users of financial statements to assess an enterprise's exposure to risk not only affects the credibility and comparability of corporate reports but also has a bearing on the stability and functioning of financial institutions and markets. Thus accounting standard-setting bodies, bank regulators and the users to whom financial reports are addressed have a common interest in increased transparency and accountability of transactions linked to new financial instruments. Regulators and legislators should create a reporting environment in which users may feel that they are being properly informed. Information should not be withheld unless the possible ill effects thereof are not only carefully weighed against advantages in terms of stability or the legitimate protection of information from one's competitors, but also checked against the moral hazard incurred by the authorities that endorse such withholding of information. Internationalisation and globalisation make the need for low thresholds to information all the greater, as well as the need for harmonized approaches to risk assessment, accounting and disclosure.

I already mentioned the call for a level playing field and that field by now is global, which suggests some inevitable curvature. The development of national accounting and disclosure standards for the new instruments is at an early stage. This provides an excellent opportunity for international co-ordination or harmonization, before positions have become entrenched. A high degree of uniformity of measurement of risks is a necessary condition, though not a sufficient one for avoiding regulatory arbitrage.

John Maurice Clark, the well-known American economist, already in 1923 pointed out that there are different costs for different purposes. I hope, therefore, that any valuation exercise will be governed by a clear view of the purposes. In the second place, I would point out that an economist's valuation of an asset would be based on the income it will generate and how to discount that future flow of income. That makes absolutist claims for methods based on retrospection a trifle vacuous, for some purposes I hasten to add. In unsettled times one experiences that the past is not a very good guide to the future. On this point too I would add what accountants have not achieved for what is on-balance they presumably will not achieve for what is off-balance in two days' time.

There may be a growing tendency towards marking to market and this is, indeed, useful as far as it goes. But the question remains what to do when there is no properly developed market, as in the field of LDC debt and certain sections of the swap and over-the-counter options markets.

Also, the issue of timely disclosure appears to be important, given swiftly changing circumstances, not to speak of the high volatility that characterises some markets. The degree to which disclosures are

complete and aggregated is also at issue as well as the practical
possibilities of dealing with the needs of users.

A great deal will have been achieved, therefore, if you reach a consensus on what commitments and contingencies should be recorded and when
and how to disclose them.

The smaller the degree of disclosure, the stronger prudential supervision will have to be. On disclosure and its relation to market
discipline and the role of implicit guarantees and explicit insurance,
much can be said and has been said. Decisions on disclosure are germane
to the way our societies run their banking and securities sectors. It
requires no flight of fancy to believe in this affecting our societies
more fundamentally."

Mr. Gautier situated the issues discussed at the Symposium in the context of international investment policies and the operation of the OECD Guidelines for Multinational Enterprises:

"Early in May, the British weekly The Economist reproduced on its cover
a print recalling (what seems to be) one of the better-known episodes of
the American Revolution: an agitated young man, on horseback in the
middle of the night, alarming his friends and relatives with the information that 'The British are coming'. What makes The Economist's cover
so interesting is that in its version of the historical event, our hero
does not limit himself to signalling the arrival of the British, but is
quoted as saying:

'The British are coming...and the Japanese, and the Germans, and the
Canadians, and the Koreans and the...'

One realises that The Economist is not just recalling the history of the
American Revolution, but is -- very effectively -- drawing the attention
of its readers to more recent events in the United States, events such
as the introduction of an amendment in the US Trade Bill suggesting that
in future foreign direct investors should be screened in order to
establish their possible contribution to the US economy before they are
allowed to come in. Another event is the recent publication of a book
-- by a couple of Harvard graduates -- America for Sale, which seems to
suggest that unless the Administration alters its attitude towards in-
coming foreign direct investment, economic life in the United States
will be dominated by foreigners who could not care less about the
American way of life.

There is a link between the recent concern over a new type of invader
and the objectives of this Symposium. At this year's Ministerial
Council, OECD Ministers agreed on a communiqué that -- in its section on
'International Investment' -- addressed the issue of a new and more
critical attitude towards foreign direct investment and expressed their
concern about signs of emerging protectionist pressures in the investment area.

The communiqué goes on to indicate the determination of Ministers to
resist such protectionism and to maintain an open investment climate.
Ministers then specified a number of measures required to achieve that

objective, measures that do not appear to be all that relevant in the context of this Symposium. However, they then concluded this section of their communiqué with a sentence that is of relevance, although that relevance may not be immediately apparent:

> 'The balance that has characterised the Organisation's approach to international investment questions, including between different elements of the Declaration, should continue to prevail.'

My interpretation of that sentence is that Ministers do realise that from the 1976 Declaration on International Investment and Multinational Enterprises, one cannot take at random one or two elements as possible candidates for strengthening OECD commitments.

One element of that Declaration, the OECD Guidelines for Multinational Enterprises, simply cannot be overlooked in attempts to maintain or strengthen an open investment climate.

It is difficult to imagine that governments will be whole-heartedly willing to offer equal opportunities to foreign investors if those investors disregard the necessity of operating as 'good corporate citizens'. The OECD Guidelines should be seen as an attempt to reflect what the expression 'good corporate citizenship' implies.

Among the many and diverse provisions of the Guidelines that deal with labour relations and the environment, consumers and taxation, there is an important chapter on information requirements -- important in the context of the international investment climate, because it may well be that doubts about the contribution foreign investors can make to the economies in which they operate stem partly from the (sometimes not totally unfounded) idea that one is dealing with an entity that is hiding more than it is disclosing.

'Hidden' assets usually do not give rise to excessive concerns, but 'hidden' liabilities do -- for anyone concerned about the enterprise, be it a partner, employee, creditor or customer.

My knowledge of 'new financial instruments' is limited but even so, I can well imagine that unless strict and, if possible, harmonized accounting standards are applied, relevant information (in the context of the Guidelines chapter on information requirements) remains un-available.

If this were to be the case, it would strengthen the hand of those who -- for nationalistic or whatever other reasons -- like the young man on the cover of The Economist, are crying: 'The British are coming, and the Japanese, and the Germans...'."

Mr. Dupont characterised the main objectives of the OECD Symposium on New Financial Instruments as follows:

"First of all, why have we chosen new financial instruments as the subject of this Symposium organised by our Working Group on Accounting Standards?

This Working Group has a twofold mandate:

-- To develop clarifications of the accounting terms contained in the chapter on disclosure of information of the OECD Guidelines;

-- To promote efforts towards increased international comparability of financial statements and harmonization of accounting standards.

The way that world economic markets are developing is making harmonization of accounting standards increasingly vital.

How can we go beyond the consensus reached on this principle in the accounting profession and the business community, and achieve concrete results? What specific approaches can be adopted? There appear to be two ways forward: eliminate past divergences and prevent further ones from occurring.

Hitherto we have concentrated our efforts on eliminating past divergences on familiar problems. This can be done in two ways. The first method is to unify standards. However, this approach runs up against many obstacles -- not only national particularities, of course, but also sometimes radical differences in national legislation and in economic and financial environments. Thus, where these obstacles cannot be instantly overcome, we resort to a second 'bridging' method, which ensures a minimum of compatibility and comparability in the presentation of financial statements.

However, our situation is not unlike that of Plato, who, having devised the main lines of his ideal city, ran into difficulty in applying them in an antique society steeped in tradition. He therefore conceived the idea of establishing his ideal city on a new island, where it would be more readily received.

The changes currently taking place in the economic and financial world perhaps offer in our field the opportunity sought by Plato. As no (or hardly any) solutions have been found to the new problems which form our new island, perhaps we can prevent divergences before they occur and thus spare our business communities the formidable consequences. In this respect, there is no better subject than the accounting treatment of new financial instruments. The explosion of the financial markets is one of the most spectacular developments of recent years. Innovative financial techniques coupled with modern information transmission and management methods have linked up or are about to link up financial markets world-wide on a round-the-clock basis. Accounting regulations must adapt to this development, which may well upset a number of principles hitherto held to be unshakeable.

The stock-market crisis last October did not alter the nature of the problems, but it did increase the urgency of the need for a new set of regulations to deal with them. The concept of realised profits, the principle of prudence and the whole system for assessing balance sheet/off-balance-sheet transactions are all issues that must be examined.

Beyond short-term solutions, which are necessary but of limited effect, there is vast scope for reflection and study in drawing up a new body of homogeneous, internationally harmonized regulations based, perhaps, on a reinterpretation of fundamental principles."

Chapter I

DISCLOSURE AND ACCOUNTING TREATMENT OF NEW FINANCIAL INSTRUMENTS

by
the OECD Secretariat

INTRODUCTION

This background report is composed of three main parts. Part I out-lines the context in which the off-balance-sheet items of banks and non-banks have developed and sets out their implications for both financial reporting and the international comparability of financial statements of multinational enterprises and, more particularly, of financial intermediaries. Part II describes in broad terms the main features and definitions of off-balance-sheet commitments -- the traditional ones encountered in enterprises and the main rules for their accounting treatment and disclosure in the accompanying notes to financial statements.

Part III deals more specifically with instruments used by banks -- their characteristics, accounting rules and problems of disclosure. The more traditional types of commitments and those resulting from new financial instruments are examined separately. The practices described are those of major international banks customarily engaging in this type of transaction, but they are also relevant for enterprises that have direct recourse to some of these instruments. It will be seen that while there might be a certain degree of inconsistency as regards the treatment of the revenue and expense resulting from transactions of this type, the major difficulties encountered relate to the disclosure of commitments in financial statements. In this part of the report, a number of suggestions for accounting and reporting of new financial instruments are considered with respect to off-balance-sheet commit-ments, with a view to improving adequacy and comparability of financial state-ments by banks and non-banking enterprises.

Lastly, the Annex summarises the fact sheets completed by OECD Member countries in June-August 1987, based on the principles applicable in their respective countries regarding accounting and disclosure of off-balance-sheet items.

The report was prepared by the OECD Secretariat as a background docu-ment for the Symposium on New Financial Instruments held on 31st May and 1st June 1988.

I. THE GROWTH OF NEW FINANCIAL INSTRUMENTS: BACKGROUND AND ACCOUNTING IMPLICATIONS

In the past decade, the international financial system has been characterised by highly volatile interest rates and exchange rates, disintermediation and growing competition between financial intermediaries, a major shift in the geographic pattern of net flows of international savings and investment, and a changing financial regulatory environment. These elements, along with the widespread application of computer and telecommunications technology, have generated and accelerated the emergence of new financial instruments which transfer risk, increase liquidity, provide new opportunities for lenders and borrowers and diversify the earning sources of financial intermediaries.

The steep rise in the volatility of interest rates created a demand for more efficient financial instruments and hedging strategies. Because of this higher volatility, banks and even commercial companies experienced a need for greater safeguards and more scope for shifting their risk exposure.

With disintermediation and growing competition among banks sharply narrowing margins on many types of conventional "on-balance-sheet" business, financial intermediaries had to respond vigorously and imaginatively in an effort to retain their customer base and increase income from new sources. The major international banks, for instance, lost their previous comparative advantage on international securities markets with respect to high-grade borrowers, and had to move into capital market activities, undertaking transactions that no longer necessarily figured in their balance sheets.

The major changes that have taken place in recent years in the geographic pattern of net flows of international savings and investments have also greatly contributed to financial innovation. Preferences of investors and borrowers in different geographical areas for specific forms of financial assets and liabilities forced financial intermediation to adjust and to develop new instruments. For instance, the reduction in investments by the OPEC countries and in the borrowing capacity of most LDCs diminished the scope for bank deposits and syndicated bank loans. Moreover, the United States, once a major supplier of funds, has now become a large-scale borrower, while Japan and Germany, with growing current account surpluses, have encouraged the use of debt instruments that can be traded on international financial markets.

The changing financial regulatory environment was also a major factor in this innovation. Internationally, the trend was towards market deregulation and reducing structural rigidities and barriers to competition. In many countries, measures were taken to reduce or abolish exchange controls and traditional boundaries limiting the types of financial activities in which banks could engage, to phase out interest rate ceilings on deposits and lending activities of key financial intermediaries, to open the domestic market to foreign institutions and to ease tax treatment. But at the same time, bank supervisors were increasingly focusing on the adequacy of financial institutions' capital base relative to their activities due to the uncertainty surrounding some international and domestic assets. The effect was (and still is) to create an incentive for banks to expand their off-balance-sheet business, which is not subject to the same stringent capital-ratio requirements as are the more traditional types of transactions.

Finally, one should not disregard the influence of the recent wide-spread application of telecommunications and computer technology to financial markets and transactions. Facilitating and accelerating national and international communications promotes competition, reduces transaction costs and stimulates the development of new international financial instruments.

The development of off-balance-sheet commitments and new financial instruments has affected the stability and the functioning of international financial institutions and markets -- as well as monetary policy -- in a number of ways. These aspects have been analysed by the Bank for International Settlements, through a study group which drafted a report in April 1986 (1). But the instruments created in recent years have also had major implications on financial accounting and reporting:

-- The accelerated growth of these instruments has not been matched by a development of the relevant accounting principles. Even if for a number of instruments fundamental accounting concepts apply, there is a lack of national standards in a great number of countries, and as regards international standards, efforts have only begun recently within the EC with the Directive on the Accounts of Banks and Other Financial Institutions and at the International Accounting Standards Committee (IASC) with its Exposure Draft on disclosures in banks' financial statements. Points of reference do not always exist, notably with respect to the measurement of income and expense related to these instruments. Even more serious is the fact that, even if management accounting systems have been introduced for these new transactions, disclosure for financial reporting purposes is not always adequately performed. Some disclosures may be required by a limited number of national accounting bodies, and additional information may be disclosed by some enterprises voluntarily or at the request of stock exchange commissions or regulators of particular industries, but in general disclosure is insufficient. Even if there exist a limited number of standards, they are often specific -- and since they were developed in an ad hoc fashion, no broad approach to disclosure truly exists;

-- Counterparties, shareholders and financial analysts have difficulty in understanding the full scope of the activities of institutions, since the development of new instruments has transformed the conventional balance sheet appreciation of banks' risks. In a great number of countries it is difficult to acquire information (whether general or specific) on a bank's exposure, owing to the lack of adequate disclosure in banks' financial reports.

In view of the growing importance of off-balance-sheet instruments in the activities of banks and some non-banks, it is essential to examine current practice with regard to the accounting treatment and disclosure of these types of transactions in order to improve the comparability of banks' and non-banks' financial statements.

In order to situate the problem in the general accounting context, it seems useful to begin by outlining the characteristics and rules for the general accounting treatment and disclosure of off-balance-sheet commitments. In the paragraphs that follow, the salient features of the new financial instruments and the main rules in this area are examined in detail, with particular reference to banks' off-balance-sheet transactions. The analysis takes into consideration Member countries' replies to the Secretariat's request for information on work currently undertaken and the fact sheets completed in 1987 on the accounting and disclosure practices prevailing in the different Member countries. Particular mention should be made of the note by the Institut monétaire luxembourgeois of 24th November 1986, providing an in-depth study of the various forms of off-balance-sheet accounts, as well as of the United States Financial Accounting Standards Board's Exposure Draft, dated 30th November 1987, on disclosures about financial instruments.

II. CONCEPT, TYPOLOGY, ACCOUNTING TREATMENT AND DISCLOSURE OF
OFF-BALANCE-SHEET TRANSACTIONS IN GENERAL

A. Concept and definition of off-balance-sheet transactions

The balance sheet expresses the financial position of an enterprise and its net worth, with all the property and claims accruing to it entered on the assets side and its debts on the liabilities side. Assets and liabilities normally correspond to items resulting from realised transactions, but some outstanding transactions may affect the financial position of an enterprise. For instance, when one enterprise guarantees the liabilities of another, this fact (or commitment) does not show up in the balance sheet, even though the possible default could cause the underwriting enterprise to run into serious difficulties. Another example is that of capital commitments that do not appear on the balance sheet but which could affect the enterprise's future liquidity, e.g. by rendering to a negative amount its working capital. The commitments of non-banking enterprises are frequently of an exceptional nature; normally they must be authorised by the enterprise's management or financial controller. In the case of banks, however, the issue of guarantees, endorsements and warranties is a normal part of business.

Because of the importance of these commitments in appraising the position, and the possible difficulties in expressing them in accounting terms in the balance sheet, they are generally mentioned -- whenever they are significant -- in the notes accompanying financial statements. In the case of banks, information on off-balance-sheet commitments is provided more systematically. Thus, an enterprise's commitments and contingencies are considered as off-balance-sheet items, i.e. rights and obligations whose effects on the amount and composition of the enterprise's worth depend on the fulfilment of certain conditions or on uncertain future events.

For the most part, present national and international accounting standards (2) distinguish between:

-- Commitments resulting from a contractual obligation;

-- Contingencies which correspond to situations (or conditions) whose ultimate outcome, gain or loss, will be confirmed only on the occurrence, or non-occurrence, of one or more uncertain future events.

In some cases, commitments and contingencies may be linked, with commitments being subject to contingencies.

The generally accepted accounting principles provide that certain commitments be reflected in the balance sheet. In effect, enterprises must examine whether the commitment in question is contingent on an act that may not necessarily take place (condition) or whether the commitment in question will inevitably be incurred at some time or other (despite possible uncertainty as to the exact date):

-- If the underwriting commitment is contingent (its realisation depending on a future and uncertain event) and at the balance sheet date there are no grounds for thinking that, for example, a guarantee would be called, no balance sheet entry is required -- it would simply need to be mentioned in the notes;

-- On the other hand, should a commitment result in foreseeable expenditure, a provision should be constituted. This would be the case, for instance, should the financial position of the company for which the guarantee was given suggest that it will probably have to be exercised and that a loss will probably result. When the guarantee comes into play, as the counterpart of the call, the enterprise will record as an asset a receivable of an equal amount on the delinquent debtor.

Lastly, in the case of guaranteed receivables or payables, the balance sheet receivables or payables, along with the guarantees, should be mentioned in the notes accompanying the financial statements.

B. Typology, accounting treatment and disclosure of off-balance-sheet transactions of enterprises in general

1. Typology

Enterprises' off-balance-sheet commitments may be broken down into three main categories:

-- Financial commitments or underwriting commitments (given or received);

-- Reciprocal commitments;

-- Pension commitments and similar obligations.

Since this last category of commitment is more specific and well-known as a result of the national and international standards instituted in this area, it will not be treated here.

Included under financial commitments are both underwriting commitments by an enterprise guaranteeing a creditor against possible default by a debtor (creditor and debtor being third parties vis-à-vis the underwriting enterprise) and commitments received by an enterprise underwriting it against a third party's insolvency or invocation of the responsibility of a third party (guarantee underwritten by an endorser on commercial paper). Underwriting commitments are valid only if they relate to contingent debts or claims (and are hence not included in the balance sheet as this would lead to double counting of assets and liabilities). Moreover, an underwriting commitment is by nature contingent, since it is only at the term of the prime obligation that it may have to be exercised.

There are normally two kinds of underwriting commitments: contingent commitments and actual commitments. A contingent commitment is equivalent to a guarantee on specific assets. The chief types of contingent commitments are bonds, sureties and endorsements. A bond is an agreement whereby a third party, the guarantor, pledges to pay a creditor if the debtor does not fulfil his obligations. A surety is a commitment by a (natural or legal) person to pay, in whole or in part, a bill of exchange or promissory note at the due date in place of the bearer. An endorsement is an enterprise's guarantee on commercial paper (acceptance or payment guarantee). Discounting of commercial paper or of export credits are examples of endorsements.

Actual commitments or sureties correspond to the earmarking of specified property as collateral security for debt payment. Such property generally consists of plant, businesses, goods, claims or immovable property. These sureties may thus be either collateral securities or mortgages.

Reciprocal commitments are commitments arising out of contracts entered into by an enterprise. They correspond to a commitment given by an enterprise to the contracting party and a commitment received from the latter. Examples of this type of commitment are: rental, leasing, delivery contracts, orders of fixed assets, and agreed discount overdrafts.

2. Main rules with respect to accounting treatment

Enterprises should disclose their commitments either in an annex to their balance sheet or in the notes to the financial statements.

In any event, irrespective of the type of commitment, the disclosure would have to be made once there are contractual obligations, e.g. at the time of signature of the bond letter or the recording of the guarantee.

The amount recorded would generally be the face value of the commitment or the amount payable or receivable by the enterprise under the terms of the contract. If advances have been paid or received, only the outstanding balance should be mentioned, assuming the advances are posted in the balance sheet. In the case of underwritten claims and debts, the guarantees should be valued at their total amount, irrespective of the balance on the corresponding claims or debts.

3. Disclosure in the notes

Broadly speaking, it would be desirable to show the amount of all significant commitments, identifying those concerning management (or the board), subsidiaries, and associated enterprises.

The different types of financial commitments are normally itemized: bonds, endorsements, sureties and collateral, leasing contracts and other commitments.

Major commitments should be clearly described (and quantified) if this is considered important for the user of the financial statements.

III. TYPOLOGY, ACCOUNTING TREATMENT AND DISCLOSURE OF BANKS' OFF-BALANCE-SHEET TRANSACTIONS

While the off-balance-sheet business of industrial and business enter-prises is relatively limited (but increasing with deregulation), the same cannot be said of banks. Owing to the nature of their transactions, financial institutions take and receive major commitments. The typology and accounting treatment is thus generally more complex, a complexity that has been com-pounded by the development of new financial instruments. The aspects that merit special study are those relating to financial commitments, since the accounting treatment relative to banks' "reciprocal" commitments and pension commitments (and other assimilated social ones) are similar to those of the general business sector. Therefore, the discussion below focuses on financial commitments and their accounting aspects.

The financial commitments of banks fall into three main categories that are not mutually exclusive: guarantees and similar contingent liabilities corresponding to situations where a bank has underwritten the obligations of a third party and stands behind the risk incurred; commitments consisting of all irrevocable arrangements and facilities that could generate a credit risk at some future time; foreign exchange, interest rates and other "market" transactions.

The first two categories of commitments are the more traditional types of off-balance-sheet bank transactions. The third category covers trans-actions associated with the rapid development of the new financial instruments referred to in Part I of this backround report. To these might be added a fourth category: trusteeship and underwriting, whereby banks may be held responsible for negligence or failure to fulfil their obligations.

A. Typology and accounting treatment

In this subsection the nature of and rules for the accounting treatment of the three main categories of commitments are studied in detail. Since, as we shall see, there are no accounting standards that fully apply in this area, the accounting treatment has been analysed with reference to the current practice of major international banks, highlighting any possible divergen-cies. Subsection B deals with problems of disclosure in the reports of accounting rules used and of the level of commitments and risks incurred.

1. Contingent liabilities

Banks' main contingent liabilities are: guarantees and other direct credit substitutes, acceptances and endorsements, documentary letters of credit and warranties.

In the case of guarantees (such as bonds or endorsements), the bank as guarantor stands behind a third party -- the beneficiary, on the order and behalf of a client (who may be a financial intermediary), the instigating party -- and carries out the client's obligations should the latter fail to do so. Asset purchase or repurchase commitments are similar in nature. The first are agreements under which banks, at the request of the holders, undertake to acquire assets at agreed prices and on set terms. The second are commitments, on similar terms, to buy back assets previously sold. An example of this type of commitment is an agreement whereby a bank assigns a loan or other asset to a third party while remaining liable for the credit risk in case of default by the borrower or depreciation of the value of the asset.

Acceptances and endorsements are commitments by banks to pay at term the face value of bills of exchange normally covering the sale of goods. It is to be noted that in a certain number of Member countries, acceptances are recorded in the balance sheet.

Documentary letters of credit guarantee payment in favour of exporters, against presentation of shipping and other documents. A distinction may be made between open, confirmed and standby letters of credit. Open letters of credit represent a commitment by the bank to pay a specified sum to the supplier of a product or service, subject to the submission within a given period of supporting documentation to the effect that the product or service has been duly provided. A confirmed letter of credit is a commitment by one bank confirming a letter of credit opened by another. A standby letter of credit is similar to an ordinary letter of credit, but is issued as a guarantee against default by one of the parties to the contract rather than as a means of payment.

In the case of warranties, banks do not guarantee existing financial commitments, but rather their customers' capacity to fulfil commitments incurred in connection with their normal business activities and specific contracts. The banks guarantee that the goods and services supplied to a third party are as specified in the contracts (bank liability is normally limited to the payment of compensation). Such guarantees may be bid bonds, performance bonds, completion guarantees in the construction sector, or advance payment guarantees.

Relative to accounting rules, banks are required for operational and management purposes, and often by statute, to keep accounts of their contingent liabilities. Since these accounting entries are not reflected in movements of funds or securities, they do not have counterparts in balance sheet accounts. Hence single-entry bookkeeping may be used. Some banks nonetheless employ double-entry bookkeeping systems, opening notional counterpart accounts in their books. In any case, the systematic entry of these commitments in the accounts is a satisfactory internal control measure and enables proper supervision of the recording of commissions paid or received on these commitments.

As in the case of commercial enterprises, the contingency must be duly recorded as soon as there is a contractual obligation, i.e. at the time of signature. The amount posted is normally either the face value of the contingent liability or the amount to be paid or received by the bank under the terms of the contract. Separate accounts should be kept for contingent commitments given and received. Last, when there is a likelihood that, owing to the default of the instigating party, the recipient will call upon the guarantor, the latter must post a provision corresponding to the amount of the commitment.

A number of specific points should, however, be noted in the case of banks. First, accounting entries are often made taking into consideration the status of the instigating party, whether a customer or financial intermediary. When several financial intermediaries decide to stand jointly in respect of a commitment, each of them, whether lead agency, participant or sub-participant, must record his share of the final risk assumed.

In the case where the assignment of paper or acceptances is not through actual endorsement but simply through transmission of notes endorsed in blank, no information on the commitment need be entered in the off-balance-sheet accounts. The same applies when paper is endorsed "without recourse" by the ceding establishment. Guarantees by endorsement must in general be entered in the books for their face value without regard to the existence of other endorsements or guarantees.

2. Commitments

This category comprises all the irrevocable facilities and arrangements. More specifically, it includes non-utilised confirmed credits (and the issuance facilities of debt securities), forward sales and purchases of assets.

Non-utilised confirmed credits are the most traditional form of bank commitments. This term covers formal commitments entered into by a bank to make funds of a specific amount available to correspondents or customers on demand. Also included under this heading are unconditional standby lines of credit, and the non-utilised portion of lines of credit extended in the framework of contingent liability transactions.

One form of confirmed credit that has come into force in recent years is the note issuance facility (NIF). A note issuance facility is a medium-term legally binding commitment under which a borrower can issue short-term paper in its own name, but where underwriting banks are committed either to purchase any notes which the borrower is unable to sell, or to provide standby credit. For bank borrowers the paper is usually a short-term certificate of deposit, while for non-bank borrowers it is in the form of promissory notes (commonly known as Euro-notes). Holders of notes (whether or not they have underwritten the facility) show them as an asset on their balance sheets, but an underwriting commitment does not normally show up.

The NIF has been successful mainly because it allows the various functions performed by a single institution in a syndicated loan to be separated and performed by different institutions. Instead of lending money, as in a syndicated loan, the NIF arranger provides a mechanism for placing notes with other investors when funds are required. Maturity transformation (assuring the borrower access to short-term funds over the medium term) is provided by the underwriting commitment, which remains off-balance-sheet unless called upon. Borrowers appreciate NIFs because of their low cost and great flexibility. An issuer may use a NIF for funding or to hold in reserve as a standby facility. A NIF that is drawn regularly may replace an alternative source of variable-rate funding, such as a floating-rate or syndicated loan. Under present market conditions, a number of NIFs have been arranged to replace existing, more expensive borrowings. When arranged as a standby, a NIF may back up other types of financing, such as US or Euro-commercial paper, or act as an emergency funding source.

Forward transactions on assets are similar to bank commitments. This type of transaction covers forward sales and purchases (agreements to buy or sell loans, securities or other assets at a later specified or unspecified date) as well as forward resales or repurchases of assets (agreements to repurchase or resell loans, securities or other assets ceded earlier, at a later specified or unspecified date). Two examples of this type of transaction are:

-- Sale and repurchase transactions on the basis of firm sale or repurchase agreements;

-- Commitments to place deposits with a counterparty at later dates and at predetermined interest rates.

From an accounting standpoint, the comments on contingent liabilities also apply to commitments. Nonetheless, a few particular points should be made.

Note issuance facilities should be entered off-balance-sheet for the whole life of the commitment during which such facilities are available. The commitments normally expire when the notes of the last issue are placed on the market (unless otherwise stipulated). Notes not placed and put back into the bank's own portfolio are to be posted under the appropriate balance sheet headings at their acquisition cost, and in some cases at less than their acquisition cost.

In the case of forward transactions on assets, commitments should of course be posted at the agreed price up to redemption. However, certain countries -- Canada, for example -- are reviewing their treatment of repurchase agreements, as they consider that agreements which are essentially "financing transactions" should be differentiated from those that are sales and repurchases. If the agreement is regarded as a financing transaction, the security would remain on the selling bank's balance sheet, with the funds received credited to the appropriate liability account. Under a reverse repurchase agreement, the funds disbursed would be recorded as loans.

3. Foreign exchange, interest rate and other market rate-related transactions

These commitments correspond to agreements relating primarily to foreign exchange, interest and other market rates such as stock indices, which are generally binding on both parties but in some cases exercisable at one party's discretion. Apart from traditional forward foreign exchange transactions, generally no exchange of principal is involved. When the transaction is unhedged, the institution is exposed to movements in interest rates, exchange rates or other market rates. Whether the transaction is unhedged (i.e. undertaken for trading purposes) or hedged (to neutralise a position exposure), the bank is vulnerable to the creditworthiness of a counterparty (his ability to fulfil his part of the agreement) and thus will be exposed to an unexpected or unintended liability should the counterparty default.

26

To improve financial disclosure, a distinction is generally drawn between the transactions related to the different rates: exchange rates (these include forward foreign exchange transactions, currency swaps, currency futures and foreign exchange options), interest rates [including interest rate swaps, interest rate futures, forward rate agreements (FRAs) and interest rate options] and, last, other market rates (including futures and options). From an accounting treatment standpoint, this distinction is not very meaningful since the underlying principles for these financial instruments, whether related to currency or interest rates, are very similar. It seemed more logical to group certain transactions and analyse those involving more specific accounting treatment. The following are thus examined in turn: forward foreign exchange transactions and currency swaps, interest rate swaps, financial futures (with special reference to interest rate futures), FRAs, options (with special reference to foreign exchange options), and caps, floors and collars.

a) Forward foreign exchange transactions and currency swaps

Forward exchange transactions are termed as forward when the contracting parties decide to defer their unwinding for reasons other than a customary lapse of time. The commitment takes the form of an obligation to deliver a sum in a specified currency against receipt of a sum in another currency, at a contractually agreed time and rate.

Forward foreign exchange transactions are entered in a memorandum account on the same day as the commitment. They are posted in an off-balance-sheet account under the heading "currencies to be delivered", normally for the amounts to be received as stipulated in the contract (i.e. at the forward rate). However, in some countries (notably in France), currencies to be delivered or received are entered at the spot rate, and the difference between the spot rate and the forward rate is posted in a premium account and will be spread over the term of the commitment in the profit-and-loss account. This is justified by the fact that the spot/forward differential is considered as an interest rate differential between the two currencies.

Since in addition to the counterparty risk the commitment also involves an exchange rate risk, it is generally valued at each balance sheet date at the forward rate applying for the term begun, the difference being posted in income using the mark-to-market technique. In countries (France for instance) where commitments are initially recorded at spot rates, these are revalued at the spot rate applying at the balance sheet date, the surplus or deficit being entered in the profit-and-loss account.

Swaps are financial transactions in which two counterparties agree to exchange streams of payments over time according to a predetermined rule which reflects interest payments and may also reflect amortization of principal. Swap markets are utilised for several reasons: to obtain low-cost financing, to obtain high-yield assets, to hedge interest rate or currency exposure generated from the structure of normal business, to implement short-run asset/liability management strategies, to earn fees, and to speculate.

More specifically, currency swaps may be defined as a combination of a spot foreign exchange transaction (spot sale of a currency A against the purchase of a currency B) and an offsetting forward foreign exchange transaction (sale of a currency B against the purchase of a currency A) undertaken with the same counterparty. The off-balance-sheet recording of the forward transaction (at the spot rate) results in a premium (the difference between the spot and forward rates) payable by one party and receivable by the other. Since the transaction is closed, it does not entail a currency exposure for the counterparties. The premium is amortized (as a profit or loss, depending on whether it is payable or receivable) over the swap arrangement period, being assimilated to an interest rate differential between the two currencies.

New kinds of swaps -- financing swaps -- have made an appearance in recent years; here, currencies are exchanged both spot and forward for the same amount (the forward rate being the same as the spot rate). For the period of the swap, interest revenue and expense is generated in the two currencies at different interest rates, depending on the currencies in question. The recording of this type of transaction is very similar to that of the traditional swap. Forward transactions are recorded off-balance-sheet, under currencies receivable and payable.

Some financing swaps may be set up without any initial exchange of principal and with reciprocal payment of interest in the two currencies. These are forward foreign exchange transactions for which, apart from the recording of interest, the accounting treatment and currency exposure are the same as in the standard case where the forward rate differs from the spot rate.

The accounting rules set out above for forward transactions and currency swaps are those routinely practised by a large number of major international banks. It is interesting to note, however, that while there is no great difference in their off-balance-sheet recording, when it comes to the impact on the profit-and-loss account, US banks use different accounting rules in virtue of Financial Accounting Standard 52 (Conversion of Foreign Exchange Transactions) if the forward currency transactions are used for hedging purposes. This is also the case in the United Kingdom.

According to FASB, a forward transaction or swap may qualify as a hedge if it reduces the exposure on a net investment in a foreign subsidiary, or on an identifiable firm foreign currency commitment or some other existing exposure (or liability). If this is the case, the gain or loss (rate differential) on the transaction is divided into two components:

-- The original discount or premium differential, i.e. the differential between the spot rate applicable on the agreement's entry into force and the forward rate specified;

-- The revaluation differential (difference between the spot rate applicable on the agreement's entry into force and the expiration date).

Normally, the initial differential is amortized over the life of the hedging transaction. In the case of the second differential, the accounting treatment varies according to the nature of the operation hedged. If it is an investment in a foreign subsidiary, the revaluation differential is included in the foreign currency translation component of shareholders' equity. In the case of hedging of a identifiable firm commitment or of a well-defined asset or liability, the differential is entered in current income.

b) Interest rate swaps

Interest rate swaps are contracts designed to hedge interest rate risks or to obtain better financing through an interest rate switch -- either between fixed and floating rates, or between two floating rates. Generally involving only one currency, they may also involve at the same time interest rate and currency swaps. The main feature of these instruments is that there is no exchange of principal. The reference figure used to calculate interest is recorded in the off-balance-sheet account. This is purely a "statistical" entry, the reference figure in no way representing the counterparty or rate exposure involved. The interest swapped is entered in the normal way by accruing it in the profit-and-loss account.

Interest rate swaps designed to hedge lending or borrowing do not raise any particular valuation problems, since they are recorded at their initial entry value. Trading swaps, on the other hand, do present valuation problems. If market references exist, the mark-to-market technique may be used. In any case, provisions should be posted against any significant adverse movement of interest rates.

c) Financial futures

Financial futures are instruments tradable on specific financial markets. These markets offer a range of diversified products -- interest rate, currency and stock index-related futures. The purchaser undertakes to accept delivery of and the seller pledges to deliver a standard quantity of a specified financial instrument at a given future date and at a mutually agreed price set in advance.

Futures can only be subscribed on these markets after payment of an initial deposit or margin proportional to the total amount of futures bought or sold. Repayment is only made at term, or earlier if the dealer unwinds his position by subscribing a similarly dated reverse agreement. In practice these deposits are often in the form of letters of credit provided by other banks or collateral securities. Periodically (and often daily), the historical price and current market price of the future are compared. As a result of this revaluation of all position exposures, profits or losses are settled. Losses lead to a mark-to-market call (variation margin) which, if unanswered, triggers automatic settlement of the position. Profits give rise to a payment.

Futures agreements are unwound with the payment or collection of a sum equal to the difference between the price at the last accounting date and the transaction price. The position is then closed. On the settlement date, if there has been no earlier unwinding of the position by a transaction offsetting the initial one, operators must fulfil their part of the agreement by delivering or receiving the financial instrument or, in some cases, by settling in cash the difference calculated on the basis of price movements.

Operators deal on these markets either for forward interest rate, currency or stock index hedging; for speculation; or for arbitrage.

The transaction is deemed to be a "hedging" transaction if it meets the following five criteria:

-- The transaction hedged must expose the operator to an interest or exchange rate risk;

-- When the contracts are concluded, the object of the transaction must be specifically identified and documented by the amount and description of the asset or liability for which the hedge was initiated;

-- From the start of the transaction and for the whole of the hedging period, the contract price should be closely correlated with the price of the asset or liability hedged, i.e. they should move according to the same criteria, in the same direction and to a commensurate extent. In the United States for example, in no way can a futures contract hedging a position exposure comprising several non-homogeneous components be considered as a hedging transaction from an accounting standpoint;

-- If an expected transaction is hedged, there must be a reasonable assurance that it will be realised;

-- In some countries, such as the United Kingdom, three major criteria are applied: intent, correlation and certainty.

A transaction is deemed to be speculative if it is undertaken for trading purposes or (in certain countries) to hedge exposures due to global interest rate mismatches (macro-hedging).

Arbitrage between maturities (purchase of a future for one maturity and sale for another), between contracts (in the case of contracts of a broadly similar nature on a single market, purchases of some contracts and sales of others with due regard to their different face values) and between different markets are considered and treated for accounting purposes as speculative positions.

On the other hand, arbitrage transactions between the spot market for the ("physical") asset and the forward market of this asset (which, by definition, implies delivery of the asset underlying the futures contract) are treated from an accounting standpoint as hedges.

Purchases and sales of off-balance-sheet contracts are recorded at the date of signature; their term and face value are entered, usually in an off-balance-sheet memorandum account. They are treated differently in the profit-and-loss account, depending on whether the transaction is undertaken for speculative or for hedging purposes. If the transaction is speculative, the adjustments recorded according to price movements (swings in the daily spread) are taken to the profit-and-loss end of each accounting period in the profit-and-loss account as unrealised. At the close of the position, the profit or loss on the outstanding contract should be taken to a profit-and-loss account as realised profit and loss.

In the case of a hedge, daily valuations of positions are entered in a suspense account until the position is unwound. At that date, the price differential settled is spread over the estimated residual life of the transaction hedged. For transactions to hedge existing assets valued at the market rate, the mark-to-market principle must be applied to ensure similarity of treatment with the income from the transaction hedged. For assets hedged, where the valuation rules require that the purchase cost or market value -- whichever is lower -- be recorded at the balance sheet date, the cumulative amount of changes in the value of the contracts recorded in the suspense account is taken into consideration in determining the necessary provision for depreciation.

In case of sale of the asset hedged before maturity, the balance on the suspense account will be charged or credited to the profit-and-loss account. If the hedging agreement is not unwound when the asset hedged is sold, then it must be redesignated as speculative.

Assuming that a futures contract hedging an anticipated transaction matures before the transaction is in fact unwound, changes in the value of the contract will continue to be deferred until the date the transaction is realised. Should it ultimately not be realised, all the deferred amounts will be posted to the profit-and-loss account on the date of expected realisation.

d) Forward rate agreements (FRAs)

Forward rate agreements (FRAs) are very similar to futures. They are transactions by mutual agreement between two contracting parties. At the date the transaction is concluded, the parties lend or borrow a notional amount at a variable reference rate with no actual funds changing hands. The parties decide on a rate -- the "guaranteed rate", according to which the transaction will be unwound at a contractually agreed date (the "effective date"). At this date, the differential between the guaranteed rate and the actual value of the reference rate is settled. This interest differential is calculated for the period from the effective date to the maturity date of the loan or of the notional amount borrowed under the terms of the contract.

In concluding such transactions, a bank may be in one of two positions:

-- That of a lender, if the counterparty guarantees it a lending rate. The bank will pay the counterparty the interest differential if, at the effective date, the reference rate is higher than the guaranteed rate, or it will receive the interest differential from the counterparty if, at the effective date, the reference rate is lower than the guaranteed rate;

-- That of a borrower, if the counterparty guarantees it a borrowing rate. The bank will pay the counterparty the interest differential if, at the effective date, the reference rate is lower than the guaranteed rate, or it will receive the interest differential from the counterparty if, at the effective date, the reference rate is higher than the guaranteed rate.

A future rate agreement may be concluded for hedging or speculative purposes. To qualify as a hedge, it must meet the same hedging criteria as those specified for futures [see Section III.A.3.b)].

From an accounting standpoint, off-balance-sheet recording is the same as for futures, i.e. with the face value and duration of the contracts recorded in an off-balance-sheet account. Treatment of the interest rate differential in the profit and loss will vary according to the use of the FRA.

If the transactions are not hedged, FRA contracts are marked to market. This means establishing the price at which the contract could be closed out in the marketplace at the balance sheet date and accounting for the gain or loss which would hypothetically ensue. Two methods can be used to determine market value, namely:

1. Determining the cost of closing out a FRA position, i.e. the rate at which an equal and opposite FRA could be purchased covering the same contract period and for the same amount of notional loan or deposit. A party to the FRA contract requesting such a quote can approach either its broker or other brokers providing such a service to third parties. That rate can then be compared to the agreed or guaranteed rate and the settlement amount calculated;

2. Estimating the interest settlement rate on settlement date for the contract period, which is then compared to the agreed or guaranteed rate and using the difference to calculate the settlement amount. It can be argued that the best estimate of this rate at the balance sheet date is a linear interpolation between the prevailing market rate for the period to settlement date and that for the period to maturity.

Each method therefore gives rise to a valuation rate which is then compared to the agreed rate to determine whether an interest payment or receipt would arise. The interest rate difference is multiplied by the underlying notional loan or deposit and then discounted back to the settlement date. This gives rise to the valuation at the balance sheet date.

The accounting treatment applicable to hedging FRAs varies according to the nature and accounting treatment of the asset and liability being hedged. In determining the correct treatment, it is important to follow the fundamental accounting concept of matching related income and expense. Thus, if a FRA is used to hedge another FRA, a futures contract or an interest rate option, it may be appropriate to mark both instruments to market. If, on the other hand, a FRA is used to hedge a cash market position, over the hedge period the gain or loss should be deferred and amortized in order to match the accounting treatment of cash market instruments. It is important to treat both sides of the hedge consistently. When a FRA is to be accounted for on a deferred basis, there are different implications depending on where the balance sheet date falls between the date the transaction is concluded (A), the contractually agreed start date (S), and the maturity date (M):

-- When the balance sheet falls between A and S, the hedge period is by definition from S to M, so that any unrealised profit or loss arising should not be recognised in the profit-and-loss account at the balance sheet date;

-- When the balance sheet date falls between S and M, the FRA will have been settled, and the profit or loss should be deferred and amortized evenly over the period S-to-M. The extent to which profits or losses are recognised in the profit-and-loss account for the period ended on the balance sheet date clearly depends on the length of time between S and the balance sheet date compared with the period S-to-M (3).

e) Options

Options are contracts conveying the right to buy or sell forward foreign currency, precious metals or any other specified asset at a fixed price during or at the end of a given period. The focus of this subsection will be on foreign exchange options, but it is to be noted that accounting treatment is very similar for all options, regardless of type.

Foreign exchange options are forward transactions conveying the right, but not an obligation, to buy or sell a specified amount of a currency against another currency up to an established expiration date -- the exercise date -- at the rate initially set, the exercise price. Option contracts may be distinguished by the nature of the underlying currency, the direction of the contingent transaction (purchase or sale) and the terms applying (at a set date or during the period between the date the contract is negotiated and its date of expiry).

Foreign exchange options may be traded either on organised markets within stock or commodity markets, or bilaterally. On the organised markets, dealing is in standardized contracts in terms of currencies, amounts and maturities; this is in contrast with bilateral (over-the-counter) transactions, whose terms are freely negotiated by the parties and are tailor-made to suit their requirements. Moreover, a central body has responsibility for the operation of organised markets. Its role is to facilitate the clearing of contracts and ensure that each transaction is successfully completed. Security on these markets is obtained through a mechanism of deposits or margins that vary according to the financial market. For instance, on the Philadelphia Stock Exchange, buyers are obliged to pay premiums immediately and sellers must lodge an amount at least equal to this premium, or a higher amount should their positions become potentially loss-making. On the London Stock Exchange, the option dealer must deposit an amount adjusted by the exposure factor, and will be credited or debited with the daily fluctuation (variation) margins on the value of the premium. Should the option be taken up, currencies are delivered spot or forward, or in the form of currency futures, depending on the market.

Options fall into two categories: call and put options. Thus market transactions may involve purchases of call options, sales of call options, purchases of put options and sales of put options.

The initial value of the option (premium) is made up of two components:

-- The intrinsic value: the difference between the price of the underlying asset (forward or spot) and the take-up price of the option if this is favourable to the buyer of the option;

-- The time value: the premium less the intrinsic value. The time value is a function of the interest rate differential between the underlying currency and the counterpart currency, and of the expected price volatility of the underlying currency and of the maturity of the option.

The premium of an option traded on an organised market is quoted. In the case of bilateral (over-the-counter) options, the revalued premiums may be calculated by means of mathematical models.

33

For the buyer of a foreign exchange option, there are three ways in which the contract may be unwound: through exercise of the option, settlement (liquidation) of the option (resale of the option or transfer to another counterparty or the original seller), or expiry of the option in the absence of its exercise, resale or transfer. For the seller of a foreign exchange or option, the option will be unwound in case of exercise of the buyer's right, repurchase or expiry at the end of the contract period.

From an accounting standpoint, treatment is at three levels: recording of the contracts off-balance-sheet, initial entry of the premiums, and treatment in the profit-and-loss account.

Although options represent only a potential commitment (to deliver under certain conditions currency A and to receive currency B), not a firm one, the risks they entail require them to be recorded in the off-balance-sheet accounts at the date the contract enters into effect. The ensuing accounting treatment distinguishes between option purchases and sales; options traded on organised markets and options traded over the counter; hedging transactions and trading transactions. The off-balance-sheet recording of these transactions is on the basis of the take-up price in each of the two currencies involved (underlying currency and counterpart currency). It is, however, important not to offset options issued with options bought by the same institutions.

Premiums, however they are settled, should be recorded in the currencies concerned in the balance sheet at the date of the contract.

As regards the profit-and-loss account, the general rule is the following: in the case of non-unwound contracts, foreign exchange options follow the valuation principle for currency transactions. At each cut-off date, the premium representing the value of the foreign exchange option is revalued on the basis of organised market prices or data available on bilateral contracts, and the premium revaluation differential is entered in the profit-and-loss account, as an unrealised gain or loss.

In case of unwinding by expiry of the option, the premium remaining in the balance sheet is taken to the profit-and-loss account as a realised gain or loss. In the case of unwinding by settlement of the option, the difference between the premium paid or received and the premium in respect to the initial settled option is posted to the profit-and-loss account, as a realised gain or loss.

As in the case of currency options, special treatment is accorded to transactions qualifying as hedges. For transactions to be so deemed, they must meet the following criteria:

-- The item hedged exposes the bank to a foreign exchange risk;

-- The bank is in a purchasing position on the contract;

-- From the date of signature of the contract, the purpose of the transaction is specifically identified and documented by the amount and description of the asset or liability for which the hedge transaction has been initiated;

-- At the outset of the hedge and throughout the hedge period, the price of the option contract is very closely correlated to the price of the hedged item, i.e. both should move according to the same criteria in the same direction;

-- If the transaction has not yet been realised, the characteristics of the proposed transaction are clearly defined, and there must be a high probability of realisation.

If these criteria have been met, the proceeds of the hedge shall be recognised in income in the same way as are those of the hedged transaction. In the case of transactions undertaken to hedge existing items valued at market price (e.g. foreign exchange transactions, foreign exchange options, etc.), the general mark-to-market principle must be applied to ensure the same accounting treatment as for the proceeds of a hedged transaction. In the case of an anticipated transaction (if it relates to a firm commitment), recognition of gains or losses is deferred until the hedged transaction is realised. If the exposure hedged is cancelled before the contract is unwound, the gains or losses deferred will be directly recognised in income. The same holds true for subsequent gains or losses.

Lastly, a distinction should be made for bilateral (over-the-counter) options. If option-pricing models exist with reference inputs provided by the market, revaluation is performed on a regular basis with revaluation gains and losses recognised currently in income. If no market reference input models are available, no revaluation can be made and premiums paid or received are therefore maintained in the balance sheet at their historical value; the entry in income is effected at the time the contract is unwound.

f) Caps, floors and collars

Caps, floors and collars are instruments guaranteeing entities against interest rate exposure. A cap is a guarantee ensuring a variable interest rate borrower that the variable rate of his loan will not exceed a fixed level for a predetermined period. The beneficiary of this guarantee pays in exchange a premium to the seller, computed on the basis of the nominal amount guaranteed. A floor is the opposite situation, enabling the entity to guarantee itself against the decrease of the variable interest rate below a certain level. Caps and floors are characterised by five parameters:

-- The nominal amount of the capital guaranteed;

-- The period of guarantee;

-- The type of variable rate hedged;

-- The maximum (cap) or minimum (floor) level guaranteed;

-- The payment of the premium (premiums are usually paid in full at the inception of the contract).

Caps and floors can be combined; the result is called a collar. This financial instrument corresponds to the purchase (or sale) of a cap accompanied by the sale (or purchase) of a floor. Entities use collars to limit their interest rate exposure within a maximum and minimum level.

As regards accounting principles -- specifically, measurement of income -- rules that apply to caps, floors and collars are similar to those governing bilateral (over-the-counter) options.

B. Problems of financial disclosure

Problems of financial disclosure in annual reports occur in three areas: information on accounting principles used, disclosure of the level of off-balance-sheet commitments, and disclosure of the risks incurred.

1. Information on the accounting principles used

The accounting practices described in Part III. A. of this background report are those generally used by large international banks, since no international standards have so far been agreed in this area. In particular, no specific recommendations have been made by either the IASC or the EC with regard to new financial instruments. Nationally, the rules used are in most cases based on the general accounting principles laid down by supervisory authorities or professional accountancy bodies. The concepts generally applied are the accruals principle (whereby revenue and costs are accrued, matched more specifically and dealt with in the profit-and-loss account of the period to which they relate) and the principle of prudence (whereby revenue and profits should not be anticipated, but are recognised in the profit-and-loss account only when realised and provision is made for all known liabilities, whether known with certainty or estimated). Only the United States [in FAS 52 on the accounting treatment of currency futures contracts (4) and FAS 80 on accounting for futures contracts (5)] and France [with the opinion of the "Conseil national de la comptabilité" on the accounting treatment of financial futures (6) and interest rate options (7), and a few documents by national banking institutions on off-balance-sheet accounts] would seem to have given consideration to the accounting treatment of the new instruments. Nonetheless, a study of the information supplied by Delegations in response to the Secretariat's request of October 1986 and the fact sheets transmitted in June-July 1987 has shown that a number of countries are intending to explore the issues involved (see Annex).

Pending the establishment of national and international standards in this area, banks and non-banking enterprises should, in application of the Section on Disclosure of Information in the OECD Guidelines for Multinational Enterprises (8), provide adequate information on the accounting methods used to record off-balance-sheet transactions that have a significant impact on financial statements. Particular mention should be made of the rules used to record the results of commitments of this type, and when they are not unwound, to value these commitments in financial statements. Is the financial instrument marked to market at the balance sheet date? What are the qualifications for it to be considered as a hedge? If so qualified, what is the treatment accorded? The following report of an international bank provides two interesting examples of the type of disclosure that could be given to transactions of this type.

"Interest rate futures: Interest rate futures contracts and forward contract commitments are a part of trading activities and are also used to hedge certain assets and liabilities, particularly loans and deposits, and anticipated transactions which will ultimately result in assets and liabilities. Gains and losses on futures and forward contracts related to trading activities are recognised in current income. Gains and losses on futures and forward contracts used to hedge assets and liabilities are generally deferred and recognised in income over the expected remaining life of the hedged asset or liability. The bank assesses monthly the changes in value of the futures and forward contracts which have been designated as hedges in order to determine whether the results have substantially offset the effects of interest rate changes on the value of the hedged item. If a high degree of correlation has not occurred, gains and losses are recognised in income currently.

Interest rate swaps: The bank enters into interest rate swaps as a source of fee income and to manage interest rate exposure. In general, income or expense, including all yield-related payments associated with interest rate swap transactions, is accrued over the life of the agreements, except for arrangement fees which are currently recognised."

2. Disclosure of banks' commitments

As noted in the Annex, at the present time, requirements for disclosure of commitments vary from country to country. In some countries there are no disclosure requirements. In others -- France, for example -- certain commitments have to be disclosed in aggregate form under the balance sheet. In countries such as the United States, Canada and the United Kingdom, commitments are disclosed in a more detailed manner in the accompanying notes to the financial statements. More recently, bank supervisors have been requiring more detailed information from institutions coming within their purview, but this information is not available to the public.

Internationally, the IASC Standard that applies is IAS 10: "Contingencies and Events Occurring after the Balance Sheet Date". This Standard concerns financial statements for all types of businesses. It states that if a contingent loss is not accrued, its financial effect should be disclosed by way of a note, unless the possibility of a loss is remote. The disclosure should contain the following information:

a) The nature of the contingency;

b) The uncertain factors that may affect the future outcome;

c) An estimate of the financial effect, or a statement that such an estimate cannot be made.

The Council of the European Communities, in its Directive of December 1986 on the annual and consolidated accounts of banks (9), requires that financial institutions show any contingent liabilities (transactions for which an institution has underwritten the obligations of a third party, e.g. acceptances and endorsement guarantees and assets pledged as collateral security) as well as any irrevocable commitments that could give rise to a risk (e.g. commitments arising out of sale and repurchase transactions). In addition, two Articles deal specifically with off-balance-sheet disclosure: Article 40 3 d) states that "credit institutions shall give particulars of the assets which they have pledged as security for their own liabilities or for those of third parties (including contingent liabilities). The particulars should be in sufficient detail to indicate for each liabilities item and for each off-balance-sheet item the total amount of the assets pledged as security; Article 41 2 h) requires that in the notes to their accounts credit institutions give "a statement of the types of unmatured forward transactions outstanding at the balance sheet date indicating, in particular, for each type of transaction, whether they are made to a material extent for the purpose of hedging the effects of fluctuations in interest rates, exchange rates and market prices, and whether they are made to a material extent for dealing purposes".

On the basis of these rules and user needs, types of disclosure that could be given in financial statements should, when significant, refer to individual types of commitments or be made in aggregate form. An example of a type of disclosure could be the following:

"In the normal course of business, various commitments and contingent liabilities are outstanding and are not reflected in the balance sheet. The management of the bank does not anticipate any material losses as a result of these transactions. A summary of significant commitments and contingent liabilities at 31st December follows:

In millions	1987	1986
Letters of credit		
. Guarantees and standby letters of credit	_____	
. Other letters of credit	_____	
Commitments to extend credit		
Securities and interest rate futures contracts		
. Commitments to sell	_____	
. Commitments to purchase	_____	
Commitments to purchase foreign currencies	_____	

With respect to interest rate swaps which are not reflected in the table above, the notional principal amount of outstanding contracts approximated at 31st December 1987 and 1986 respectively ------ and ------."

3. Disclosure of banks' risk exposure

Information disclosed in notes, such as significant accounting policies or the details of commitments and contingent liabilities, is essential for creditors' and investors' understanding of a company's financial situation. However, descriptions of accounting policies or point estimates communicate only partially the information users need about future benefits or losses. Additional disclosure is generally necessary to help the reader of financial statements assess the uncertainties that are present and the potential effects on the entity of the different possible outcomes. Assessing downside risk is essential for investors and creditors, but knowing the upside potentials is almost as important. For instance, in the case of a bank that deals heavily in futures, options or collars, there is an upside potential of producing gains and, through hedging, stabilizing an entity's financial position in an unstable market environment. But there are also risks of sudden loss or failure if speculative positions are taken or if apparent hedges prove to have been speculative. Specific notes on the different instruments are useful to analyse risk, but they are in most cases incomplete. Since for most diversified institutions risk exposures among assets, liabilities and off-balance-sheet activities are integrally related, analysis of only one instrument can result in misleading conclusions. An analysis taking into consideration instruments globally portrays more faithfully an entity's position towards risks.

By and large, balance sheet business as well as off-balance-sheet activity gives rise to the following types of risk: credit risk, financing and liquidity risk (market risk), interest rate and exchange rate risk, and management and internal control problems.

Credit risk relates to the situation where a contractor fails to honour his commitment at maturity date. Included in this category are counterparty risk, settlement risk, potential country risk, and cross-border problems.

Financing and liquidity exposure is the risk that a bank will be called upon to provide funds at a time when it cannot easily do so, either because the individual bank is unable to fund itself at market rates or because of the general conditions in the interbank market. In the case of NIFs, for instance, banks' underwriting commitments may be obliged to acquire an asset whenever the borrower chooses to call funds.

Interest rate and foreign exchange exposure is the risk that interest rates or exchange rates may change after the date of the bank's commitment; this risk concerns for example swaps, options and futures and forward foreign exchange transactions.

Management and internal control (as well as computer security) exposure is the risk that transactions may take place before limits and proper internal controls are in force or may exceed those limits and controls, and that the computer system may become inoperative.

International accounting bodies have recently issued standards or exposure drafts emphasizing the necessity of risk disclosures. For instance, the IASC has recently prepared an Exposure Draft on disclosures in banks' financial statements (10). In this draft, the IASC recommends that banks disclose the necessary information to assist the user of financial statements in assessing the liquidity, solvency and risk exposure of banks' assets and liabilities. This draft Standard also provides that, in addition to the information on commitments specified in IAS 10 (2), banks be required to specify the nature and scale of any irrevocable commitments that might give rise to a credit risk, as well as the nature and scale of their off-balance-sheet business.

In order to furnish useful information to shareholders, creditors and analysts, certain international banks are voluntarily providing disclosures based upon the information actually used by management in running their businesses. These are usually narrative presentations (covering recognised and unrecognised financial instruments) of their approach to managing and controlling data, accompanied by tabular disclosures. The following is an example of an interest rate sensitivity disclosure that has the potential benefit of providing a useful summary indicator of management's control and of the degree to which an entity is exposed to loss or gain from fluctuations in interest rates:

"Management of interest rate risk

The Sources and Uses of Funds Committee of the bank meets regularly to review and manage the risk associated with interest rate sensitivity.

Management reviews regularly major exposures to interest rate risk both in US and foreign currencies on a global basis by forecasting rate developments and by measuring the effect of possible outcomes on net interest earnings. The bank manages the relationship between repricing dates or maturities ("rollover dates") of its assets and liabilities in a manner which aims to increase net interest earnings while taking into account vulnerability to unanticipated interest rate movements. By maintaining interest rate sensitivity gaps, in which groups of interest-earning assets are funded with interest-bearing liabilities having different rollover dates, benefit may be realised from rate changes; however, net interest earnings can be reduced if rates move in an unanticipated direction. Interest rate and currency swaps, interest rate futures and options, and similar agreements are important in the bank's management of exposure to interest rate movements.

Certain interest rate sensitivity data for the bank at 31st December 1987 are presented in the table on the next page. Amounts denominated in foreign currencies have been translated into US dollars and constitute...per cent of the interest-sensitive assets appearing in the table. The effects of interest rate and currency swaps and interest rate futures used to manage exposure to interest rate movements are reflected in the table.

Management considers a portion of net non-interest-bearing deposits to be stable and hence a consistent source of funding. These non-interest-bearing deposits and stockholders' equity reduce the amount of purchased funds the bank needs to fund its longer-term interest-earning as well as non-interest-earning assets.

The following table indicates only a one-day position. Major changes in position can be, and are, made promptly as market outlooks change. In addition, significant variations in rate sensitivity may exist within the periods presented and among currencies."

Similar narrative disclosures are made in certain annual reports on credit risk, liquidity risk, or foreign exchange exposure.

INTEREST RATE SENSITIVITY TABLE
(By rollover dates)

In millions: 31st December 1987	Within three months	After three months but within six	After six months but within one year	After one year but within five	After five years	Non-interest-bearing funds	Total
ASSETS							
Interest-bearing deposits with banks.							
Investment securities.							
Loans and lease financing							
Other assets*							
Total assets							
SOURCE OF FUNDS							
Interest-bearing deposits							
Other money market liabilities							
Long-term debt							
Non-interest-bearing deposits							
Other liabilities							
Stockholders' equity .							
Total source of funds							
Interest rate sensitivity gap							
Cumulative interest rate sensitivity gap							

*   Net trading account assets amounting to $4.6 billion at 31st December 1986 are included in "Other assets maturing within three months".

It is important to mention that regulatory bodies such as central banks are endeavouring to control banks better and ensure that risks are correctly covered. An important step was taken in this field recently with the publication in December 1987 of a report by the Basle Committee on Banking Regulations and Supervisory Practices (11). It contains proposals for achieving convergence of national supervisory regulations and practices in respect of capital adequacy measurement and standards for banks engaged in international business. The proposed framework incorporates a definition of capital that gives special emphasis to equity capital and retained earnings, but -- even more interesting -- it includes a method of measuring capital adequacy based on a system of relative risk-weightings applied to all balance sheet assets and off-balance-sheet engagements. In particular, these weightings address relative credit or counterparty risks, but national supervisory authorities have the possibility of incorporating aspects of foreign exchange and interest rate risk into the measure. When conceptualising its capital adequacy ratio, the Committee covered comprehensively all categories of off-balance-sheet instruments, including recent innovations.

On the same lines, efforts are made nationally by central banks to measure risks better. An interesting example is that of the French Banking Commission, which published in March 1987 a report (12) on the different risks arising from new financial instruments. In this report, the Commission analyses the different risks and instruments concerned, and gives recommendations as to the management of risks.

Regulatory requirements apply mainly to the management of banks, or to the reports which are transmitted to central banks, and generally not to published financial statements for shareholders, investors or creditors. However, they contribute greatly to the research performed by accounting bodies on risks, which is presently developing world-wide. In this area, particular mention should be made of the US Financial Accounting Standards Board's programme on financial instruments. More specifically, the Exposure Draft (13) published on 30th November 1987 is certainly at the present time the first comprehensive document developing the type of information that should be disclosed in financial statements on the risks of financial instruments.

Noting that many financial instruments are currently not adequately reported in financial statements, the FASB considered methods for better disclosure of the potential favourable or unfavourable effects of instruments, whether recognised or unrecognised as assets or liabilities. Analysing the type of objectives of disclosures, the instruments concerned, and the risks that had to be covered, the FASB proposed that minimum disclosures applicable to all financial instruments and entities be made on credit risks, future cash receipts and payments, interest rates and market values (14).

The FASB Exposure Draft represents an important step in the field of adequate disclosure of financial instruments. Efforts in this direction can only be encouraged, and national and international accounting bodies should take the Exposure Draft into consideration, along with the work now being performed by certain other countries or regulatory authorities, so that risks are correctly disclosed in the annual (or interim) reports of enterprises.

IV. GENERAL CONCLUSIONS

National and international standards do not seem to have kept pace with the recent expansion of off-balance-sheet commitments that has resulted -- in large part -- from the emergence of new financial instruments, as pointed out earlier in this report. Even if the existing guidelines and general standards broadly apply, the specificity of some of these instruments calls for the establishment of specific rules so as to improve the comparability of banks' and non-banks' financial statements.

Pending this standardization and in order to improve the quality of financial statements, as recommended in the OECD Guidelines for Multinational Enterprises (15), it is essential that particulars of off-balance-sheet transactions be disclosed in annual (or interim) reports of enterprises. Information should cover the accounting methods used (with particular reference to the treatment of such transactions in the income statement, whether for hedging or trading purposes), the amounts of the different types of commitment and information on the risks incurred, on an overall basis and for all financial instruments.

Harmonization of accounting practices and better disclosure would help to stimulate international investment, improve communication, reduce accounting costs and enhance management effectiveness. It is hoped that the OECD Symposium on New Financial Instruments and the contributions published in this volume, will act as a catalyst to induce further action by all those concerned with the quality, comparability and reliability of information on new financial instruments.

NOTES AND REFERENCES

1. *Recent Innovations in International Banking*, Bank for International Settlements, April 1986.

2. *IAS 10: Contingencies and Events Occurring after the Balance Sheet Date*, International Accounting Standards Committee.

3. See Ernst & Winney, *Forward Rate Agreements*, February 1987.

4. *FAS 52: Foreign Currency Translation*, Financial Accounting Standards Board, December 1981.

5. *FAS 80: Accounting for Futures Contracts*, Financial Accounting Standards Board, August 1984.

6. *Avis relatif à la comptabilisation des opérations sur le marché à terme d'instruments financiers*, (MATIF), Conseil national de la comptabilité, July 1986.

7. *Avis relatif à la comptabilisation des options de taux d'intérêt*, Conseil national de la comptabilité, July 1987.

8. *OECD Guidelines -- International Investment and Multinational Enterprises, Revised Edition*, OECD, Paris, 1984.

9. *Council Directive on the Annual Accounts and Consolidated Accounts of Banks and other Financial Institutions*, EEC, December 1986.

10. E29, "Disclosures in the Financial Statements of Banks", International Accounting Standards Committee.

11. "Proposals for International Convergence of Capital Measurement and Capital Standards -- Basle Committee on Banking Regulations and Supervisory Practices (Consultative Paper)", *Bank for International Settlements*, December 1987.

12. *Les nouveaux instruments financiers et le risque bancaire (Livre Blanc)*, Commission Bancaire -- Banque de France, March 1987.

13. Exposure Draft "Disclosures about Financial Instruments", Financial Accounting Standards Board, November 1987.

14. For details on the FASB Exposure Draft see in particular the contributions by D. Mosso and J. Goodfellow in the present publication.

15. *Harmonization of Accounting Standards -- Achievements and Prospects*, OECD, Paris, 1986.

ANALYSIS OF THE FACT SHEETS SENT IN ANSWER TO THE OECD SECRETARIAT IN JUNE-AUGUST 1987 ON OFF-BALANCE-SHEET ACCOUNTING PRACTICES

QUESTIONS	AUSTRALIA	AUSTRIA	CANADA	DENMARK	FINLAND	FRANCE	IRELAND	JAPAN	LUXEM-BOURG	NETHER-LANDS	SWITZER-LAND	UNITED KINGDOM	UNITED STATES
I. ALL ENTERPRISES: DISCLOSURE AND ACCOUNTING TREATMENT OF OFF-BALANCE-SHEET ITEMS													
· Are these items disclosed in the financial statements? (*)	Y	Y	Y			Y (4)	Y (5)	Y	Y	Y (6)	Y	Y	Y
· Are they disclosed below the line of the balance sheet?	N	Y (1)	N		N	Y		N		N	Y (8)	N	N
· Are they disclosed in the notes to the accounts?	Y	Y (2)	Y (3)	Y	Y	N	Y	Y		Y (7)	Y (8)	Y (9)	Y

* Financial statements are understood to include the notes to the accounts.

1. In one condensed figure. Partly: endorsements, guarantees, letters of credit.
2. Split up: endorsement, guarantees.
3. Where material.
4. Partially.
5. No mandatory requirement.
6. Partly; present requirements cover mainly traditional instruments.
7. There is a legal requirement to disclose important financial commitments that are not included in the balance sheet.
8. According to Art. 670 of the Obligations Code, endorsements and other guarantees should be mentioned in the statements or in notes, in an aggregate amount for each category.
9. Contingent liabilities and commitments for which no provision has been included in the balance sheet are required to be disclosed in notes to the accounts under SSAP18 and the Companies Act 1985. Contingent gains are only disclosed if it is probable that the gain will be realised.

QUESTIONS	AUSTRALIA	AUSTRIA	CANADA	DENMARK	FINLAND	FRANCE	IRELAND	JAPAN	LUXEM-BOURG	NETHER-LANDS	SWITZER-LAND	UNITED KINGDOM	UNITED STATES
. Is there a distinction made between:													
— Commitments resulting from an agreement?	Y (1)	N	Y (4)		Y	Y	Y	N	N	Y	N	Y (14)	Y
— Contingencies?	Y (1)	N	Y (4)		Y	N (6)	Y	N	N	Y	N	Y (14)	Y
II. BANKS: TYPOLOGY AND ACCOUNTING TREATMENT OF OFF-BALANCE-SHEET ITEMS													
1. Is there a distinction made between:													
— Contingent liabilities?	Y	Y (3)	Y (5)	Y	Y	Y	Y (8)	Y	Y	Y	Y (12)	Y (15)	Y
— Commitments?	Y	Y (3)	Y (5)	Y	Y	Y	Y (8)	N	Y	Y	Y	Y (15)	Y
— Foreign exchange, interest rates, other transactions?	Y	Y (3)	Y (5)	Y	Y	N (7)	Y (9)	N	Y	Y (11)	N (13)	Y (15)	Y
2. Regarding contingent liabilities, is there a distinction made between:													
— Guarantees?	Y (2)	Y (3)	Y (2)	N	Y	Y	N (10)	Y	Y	Y	Y	Y (16)	N (17)
— Acceptances and guarantees by endorsement?	Y (2)	Y (3)	Y (2)	N	Y	Y	N (10)	Y	Y	Y (2)	Y	Y (16)	N (17)

1. Clauses 2 and 22 of Schedule 7 of the companies regulations require companies to disclose separately commitments for expenditure and contingent liabilities, where those amounts are material.

2. Guarantees and bill endorsements are shown as contingent liabilities in the notes to the accounts or as an off-balance-sheet item as in the Netherlands, but in Australia this distinction applies only to reports submitted to the Reserve Bank of Australia. Bill acceptances are shown on the balance sheet.

3. This distinction only applies to reports submitted to the Austrian National Bank.

4. Section 3280 of the CICA Handbook covers commitments and Section 3290 covers contingencies.

5. Memorandum items accounting is used for these three categories of transactions. Letters of credit and guarantees must be reported in the footnotes of banks' financial statements.

6. Only written contingencies are reported.

7. These appear only on statements sent to the regulatory authorities.

8. In notes to the accounts.

9. Reference is made to the existence of these items but rarely to the amounts involved.

10. These are usually grouped under one total.

11. Internally, but not disclosed.

12. This distinction is made if Art. 24 of the Banking Law requests it.

13. These should be accounted for but not published.

14. Commitments for capital expenditure, unprovided pension commitments and other financial commitments (such as lease rentals, intra-group letters of support or forward purchases) are shown separately from contingencies.

15. Reference is usually made to the existence, but not the amount, of contingent liabilities and commitments arising in the normal course of banking business, including those from financial futures contracts, forward contracts for the purchase and sale of foreign currencies, option and swap contracts and other facilities to customers.

16. Guarantees are usually shown separately, and acceptances are generally quantified in a note to the accounts.

17. If a contingent liability is both probable and reasonably measurable, it must be included in the accounts. Otherwise only footnote disclosures (including the nature of the item) are required.

47

QUESTIONS	AUSTRALIA	AUSTRIA	CANADA	DENMARK	FINLAND	FRANCE	IRELAND	JAPAN	LUXEM-BOURG	NETHER-LANDS	SWITZER-LAND	UNITED KINGDOM	UNITED STATES
Is there a distinction made between:													
-- Customers?	N	N (3)	N	N (9)	N	Y	N	N	N	Y (17)	N	N	N
-- Financial intermediaries?	N	N	N	N	N	Y	N	N	N	Y (17)	N	N	N
3. Among commitments, is there a distinction made between:													
-- Confirmed credits?	N (1)	Y (4)	N (6)	(10)	Y	Y	N	N	Y	Y	N	Y (18)	Y (23)
-- Forward sales and purchases of assets?	N (1)	Y (5)	N (6)	(11)	Y	N	N	N	Y	Y (17)	N	Y (19)	Y (23)
-- The unpaid amounts on securities?	N (1)	Y (5)	N (6)		N	N	N	N	Y	Y	N	N (20)	Y (23)
Are note issuance facilities and revolving underwriting facilities commitments included among confirmed credits?	Y (5)		N (7)	(12)	Y	Y	Y (15)	N	N	Y		Y (21)	Y
4. Is there a distinction made between:													
-- Foreign exchange rate transactions?	N (2)	Y (5)	Y (8)	N (13)	Y	Y (14)	N (16)	N	Y	Y	N	Y (22)	Y
-- Interest rate transactions?	N (2)	Y (5)	Y (8)	N (13)	Y	Y (14)	N (16)	N	Y	Y (17)	N	Y (22)	Y

48

1. Generally not disclosed.

2. Generally not disclosed; however, some banks provide listed information on foreign exchange transactions.

3. Internal distinction for guarantees.

4. Only NIFs and RUFs.

5. This distinction applies only to reports submitted to the Austrian National Bank.

6. Distinctions are made internally, although forward sales and purchases of assets may be disclosed where material.

7. Memorandum accounting only. They are reported separately on regulatory returns. Public disclosure to date has been at the discretion of the banks.

8. Banks have internal accounting guidelines for each type of investment. Public disclosure to date has been at the discretion of banks.

9. None as regards accounting principles.

10. Unused parts are not booked.

11. Only rules for currency and funds, as these transactions are treated as analogous with forward transactions.

12. These are treated as guarantees.

13. Both types are treated as analogous with forward transactions provided that rules are laid down.

14. Only applicable to reports to regulatory authorities.

15. But the amount involved could not be identified separately.

16. The existence of newer financial instruments is referred to in the notes, but the extent of the activity is not identified.

17. Internally, but not disclosed.

18. Usually classified as a trading contingency but not disclosed separately from guarantees.

19. May be treated as on- or off-balance-sheet, depending on the terms of the transaction.

20. Would be reflected in a note on contingent liabilities if material.

21. Included under guarantees and similar obligations.

22. The existence but not the amount of foreign exchange transactions, where these are material, is evident from a note. Interest rate transactions are not normally mentioned. The majority of off-balance-sheet instruments can be divided into those related to exchange rates and those related to interest rates, but no separate disclosure is made.

23. If individually significant.

QUESTIONS	AUSTRALIA	AUSTRIA	CANADA	DENMARK	FINLAND	FRANCE	IRELAND	JAPAN	LUXEM- BOURG	NETHER- LANDS	SWITZER- LAND	UNITED KINGDOM	UNITED STATES
-- Other transactions?	(1)	N				Y	Y	N	N	Y	Y (10)	Y	Y (14)	Y (19)
Are forward foreign exchange transactions registered in the financial statements:														
-- At the spot rate?		Y (2)	Y (5)	(7)	Y	Y		N	N	Y (11)	Y (13)	Y (13)	N	Y (20)
-- At the forward rate?		N	Y (5)	(7)	N			Y (8)	N	Y	Y (12)	Y (13)	Y (15)	Y (21)
When registered at the spot rate, is the difference spread over the term of the commitment in the income statement?		Y (3)	N	(7)	Y	Y		N	N		Y	Y		Y (22)
For traditional currency swaps, is the premium spread over the swap arrangement period?	(1)	Y	Y		Y	Y		N	N	Y	Y	Y	Y (16)	Y
Is there a distinction made between pure currency swaps and hedging swaps?	(1)	Y (4)	Y (6)		N	N		Y (9)	N	N	Y	N	Y (17)	Y
-- For hedging swaps, is the gain (or loss) on the swap amortized over the life of the hedging transaction?		Y	Y		Y	N		Y	N		Y	Y	Y (17)	Y (23)
Is the accounting treatment different for hedging and trading interest rate swaps?	(1)	Y	Y		N	N		N	N		Y	N	Y (18)	Y

1. Generally not disclosed.

2. If different from spot rate stated according to period.

3. In principle, for outright transactions, losses are recorded in the income statement but profits are not.

4. Distinction only in internal reporting.

5. Generally, forward exchange contracts are valued using the current exchange rate, subject to appropriate adjustments to reflect the gain or loss in showing the forward unmatched positions. The adjustment should be calculated using a forward rate quoted in the market at the balance sheet date.

6. Gains and losses attributable to an economic hedge of a "net investment position" as a foreign operation should be charged on credit to re-tained earnings, as an offset to the gains and losses arising from the "net investment position".

7. A distinction is made for covered transactions.

8. Forward foreign exchange transactions are translated at appropriate forward rates of exchange, ruling out balance sheet data. Profits and losses arising from this translation are included in trading income. The amount involved would not be disclosed.

9. But the amount would not be disclosed. It is normal practice for banks to refer to their investment in swap activity but not to disclose the amount of turnover.

10. Internally, but not disclosed.

11. If relating to deposit swaps in connection with moneys invested and borrowed.

12. All other.

13. The general practice is to record in the accounts at the forward rate and to re-evaluate at balance sheet date at the spot rate.

14. Other banking transactions are mentioned but amounts are not disclosed.

15. With the exception of hedge transactions and deposit-linked swaps, forward rates are generally used.

16. Premium/discount (arbitrage) arising on deposit-linked swaps is taken to income over the life of the swap as interest income/expense.

17. Exchange differences relating to hedges are normally released to the profit-and-loss account so as to reflect the underlying hedge.

18. Trading swaps are either marked to market or accounted for using an accruals method.

19. Such as litigation claims, income tax disputes, and gain contingencies.

20. For a hedge transaction.

21. For a speculative transaction.

22. For hedges involving asset or liability position.

23. Recognised in income in the same way that the result of the change in currency rates is recognised in the hedge item.

QUESTIONS	AUSTRALIA	AUSTRIA	CANADA	DENMARK	FINLAND	FRANCE	IRELAND	JAPAN	LUXEMBOURG	NETHERLANDS	SWITZERLAND	UNITED KINGDOM	UNITED STATES
-- In the first case are they reported at their acquisition cost at the closing date of the balance sheet?		(1)	Y	(4)	N	N	Y (7)	N	(9)	Y	(11)	N (12)	Y
-- In the second case are they revalued at current value?	Y (2)		Y (4)	(4)	N	N	Y	N	(9)	Y	(11)	Y (13)	Y
5. Regarding futures, is there a distinction made between trading and hedging transactions?				Y (5)	N								
-- For trading transactions, is the gain or loss recorded in the income statement at the end of each intermediary period of accounting, following the mark-to-market principle?	Y		Y	Y (4)	N	Y	Y	N	(9)	Y	(11)	Y	Y (16)
-- For hedging transactions, is the gain or loss accounted for only when the position is unwound and amortized over the life of the hedging element?	Y		Y	(4)	N	Y	Y	N	(9)	Y	(11)	Y	Y
-- Are there specific criteria for a future to be deemed a "hedging" transaction?	Y	Y (3)	Y	(6)	N	Y	Y (8)	N	(9)	Y (10)	(11)	Y (14)	Y
-- Is the FRAs accounting treatment similar to that of futures?	Y		Y	(4)	Y	Y	Y	N	(9)	Y	(11)	Y (15)	Y (17)

52

1. For example, costs of own issues reduced by interest swap income.
2. Marked to market.
3. Internal criteria.
4. There are no established rules.
5. Covered futures are not included in the balance sheet. Uncovered futures are included analogous with uncovered forward transactions.
6. The covering rules are analogous with the covering rules for forward transactions.
7. Profits and losses are amortized alongside the underlying hedge transaction.
8. But not detailed. In general, a future would be considered a hedge when used to offset or unwind an exposure on position within the bank's own portfolios.
9. No existing rules at present.
10. Hedging as undertaken by the treasury department is usually macro-hedging to balance positions.
11. Not applicable.
12. Acquisition cost, if any, is deferred and spread over the period of the transaction.
13. Usually, but may also be accounted for using an accruals method.
14. A transaction is normally classified as a hedge if it satisfies the following criteria:
    a) Intent: the financial future should be intended and designated as a hedge and its purpose and timing identified and recorded at the time of the transaction;
    b) Correlation: there should be a high correlation between movements in the market value of the item hedged and the financial future;
    c) Certainty: there should be a reasonable expectation that where the financial future anticipates a commitment due to crystallise at some future date, the commitment will be fulfilled.
15. Not if the FRA transaction is speculative, in which case the discounted proceeds will usually be taken directly to the profit-and-loss account.
16. See FAS 80, para. 3.
17. See FAS 80, para. 4.

QUESTIONS	AUSTRALIA	AUSTRIA	CANADA	DENMARK	FINLAND	FRANCE	IRELAND	JAPAN	LUXEM-BOURG	NETHER-LANDS	SWITZER-LAND	UNITED KINGDOM	UNITED STATES
-- Is the accounting treatment for options similar to that for futures?	Y	Y (2)	Y	(5)	Y	Y	Y (7)	N	(9)	Y	n.a.	Y (11)	Y
-- Are foreign exchange options and interest rate options treated in a similar manner for accounting purposes?	Y	Y	Y	(5)	Y	Y	Y	N	(9)	Y	n.a.	Y	Y
III. BANKS: PROBLEMS OF FINANCIAL DISCLOSURE													
Is detailed disclosure of information required on the accounting principles used for:		(3)											
-- The accounting treatment of traditional off-balance-sheet commitments (including forward foreign exchange transactions)?	N (1)	N	(4)	N (6)	N	N	N (8)	N	N (10)	N	N	Y (12)	Y
-- The accounting treatment of new financial instruments such as:													
-- Swaps;		N	(4)	N	N	N	N (8)	N	N (10)	N	N	Y (12)	Y
-- Futures;		N	(4)	N	N	N	N (8)	N	N (10)	N	N	Y (12)	Y
-- Options?		N	(4)	N	N	N	N (8)	N	N (10)	N	N	Y (12)	Y

1. Banks generally provide a statement on translation of foreign currency amounts. However, little information is provided on off-balance-sheet business.

2. Like futures for hedging.

3. Treatment checked by external and internal auditors, but not disclosed so far.

4. Although not currently required by the regulatory authorities, accounting practices are generally disclosed when significant.

5. General rules have not been laid down. The inspectorate's annual guidance states that uncovered currency options are booked analogous with uncovered forward transactions, but in such a way that a currency forward transaction cannot be covered by a contrary currency option transaction.

6. Most contingent liabilities are included in the balance sheet.

7. Accounting policies are evolving in this area. Option risk is assessed on a mark-to-market basis with premiums being taken to the profit-and-loss account on a phased basis.

8. While reference to the accounting treatment is made, it would be erroneous to describe it as detailed.

9. No applicable rules.

10. Available for the information of authorities.

11. Options are normally marked to market. Alternatively, the premium on a foreign exchange option is released to the profit-and-loss account as the option is exercised or expires or as the position is closed out. In the case of an interest rate option, the premium is amortized over the maturity of the contract if the option is exercised or taken to income once it has expired.

12. For all items that are considered material in relation to the results for the year or on the financial position, accounting policies are required to be disclosed according to SSAP2. Where applicable, these would include off-balance-sheet commitments (including foreign exchange controls, swaps, financial futures and options). Where details are not published in financial statements, relevant information is made available to the regulatory authorities.

QUESTIONS	AUSTRALIA	AUSTRIA	CANADA	DENMARK	FINLAND	FRANCE	IRELAND	JAPAN	LUXEM-BOURG	NETHER-LANDS	SWITZER-LAND	UNITED KINGDOM	UNITED STATES
Are off-balance-sheet commitments detailed in the financial statements to be published?		(4)	N		Y	Y	Y (7)	N		N	Y	N (17)	Y
Is there a disclosure of:													
-- Contingent liabilities?	Y	Y	Y (5)	Y	Y	Y (11)		N	Y	Y (13)	Y	Y	Y (20)
-- Commitments?	N (1)	Y	Y (6)	Y	Y	Y (11)		N	Y	Y (14)	Y	Y	Y (21)
-- The commitments for:													
-- Forward currencies?	N	N	N (7)	Y	N	N		N	N	N	N	N (18)	Y
-- Currency swaps?	N	N	N (7)	N	N	N		N	N	N	N	N (18)	Y
-- Interest rate transactions?	N	N	N (7)	N	N	N		N	N	N	N	N (18)	Y
-- Futures?	N	N	N (7)	N	N	N		N	N	N	N	N (18)	Y
-- Options?	N	N	N (7)	N	N	N		N	N	N	N	N (18)	Y
Are the capital ratios disclosed?	N (2)	(3)	Y (8)	Y (10)	Y (10)			Y (12)	N	N (15)	N	Y (19)	N
Is there any disclosure of the global risks of foreign exchange exposure, of interest rate exposure, of liquidity exposure?	N	N	N (9)	N	N	N		N	N	N (16)	N	N	N

1. Most banks provide information on leasing and capital expenditure commitments. Some provide information on other commitments.

2. Some banks provide information in summary form.

3. Capital ratios can be calculated from the notes to the balance sheet.

4. Sometimes items are detailed in the notes; sometimes they are detailed in the analysis section of the report.

5. Letters of credit and guarantees are described in the notes.

6. Should be disclosed if significant in relation to the current financial position or future operations.

7. Sometimes there is coverage in the analysis section of the annual report (such disclosure is discretionary -- requirements for disclosure under review).

8. Such a disclosure is not a requirement of the regulatory authorities.

9. In some instances there may be a general discussion in the annual report.

10. Voluntarily in notes.

11. Contingent liabilities and commitments are usually grouped together.

12. Disclosed in annual reports.

13. At present, disclosure of the following amounts is required:
    -- Contingent liabilities on account of pledges and guarantees;
    -- Contingent liabilities on account of irrevocable letters of credit;
    -- Recourse liabilities in respect of bills discounted.

14. Off-balance-sheet disclosure requirements for banks concerning the amount of irrevocable commitments have recently been instituted.

15. However, monthly returns are provided to the supervisory authorities as a basis for solvency and liquidity tests.

16. All information except that relating to interest rate exposure is given to the supervisory authorities.

17. Details of off-balance-sheet commitments are generally restricted to footnote disclosures, usually including the total amounts of acceptances, and guarantees and similar obligations.

18. Although the extent of these commitments is not normally quantified, their existence is disclosed if the amounts are considered material.

19. While there is no requirement to disclose capital ratios, some banks provide certain key ratios by way of supplementary financial information.

20. FAS 5, paras. 10-12.

21. FAS 47, para. 7.

Chapter II

NEW FINANCIAL INSTRUMENTS: MAIN TRENDS AND ECONOMIC AND FINANCIAL POLICY IMPLICATIONS

THE IMPORTANCE OF NEW FINANCIAL INSTRUMENTS
FOR ACTIVITIES OF BANKS

by
David F. Lomax
Group Economic Adviser,
National Westminster Bank PLC

Introduction

The implications for the banking system of the new financial instruments have been profound, and the effects are still being felt. Indeed, the emergence of these instruments has forced a restructuring of banks and, in many cases, a complete reconsideration of their basic strategy.

The new financial instruments are mainly:

    i) Futures;

    ii) Options;

   iii) Swaps;

    iv) Note issuance facilities and revolving underwriting facilities;

    v) Forward rate agreements (FRAs); and

    vi) Commercial paper.

There has been no single reason for the creation of new instruments; they serve a wide range of purposes. A series of developments has created conditions that have transformed the financial instruments available in the marketplace.

New factors

It is difficult to identify any single factor as being the most important. Nevertheless, I am inclined to the view that changing technology may have had that role. In previous years we had seen the intensification of technological use in foreign exchange dealing rooms and in the treasury function. This created a large body of people with experience in handling this kind of financial transaction, together with the technology to effect the calculations quickly, accurately, and on a massive scale. This technology could be used at extremely low marginal cost to support new markets. In some fields the concepts of the markets were previously well-known, such as options or FRAs, but it was simply impractical to run a market on a significant and controlled scale before the computer hardware to support it was available.

A second pressure was the marketing and competitive structure of the banking industry. With the globalisation of international finance, many banks and innovative investment houses moved into other markets, taking their ideas with them. The mode of marketing in banking is in some fields through innovation. Those finance houses attempted to think of new products which they could take to their customers and use as the justification for being given their business.

The traditional relationship between a bank and its customer had been a one-to-one link, with the bank and the customer meeting across a table to negotiate a loan or some other deal. But in the new structure, the innovative finance house put itself between the bank and its customer, suggesting ideas to the customer, and expecting the banks to compete on price and quality to provide whatever financial instruments the customer wished. This new marketing structure thus accelerated the introduction of innovations, and at the same time forced more competitive pricing.

During the mid-1980s, the margins on wholesale business were reduced significantly. This stemmed from many factors. There was excess capital in banking, in particular as the Japanese banks benefitted from the enormous commercial success of Japan, and began to take their due place in the world banking scene. Corporate treasurers became increasingly concerned about price, and about being seen to obtain the best deal in the marketplace. They began to measure their success in pricing in terms of basis points, or hundreths of a per cent. The advent of new bankers in the marketplace and of extra capital in banking gave them plenty of scope for testing their bargaining.

During this period the banks were slowly coming under greater regulatory pressure, in particular as regards their capital ratios. This, combined with the low margins on wholesale business, led them to look to new sources of income, and preferably ones which were not on the balance sheet, and thus were not (at that time) subject to capital ratios. New financial instruments provided an excellent means of achieving both fee income and off-balance-sheet business.

Seeing the development of new markets, such as the futures markets in the United States, banks elsewhere supported the development of such markets as a means of achieving income, and hopefully of generating customer business.

Taken together these factors were fully adequate to generate a period of major innovation in the banking markets, which has also to some extent transformed the relationship between banks and their major customers.

The new instruments

What then are the qualities of the new instruments which led to their adoption? These innovations were of genuine importance in improving the quality of service available to the corporate sector and other financial customers. This improvement in service has been the underlying reason why the innovation has been sustained, and why the new instruments have become well-established. There are five main benefits from these new instruments:

i) They are cheaper. This condition may vary according to market circumstances, but instruments like commercial paper are likely to be cheaper than bank loans, partly because of their marketing structure, and partly because they bring into play a wider range of potential lenders or investors. Swaps in particular are, by their structure, almost certain to lead to a reduction in the cost of finance to borrowers;

ii) They make available a wider range of financial sources to the customer (or certain relatively unfamiliar markets may be tapped at a much lower cost than would otherwise be the case). This applies particularly to swaps, under which the participants borrow in the markets in which they have the greatest acceptability, and then swap the resulting financial commitments. A swap will not take place unless a financial gain is achieved, so all swaps lead to some combination of tapping wider markets and/or obtaining cheaper money. Thus, the archetypal swap between the World Bank and a Swiss corporation means that the World Bank obtains Swiss francs to an extent which might not easily have been available to it, together with low-cost Swiss franc financing, while the Swiss corporation obtains dollars at a rate much lower than it would otherwise be able to obtain;

iii) They provide instruments for hedging risk. This is the clear benefit of the futures markets, of the use of options, and of the use of FRAs. In the case of futures and FRAs, the customer is bound to a contract, and so may forgo a profit if the markets move in this favour. In the case of options, the customer pays a fee, and that is his greatest cost. If markets move against him, he may exercise the option and save himself the loss. If markets move in his favour, he may benefit from that movement, subject to the cost of the fee. With the recent volatility in interest rates and in particular in exchange rates, sophisticated companies have had to investigate far more closely the potential for hedging their risks;

iv) They may involve maturity transformation, thus improving the mix of cost and availability of funds. This applies in particular to note issuance facilities and revolving underwriting facilities, both of which combine periodic raising of funds at short-term interest rates with a commitment to the long-term availability of funds. The customer thus has the assurance of long-term availability, while being able to obtain the funds at a price associated with the interest rates in the short-term markets;

v) The new techniques may increase the liquidity of financial instruments, and thus widen the range of sources of finance. Again, this applies in particular to the various forms of securitisation, which means that a wide range of investors will be able to provide the finance, and not just the traditional banks.

The banks

The banks have thus had to adjust to a genuine and substantial change in the quality of instruments available to their customers. What are the business implications for banks of this sharp change in commercial conditions? To understand this point, it is necessary to realise that the exact question banks ask is not how they should cope with the new financial instruments. It is, rather, how they should decide which markets to be in, and how to be profitable in those markets, given the entire commercial background. In this regard, the dominant feature is in my view the extreme competitiveness of the wholesale markets, both the capital and banking markets. The first question a bank thus has to ask is whether it wishes to remain in those markets. Many substantial banks around the world appear to be deciding that they do not wish to be substantially in those markets, or if they are to be in those markets, they intend to be only in particular niches where they may be guaranteed an adequate profit.

For banks that decide to remain in the wholesale markets, having a full capability with these new instruments is absolutely vital to remain credible there. Nevertheless, that is by no means the whole picture.

The broad thrust of the competitive situation is that banks seek to differentiate themselves from each other, and to obtain prominent or lead positions, through acquiring special skills and strong positions in certain markets. Thus banks are acquiring skills in project finance, taxation and financial engineering, for example, which they make available to customers. Likewise, banks with certain competitive advantages, such as placing power or computer skills, will endeavour to obtain market positions based on their special strengths. Also, one should not ignore the importance to banks of obtaining profits from their traditional business in the capital and wholesale markets, such as bond and share issues, stockbroking, and foreign exchange trading. Maintaining a profitable presence in these traditional markets is as vital a matter as making the appropriate impact in the new markets. Nevertheless, a fully effective presence in the new markets is essential if banks are to be credible participants in the modern wholesale markets, and the banks' use of these markets takes several forms.

Banks' use of new instruments

Banks may use these markets for their own funding, to reduce the cost of funds and/or to tap additional markets. These functions are analogous to the use made of those markets by the corporate sector and other customers. In view of the narrow margins now available in the wholesale markets, any cost reductions which banks can achieve through this means are valuable, and in this field banks are as determined and aggressive as companies in obtaining reductions in their cost of funds.

Banks will provide these instruments to customers, as a customer service. Thus in approaching a borrower, or approaching a customer regarding any traditional service, banks will expect to have on offer the most sophisticated combination of instruments so as to satisfy the customer's requirements more effectively.

As a follow-up to this service, banks may create markets professionally in these new instruments. This is a source of income. It also enhances the quality of the markets available to customers, providing liquidity to those instruments. If banks did not make these markets, then the pricing to customers of instruments would be less keen, since the instruments would not be so liquid. Banks make markets in options, swaps, and FRAs, as well as in more traditional instruments.

Banks also use the instruments to hedge their own risks -- on the balance sheet, for instance. Moreover, in offering these new products to their customers, and in making a market in some of these products, banks are taking on new risks. These further risks also require protective action, and new instruments have to be used widely in hedging the bank against both traditional and non-traditional risks.

The banks may manage the infrastructure of a market, or help police it as part of the financial infrastructure. An example of this is the backing given by the London clearing banks to the London International Financial Futures Exchange (LIFFE), through the ownership of the International Commodities Clearing House (ICCH), as well as their being founder General Clearing Members (GCMs) of the Exchange.

In some cases these new instruments are intrinsically riskier and there can be no perfect hedges. This is very much the case where the hedging strategy has to be based on assumptions about the volatility of the market, and particularly the case with options. Moreover, hedging techniques may require assumptions about continuous pricing and the liquidity of the market, which may not be borne out in practice. The events of 19th October 1987 showed that many assumptions about volatility, continuous pricing and liquidity were considerably in error at the precise moment they were called into question. Banks which have made mistakes in assessing the fundamental characteristics of instruments, or in supervising their exposure in these markets, have suffered substantial losses. Nevertheless, banks are forced to operate in these riskier markets if they wish to be credible in wholesale business. It is therefore of vital importance that the established banks with a long-term perspective operate the strictest controls over the conduct of their own business.

Regulatory costs

A significantly greater consideration now for banks, as they structure their entire business, is the regulatory cost. The agreement at the Bank for International Settlements on the convergence proposals for capital supervision, combined in Europe with the expected proposals from the European

Commission, will create a mandatory framework for banks' prudential control. The ratios have already been set out in some detail as regards business on the balance sheet, and progress is being made regarding the ratios to apply to off-balance-sheet business. Banks will be assessed on both credit risk and position risk. These ratios will have influence over the minimum prices that banks will need to charge so as to cover their capital costs. The application of these controls on a continuing basis to sophisticated activity in a wide range of wholesale and capital markets will require a corresponding strengthening of the banks' control systems. Moreover, this development will also affect the character of the management of the banks, in the sense that greater continuing emphasis will have to be placed on monitoring a bank's positions and the business it undertakes.

At present there is a slowdown in the pace of innovation, for two main reasons. First, the major innovations of the greatest commercial advantage have probably been achieved in recent years, and there is less to aim for. Second, the existing new instruments have created a range of problems for banks, as regards setting up the internal technological infrastructure, creating viable business units, and in particular in establishing and maintaining effective controls. The market is thus now going through a phase of consolidation, which coincides with the slower activity in some of these securitised markets, following Black Monday of October 1987.

Relationship banking

The greatest pace of innovation in recent years coincided with the move of bank customers, and in particular of corporate treasurers, towards an attitude of requiring transaction banking, rather than relationship banking. Traditionally banks have had continuing relationships with their customers, based in part on the view that in most cases bankers are lenders of last resort to companies and would be called upon for finance in case of difficulty. This situation was seen markedly in the United Kingdom during the recession of the early 1980s. The traditional banking relationship has associated this underlying commitment of banks to their customers with companies providing them with a continuing range of business. But during the mid-1980s, that consideration moved into the background; companies became concerned far more with the pricing of individual transactions, and they would put business with whoever gave them the best price.

There is now a modest move back towards relationship banking, with banks making it clear that if they are to be expected to have a continuing commitment to companies, then they expect some form of continuing business. Moreover, companies have realised that they may obtain fully competitive prices, while still retaining links with a particular bank or with a group of banks. However, the links are less close than would have been the case, say, fifteen years ago. Furthermore, companies still expect the finest pricing, and so far little pricing advantage has been seen for banks in the new situation.

Conclusion

 I have so far discussed the impact of these new instruments on various forms of bank business. More fundamentally, banks are now having to reconsider their entire approach to the capital and wholesale markets. Banks have traditionally incorporated three elements in their business structure: a capital markets division or subsidiary, a treasury function, and a wholesale or corporate banking function. One of these elements has been both function- and market-oriented (the capital markets business), one has been function-oriented (treasury), and one has been marketing-orientated (wholesale lending). The previously clear distinctions between capital markets, treasury and wholesale business have now been eroded. Marketing to the corporate sector requires both capital market and treasury skills. At the same time, the instruments and the skills traded in the capital markets function and the treasury function now overlap to a very substantial extent -- in fact, a far greater extent than hitherto. There is no natural division between these phases of business, yet to pull them all into one could create other difficulties. At the same time, the restructuring of this element of business is likely to affect the entire internal structure of a bank, and thus lead to restructurings elsewhere. It is no exaggeration to say that the advent of new financial instruments has been part of a process which has precipitated major rethinking by banks, both of their strategic business direction and their own fundamental internal structure.

THE USE OF NEW FINANCIAL INSTRUMENTS BY NON-BANKING ENTERPRISES

by
John Grout
Director of Treasury, Cadbury Schweppes Co. Ltd;
Business and Industry Advisory Committee to the OECD (BIAC)

 To begin with, new financial instruments are not universal -- some companies deem them inappropriate or are simply unaware of them, or have not yet identified all the commercial and financial risks to which they are significantly exposed, let alone decided how to manage those risks. However, for those non-banks that do use new instruments, risk management is indeed a key motive.

 Most of these new financial instruments can be created from older instruments. Just as a forward exchange contract to buy a foreign currency can be proxied by buying spot and depositing the currency, so can an option be modelled by a suitably traded forward currency contract portfolio. In this case, though, there is a risk that the cost of trading that portfolio will be excessive, or that it will be impossible to trade at some time.

 Thus if a company estimates the notional cost of that risk and finds that a bank or other counterparty is willing to provide the option at an actual cost lower than the notional cost, it profits the company to buy the option -- the new product -- rather than use old-fashioned forward contracts to make a proxy for it. My own company uses a mathematical model that is different from those used by banks. It is less sensitive to short-term volatility. Therefore, we buy currency options when exchange volatility has been low (that is, when bank and traded options are low in cost) and generate them ourselves from the earlier instrument when volatility is high and bank or traded options are expensive.

A traded portfolio of forward exchange contracts entails various risks in relation to the banks we trade with and to the credit limits involved. The trading fits within our general trading-room and risk-control systems, which function in real time and for which accounting data is, at best, a back-check.

Generating the proxy of the option creates work for us -- trading a portfolio and monitoring bank credit limits -- and it leaves us with a risk of excessive costs. It is for this reason that many companies continue to buy options instead of modelling them.

My company uses options in much of its trading and financing, and considers them very good value for money. For example, as a chocolate confectioner, my company is engaged in a business with a high commodity content -- the commodity in this case being cocoa. Like our competitors, we must buy cocoa on world markets. The exchange rate at which we convert the world market cocoa price, which moves with a basket of currencies, into a functional currency is vitally important to our performance. We separate this currency aspect of cocoa purchasing from the management of the risk of the cocoa price moving in its basket of currencies. If we buy currency forward -- say a year -- today, we have certainty of that rate but we lose the possibility of getting a better rate. If our competitor waits a month and gets a better rate, we are disadvantaged. Of course he could wait two months -- or the whole year! If we wait, he could meanwhile lock into a better exchange rate. The only partial solution is the option -- or, more accurately, sets of options.

But if in modelling options we use forward currency contracts -- themselves a secondary product -- why don't we model the forward contracts by, for example, buying spot and depositing? The answer partly involves the relative liquidity of markets and differential buy/sell spreads. However, the most important reason is that if the purchased foreign currency is deposited, the deposit will appear on the corporate balance sheet -- and so will the borrowing of the other currency needed to pay for the foreign currency. Not only will this gross up the balance sheet, but there will be a credit exposure for the full sum on the bank with which the currency is deposited. If a forward exchange contract is entered into, nothing comes on to the balance sheet and the maximum credit risk with the bank is any profit derived from the contract at any time -- except on the day of delivery when there is full exposure.

Obviously, trading forward contracts to model currency options means building up very large offsetting positions which, using the underlying buy-and-deposit and borrow-and-sell methods, would quickly overwhelm the balance sheet.

This leads to an important point regarding financial reporting: if I had to disclose my currency positions and maturities, my competitors would be able to deduce quite a lot about my cocoa buying position -- which we regard as a key commercial secret.

Let us now turn to the subject of interest rate risk. This turns up in companies both in trading (examples are where capital goods or engineering projects involve long payment periods and contango in commodities trading) and in financing -- both debt and surplus funds management.

In the past, there were two ways of hedging interest rate risk: going out and issuing a bond or doing a borrowing for the interest period, or buying a bill or a bond for the period. To fix a rate in advance, one would have to do both -- for example, buying a three-month bill and issuing a six-month bill in order to fix a three-month rate starting in three months. This models a forward-forward agreement which has the advantage of not appearing on the balance sheet until the start of the target period. A forward rate agreement (FRA) has the advantage of being settled net in cash at the forward date, with the gross sums never appearing on the balance sheet at all.

By regularly creating new borrowings and investments, or forward rate agreements in proxy from them, one can model an interest rate option. If this is done for successive future periods, an interest rate cap or floor is modelled. This is scarcely possible using the underlying borrowing and deposits because of the huge balance sheet effects and the excessive trading costs (spreads) generated. The FRA and the interest rate option, cap and floor come into their own.

Using interest rate caps and floors, one is able to adjust trading and financing interest rate exposure regularly to a risk profile considered appropriate without involving the balance sheet.

The great advantage of the cap/floor is that it has the characteristic of an option: if it is in the money at the relevant date, it will pay out. If it is not it will not, but there is no further cost to the buyer.

On the other hand, the swap is an outright contract to exchange money flows. It is common to exchange the fixed interest on a notional principal for the floating interest on the same sum -- a simple interest rate swap. A currency swap can exchange flows in different currencies; like other outright contracts, they have to be traded if they are to model or provide a proxy for an option. In passing, I note that options on swaps ("swaptions") are now available.

We have used straight interest rate swaps at Cadbury Schweppes, but the company I was with previously made extensive use of mixed swaps -- for example, swapping fixed rate dollars for floating sterling.

However, swaps do more than exchange flows. By proxy, they enable a company without a strong credit standing or without the need to raise large sums in marketable securities to benefit from the availability of long-term bond market rates. They extend the possibilities available to the treasurer of the middle-sized company. Thus, a company needing to raise only as much medium-term money as it would take to purchase one bond issue -- say $100 million -- can take the rates applicable to five bond issues of $20 million each -- not a marketable amount -- while actually funding from short-term markets. Thus interest rate fixing is separate from the funding decision.

In the same way, it is possible to separate the nominal funding of the company from the assurance of liquidity by borrowing in short-term markets, such as commercial paper, bankers' acceptances or advances from a tender panel of banks, backed by assurance of liquidity from five- or seven-year standby multiple-option facilities.

The existence of swaps means that having taken fixed- from floating-rate flows, one can go back to floating rates by doing a reverse swap. There may be a gain or loss in this. However, because of the medium- to long-term nature of the swaps, doing this more than a couple of times soon builds up quite large credit exposure for the company, and as few companies mark large credit limits for banks, this is a considerable constraint.

Why do companies usually mark a much smaller credit limit for a bank than the bank marks for a company? The reason is that a company may deal with only a few banks -- perhaps a hundred all told. A bank, on the other hand, will have many clients. The portfolio effect is thus much greater for the banks, the riskiness of any one new commitment not materially changing the risk of the portfolio. A company does not benefit from this effect. This is reinforced by the lack of sectoral diversification for the company; all its counterparties are banks, while a bank has counterparties in many different areas of business. I also note that the number of banks of AAA credit status is now very small. Only the authorities maintain our confidence in the system as a whole.

In short, with the new financial instruments we are generally concerned with unbundling: separating market risks from credit risks, liquidity from interest rate risk or -- in the case of Cadbury's cocoa buying -- cocoa price risk from the associated currency risk. We then transfer the risk away from the company and on to other economic agents.

This is done more today than in the past for several reasons. First, in the United Kingdom, the lifting of exchange controls enabled companies to manage risks in new ways -- or, in some cases, to manage them (rather than simply respond to them) for the first time. Second, there is greater aware-ness of the risks of volatility and, in many countries, the risks of infla-tion. Third, the technology now exists for us to monitor both old risks and new risks introduced by hedging activities. Fourth, by assuming risk from others, a company can earn income for itself -- a different economic role, and I venture to suggest that here different accounting rules should apply.

Finally, there is pressure from the banks. Capital adequacy rules can add substantial costs. Therefore, banks tend to prefer less credit-exposed contracts or off-balance-sheet contracts with clients. They provide back-up lines of credit (note issuance facilities, revolving underwriting facilities, etc. for commercial paper issues, for example) rather than lending (disinter-mediation). As we have seen, they also engage in forward exchange agreements -- in respect of which the net difference is exchanged on maturity, not the gross currency amounts each way. Pressure also comes from banks in the form of pure salesmanship; new instrument varieties are fashioned with fancy names, sometimes at "zero cost" to the buyer. These are usually not worth-while, adding no value to what was there before, and often involve inefficient instruments such as out-of-the-money options.

The size of the market for the new instruments must not be under-estimated. The Economist of 28th May 1988 reports that $500 million of interest rate options and $10 billion of foreign exchange options are written daily by banks. These figures include interbank deals, but it is very impor-tant that 20 per cent of those foreign exchange options -- i.e. $2 billion daily -- were initiated by non-banks (compared with only 5 per cent of ordi-nary forward exchange contracts).

These instruments allow us to pass risks on to those -- specialists, banks or others -- who, rightly or wrongly, feel best able to handle them at any given time. They also permit us access, directly or by proxy, to markets we could not otherwise use. They contribute greatly to the efficient func-tioning of commerce.

ECONOMIC AND FINANCIAL POLICY IMPLICATIONS

by
Gavin Bingham
Monetary and Economic Department, Bank for International Settlements
(BIS)

"The business of banking ought to be simple; if it is hard it is wrong."
W. Bagehot

The proliferation of new financial instruments over what is now a span of decades raises a host of questions bearing upon economic and financial policy. The purpose of this paper is to set out some of the issues in a structured manner and to comment on them briefly (1). Accordingly, both the description of new products -- swaps, futures, contingency contracts like NIFs (note issuance facilities) and MOFs (multi-option facilities), warrants, options, etc. -- and the explanation of the reasons for their emergence are given short shrift. [Information on some of the new instruments, however, is provided in the annex tables (2).]

The issues are considered under three headings: efficiency, stability and equity, with a final section providing some observations on disclosure and information. There is, admittedly, considerable overlap between the three categories, but this taxonomy does help to focus attention on several basic questions relating to disclosure and accounting. Moreover, it permits the new financial products to be seen as reflections of some fairly broad and funda-mental changes taking place in financial markets, changes associated with technological progress, regulatory shifts, increased competition and greater internationalisation.

It may be useful to set out at the beginning two propositions under-lying much of the subsequent analysis. The first proposition is that the new financial instruments are, in fact, not all that new. Rather than constitut-ing completely novel products, most of them simply make it possible for finan-cial services to be provided in new combinations or at lower cost or by new institutions. A currency swap, for example, is very much like a back-to-back loan. And the assumption of contingent claims is the stuff and substance of classical commercial banking. Traditional commercial bankers have always stood ready to extend further credit to sound customers confronting unexpected liquidity needs, although this commitment has often not been explicitly embodied in a contract.

The second proposition is that even though the new products themselves may not be much different from earlier ones, they may set off a train of larger changes in the functioning of financial markets or in the management of risk that have far-reaching implications for efficiency, stability and equity. It is therefore essential to look beyond the specific instruments and to assess their impact on the overall operation of the financial system. It is here that Bagehot's dictum above becomes apposite. Managing the specific risk to which each individual new product relates may ultimately be fairly simple, but given the fact that the basic functioning of the financial market is altered, the business of banking is no longer as simple or straightforward as it once was. In particular, the dangers relating to the fallacy of composition and the illusion of liquidity grow as greater emphasis is given to actuarial methods when managing risk and to holding marketable assets when meeting liquidity needs.

1. Efficiency

A basic question that arises under this heading is whether the new financial instruments foster efficiency in the financial system and in the economy more generally. In this context, efficiency can be seen to have two dimensions, the first being whether the allocation of finance -- and indeed of labour, capital and other resources -- is "optimal" in some not necessarily well-defined sense, and the second being whether the allocative function is performed with the minimum claim on real resources.

There are a number of reasons for thinking that the new financial instruments promote allocative efficiency; most are linked with the propositions that pricing in the financial market is improved, that a wider range of products is available or, what amounts to much the same thing, that more contingencies can be managed. The impact of interest rate swaps is but one example of how these instruments result in better pricing. Swaps enable borrowers wanting fixed-rate funds and those wanting floating-rate funds to obtain finance more cheaply when the two parties enjoy specific comparative advantages in different markets. The gains generated by swap transactions are identical to those arising from trade in commodities. Not only are there obvious benefits for the individual participants (including the organiser who earns a fee), but the market also functions more efficiently in the sense that a single price tends to prevail for a common financial product.

New financial instruments may also improve pricing by increasing competition. For example, by lowering the cost of covering exchange risk, they make it easier to invest or borrow in previously inaccessible markets, thereby vastly extending the size of the marketplace. Greater competition also tends to compress the gap between borrowing and lending rates, which obviously benefits both creditors and debtors. In addition, it encourages the explicit market-related pricing of financial services that were sometimes previously provided free of charge. One further reason why keener competition and improved market access may promote efficiency is that success becomes less a function of the ability to lobby regulators and legislators and more one of the ability to meet the needs of customers. Particular institutions no longer enjoy near-monopoly powers in a stagnant market setting.

A final way in which new instruments may augment allocative efficiency and welfare is by making it easier to obtain a financial asset or liability that is closely tailored to the specific needs of the lender or the borrower. If, for example, borrowers can only obtain a standard product, they may have to curtail their investment or production because the risk or cost of their funding is then higher than it would otherwise be. Similarly, the new contracts allow the covering of risks that were previously "uninsurable" and facilitate the creation of synthetic products when appropriate ones cannot be found from among the enormous range now available.

There are, however, some arguments to the effect that financial innovation may be inimical to efficiency. Let us consider three. The first is that financial innovation and the more intense competition associated with it may distort resource allocation by leading to mispricing and imprudent credit decisions. The perpetual floating-rate note (FRN) market provides one example of the serious mispricing of some financial products. Moreover, keen competition between banks was one, although not the sole, cause of the massive build-up of LDC debt. The most dramatic recent illustration of prices being out of line with fundamental factors is the stock-market collapse. The size and speed of the correction constitute prima facie evidence that asset prices "overshot". Once again the new financial instruments were not the sole cause, but it is difficult to avoid the conclusion that they facilitated the overshooting, if only by lowering transactions costs and increasing the ease and speed with which financial prices can adjust compared with the prices of goods and production inputs such as labour.

The second argument is essentially physiocratic in inspiration and holds that resources are wasted when they are used to conduct financial transactions having no direct link either with production or with the process of saving and investment. Many of the new financial instruments or techniques are clearly derivative and appear to be only distantly related to the production of goods. In addition, novelty is sometimes largely illusory, with the essential features of the new instrument mimicking those of others available in the market. New instruments are on occasion little more than a marketing device or a means of circumventing proprietary claims laid by other market participants to a particular innovation. The assumption underlying this physiocratic argument, which often lurks behind some of the criticism of "short-termism", is that portfolio-churning, arbitrage and other "incestuous" financial transactions are basically redundant rather than being indispensable for the smooth and effective operation of the market.

A final reason for thinking that efficiency may be reduced by the new instruments stems from the proposition that they amplify instability in the financial system, a proposition considered at length in the following section. There are several ways in which greater instability may lower efficiency. For example, failures of banks and other intermediaries tend to deprive small borrowers of credit, at least temporarily. They are not able to tap securities markets directly and need time to establish new banking relationships. In the meantime they suffer from credit-rationing and may not be able to implement viable projects which in the presence of complete and reliable information would otherwise have been financed. Moreover, by undercutting the scope for discretionary monetary policy, the new financial instruments dull the edge of one of the major policy instruments used in the pursuit of the stability of prices and underlying economic conditions. If macro-economic policy is unable to ensure a stable overall environment, narrow financial decisions will be subject to uncertainty and, ultimately, error.

2. Stability

The basic question is whether the new financial products reduce or increase risk, particularly risk to the stability of the financial system as a whole. Here again a slew of arguments pro and con have been advanced. One of the reasons for thinking that risk has been reduced and stability promoted is simple and straightforward. A principal driving force behind the emergence of many of the new instruments has been the desire to improve risk management. Futures and options, for example, make it easier to hedge interest rate, exchange rate and other financial risks and were devised in response to increasing volatility of interest and exchange rates. To be sure, it can be argued that this was very much a second-best solution and that it would have been far better to have had more consistent and far-sighted economic policies, thereby obviating the need for the new products, but once interest and exchange rate risks had become a fact of life, the new instruments provided a means of dealing with them.

How do the new instruments augment stability? In the first place they allow equal and opposite risk positions to be offset. Take, for example, exporters in the United States and Germany which have equal and opposite open positions in Deutschmarks and dollars. Forward market operations between these two parties will reduce risk exposure both individually and in the aggregate. In other cases the new financial instruments do not eliminate risk but merely transfer it. Nonetheless, for the financial system as a whole this shift may be beneficial if risk is passed on to those who, because of superior information, larger reserves or holdings of negatively correlated claims, are better able to bear it. On the other hand, risk may sometimes be shifted to those who, because of a greater risk preference, are more willing to assume it but not necessarily better qualified to manage it.

In other words, the new instruments make it easier to manage some types of specific risk. They can be employed to reduce or increase risk exposure; in themselves they are neutral with respect to risk. As with any tool, whether they are harmful or useful depends upon how they are used.

By easing access to new markets and broadening the range of activities undertaken by financial market participants, the new instruments facilitate, if they do not automatically generate, greater portfolio diversification, which can on the whole be expected to reduce risk. This is offset, at least to some degree, by the fact that ease of access to new markets may allow financial intermediaries to shift business to centres where regulation is minimal and the potential for disruption greater. Moreover, greater financial integration causes shocks to spread more widely and more quickly from one market to another and from one country to another.

However, the meagre available evidence on the October 1987 stock-market break suggests that despite some repatriation of capital, explicit cross-border transactions were not the principal channel for the transmission of the shocks to each and every equity market. Instead, parallel decisions by entities increasingly affected by similar events and sensitive to price signals in foreign markets appear to have been a more important cause of the simultaneous and large corrections of prices on the world's stock exchanges.

In some countries, the new financial products may nonetheless have increased interaction between different and formerly independent markets which were stable in isolation but not when joined. The interaction of portfolio insurance with arbitrage between spot and stock index futures markets having different and ultimately incompatible rules and institutions is believed to have been one of the factors contributing to the size and speed of the equity price collapse in the United States, though not in other countries.

The mispricing of financial products generated by intense competition in unfamiliar areas, which may hamper efficient resource allocation, can also increase risk. This can occur in essentially two interrelated ways. Firstly, the pricing of the individual financial instruments may not reflect the risk/return configuration associated with the particular asset. Secondly, the profitability of financial institutions may be squeezed so much that they are unable to set aside the reserves they require or to raise additional equity capital. Narrower margins in themselves do not necessarily denote mispricing. If lower returns are associated with lower risk, owing in part to greater scope for managing risk with the aid of the new financial products, neither the institutions nor the financial system are endangered by compressed profits. However, by preventing the build-up of reserves and capital, lower profits may reduce the ability of banks and other institutions to withstand unexpected shocks. Many of the new instruments improve the capacity of institutions to manage individual types of risk -- e.g. exchange rate or interest rate exposure risk -- but they may make the management of the aggregate risk faced by the institution more difficult. This is because the interlinkages between individual types of risk become more complex and possibly more volatile.

A noteworthy feature of many of the new financial products is solid reliance on actuarial or probabilistic techniques for managing risk. This marks a significant shift in the relative importance of the various ways in which banks and other financial institutions contend with risk. Although there has always been a clear actuarial dimension to banking in that reserves are held against bad debts and to meet liquidity needs, bankers have traditionally relied heavily on credit analysis and continuous monitoring and control. In other words, they have reduced risk by collecting and processing proprietary information on specific customers that is not available to the market. The greater emphasis given by banks to risk management through diversification is a reflection of a larger trend: the homogenisation of financial business in general. The distinction has become hazy not only between different types of banks or between banking and securities market activities but also between insurance, banking and capital market activity.

In this environment diversification has an important role to play in managing risk, but its limits should be recognised. Firstly, there are some types of risk that are not diversifiable. Shocks that have an identical impact on all entities cannot be managed by diversification alone; it is essential to hold adequate reserves to absorb not only the virtually inevitable and actuarially predicted losses affecting specific items in the portfolio but also the losses arising from unexpected general shocks. Secondly, managing risk through probabilistic methods is complicated by discontinuities, and these occur with greater frequency when the financial system is evolving and new instruments are emerging. Thirdly, diversification should not supplant risk management procedures based on the acquisition of information and the putting in place of monitoring systems and incentives to discourage highly risky actions.

Another way in which financial innovation has a bearing on stability is by altering liquidity management strategies. Although it is extremely difficult to sell some customised financial products in the secondary market, on balance financial innovation has, by lowering transactions costs, stimulated the growth of the markets for negotiable paper -- a trend sometimes referred to as "securitisation". This in turn has meant that liquidity needs are today met by holding not only cash and portfolios of claims whose cash flows correspond to the expected pattern of payments, but also assets which the holder believes can be sold quickly, easily and at low cost. In such conditions, the continued functioning of secondary markets is essential for the maintenance of liquidity.

As risk management comes to depend increasingly on probabilistic techniques, and liquidity on the presumed ability to sell claims in secondary markets, it becomes more and more important to avoid the fallacy of composition. The new techniques that may provide adequate protection for the individual cannot protect the system as a whole. For example, liquidity will prove ephemeral if all agents attempt to sell their asset holdings simultaneously on the secondary market, and the purported protection of a diversified portfolio will vanish if herd instincts predominate. What works for the individual does not necessarily work for the system. The turbulence in the financial market in 1987 has demonstrated the illusory nature of secondary market liquidity and the potential folly of relying excessively on diversification to mitigate risk.

3. Equity

Three issues arise under the heading of equity and fairness: investor protection, insider trading, and the "level playing field" proposition.

To consider investor protection first, a distinction should be made between the small saver with a modest portfolio and possibly only sporadic interest in its management, and the large institutional investor whose principal vocation is asset management. By making it easier for small and unsophisticated investors to enter new and unfamiliar markets and to assume unknown and potentially substantial risks, the new financial instruments may have increased the need for investor protection. For example, small investors sometimes use the futures exchanges for speculative position-taking, whereas large investors often use them for implementing hedging strategies. In any case, institutional investors should have greater capacity and incentives to look after their own interests. In their case, caveat emptor is a reasonable precept.

Recent regulatory decisions seem to take this fact into account. For example, one of the main concerns of the new financial services legislation in the United Kingdom was the protection of unsophisticated investors, while wholesale markets in which large institutional investors operate are exempt from some of its provisions. Moreover, largely because such cross-border financial business is dominated by banks and other institutions, investor protection as such is conspicuous by its absence from the agenda for international harmonization.

The question of insider trading is somewhat different and affects all investors, large and small, dealing with financial market intermediaries. As far as efficiency is concerned, insider trading has several somewhat opposing consequences. To the extent that it causes previously private information to be embodied in the price of the financial asset more quickly than it otherwise would be, it promotes efficiency. But to the extent that it entails price-rigging and market manipulation, it may reduce efficiency. In addition, by undermining the confidence of investors and "outsiders", it may discourage participants from entering the market, thereby reducing liquidity and potentially raising costs.

The insider question can be viewed as essentially one of fiduciary responsibility and proprietary rights. To what extent can and should an agent take advantage of his principal? To what extent does the buyer have a proprietary claim on the information on which his decisions are based? One normative answer is that in no circumstances should the agent exploit the information he obtains directly or indirectly. Another answer is that insider trading benefits may be given to the broker or agent by the principal in lieu of a fee. The principal, by implicitly sanctioning insider trading, may even subsequently gain by receiving advice that reflects the agent's privileged access to information in other areas. While there is no simple solution to the problem, in part because the distinction between proprietary and public information is so blurred, attempts have recently been made in a number of countries to place limits on the scope for insider trading largely because it easily shades into fraud.

A final question relating to equity and fairness is how to make sure that different types of financial intermediaries are treated in an even-handed manner. There is both a domestic and an international dimension to this question, but the basic idea in both areas is to balance rights and obligations so that no particular institution or class of institution is seriously disadvantaged. The gradual relaxation of restrictions on the type of business in which financial institutions can engage (reflected in the slow but certain disintegration of the commercial/investment banking distinction in the United States and Japan) and on the range of markets in which business can be conducted (reflected in the abolition or relaxation of exchange controls in almost all developed countries) shows that officially sanctioned barriers to entry are ceasing to be a source of quasi-monopoly profits and that equal treatment in different markets is increasingly topical.

It should be recognised that in these conditions national authorities sometimes act to promote the interests of their own domestic institutions in international markets. This has been reflected in the recent wider use of reciprocity clauses in place of the more general "national treatment" provisions of the OECD Codes. While reciprocity may bring about fair and equal treatment bilaterally and can be used to pry open markets that would otherwise remain closed to international competition, it can also create a complex network of subtle inequalities on a multilateral plane. The principle of national treatment is intended to guarantee equality within a particular jurisdiction, but it can give rise to differential advantages for different types of financial institution operating from different home countries. For example, the principle of national treatment will allow a Japanese securities house to conduct both banking and securities business in Germany (as long as it obtains a banking licence), whereas a German bank with a Japanese banking permit will not be able to conduct securities business directly in Japan but will have to do it through a subsidiary.

Partly because there is a tendency for business to migrate to the least regulated markets, it is important to attempt to forge certain minimum rules, at least in the major markets. It is worth noting in this context that a certain type of regulation, namely that which fosters the integrity of the market without at the same time greatly restricting freedom of manoeuvre, is positively welcomed by those subject to regulation.

4. Disclosure

How does disclosure relate to this broad range of economic and financial policy issues? Clearly it has an important role to play in promoting the transparency of the market. By ensuring that an adequate amount of reliable information is available to interested parties, disclosure fosters market efficiency. Secondly, disclosure facilitates risk assessment. It helps market participants and regulators to cut through the acronyms and novel packaging to the basic principles underlying the new instruments. Acting to guarantee that such information is available through various disclosure requirements is not, moreover, an idle endeavour, because many of the new activities are off-balance-sheet and outside the purview of established accounting and disclosure conventions. In addition, disclosure can help to prevent problems by encouraging managements to put in place comprehensive monitoring and control systems. A sine qua non for disclosing information to either regulators or markets is collecting it, and often such information, even though initially compiled only with reluctance, can be put to good use within the financial institution.

Disclosure also has a bearing on the question of the international competitiveness of different financial centres. It is costly to provide information to the financial markets or regulatory authorities, and issuers sometimes bypass markets with strict disclosure requirements, preferring those with less onerous ones. Lenient disclosure requirements for issuance and listing are one reason why the Euro-bond market has grown so rapidly during the current decade, but also one reason why issuing activity in that market is in effect restricted to large and well-known borrowers.

Disclosure should not be seen as a panacea for all the problems discussed above. For example, when the new products alter the functioning of the entire financial system by increasing interdependence among various markets and by encouraging reliance on the sale of assets in secondary markets to meet liquidity needs, disclosure of the internal affairs of individual firms will in itself do little to prevent action by virtually all market participants almost simultaneously. Avoiding the fallacy of composition becomes essential for minimising the threat of financial instability. Disclosure has a role to play, but it is necessary to supplement it both with other regulations and with consistent and co-ordinated macro-economic policy.

NOTES AND REFERENCES

1. The author thanks J.S. Alworth, C. Borio, C. Butler, M.G. Dealtry, H.W. Mayer and P.F. O'Brien for their helpful and perceptive comments.

2. The tables are taken from H. Bockelmann, <u>Die neuen Finanzinstrumente -- Chancen und Risiken</u>, Colloque du Groupement International pour l'Etude des Problèmes de l'Epargne, Zurich, 20th May 1988.

Table 1

NEW FINANCIAL INSTRUMENTS IN INTEREST RATES AND FOREIGN EXCHANGE

Instrument	Date of first appearance	Date of market maturity	Trading volume or new contracts, 1987 (transactions in millions)	Outstanding positions or open interest at end-1987 (in billions of dollars)	Intermediaries (arrangers)
FUTURES					
Foreign currency on exchanges	1973	1979-81	20.5 (1)	11.9 (1)	Organised exchanges
Interest rate on exchanges	1975	1979-81	97.5 (1)	345.6 (1)	Organised exchanges
Equity indices	1981	1983-84	25.5 (1)	17.2 (1)	
Forward rate agreements	Early 1980s	1985-86	n.a.	n.a.	Commercial banks
OPTIONS					
Foreign currency, traded on exchanges	1978 (2); 1982 (3)	1985-86	7.0 (1)	32.1 (1)	Organised exchanges
Interest rate, traded on exchanges	1980 (2); 1985 (3)	1986	23.3 (1)	115.7 (1)	Organised exchanges
Over-the-counter foreign currency options	Existed for many years	1984-85	3.1 (4)	n.a.	Commercial and investment banks
Over-the-counter interest rate options	Existed for many years	1984-85	n.a.	n.a.	Commercial and investment banks
SWAPS					
Foreign currency swaps (5)	Late 1970s	1982-83	40-45 (e) (6)	100-150 (e)	Commercial and investment banks
Interest rate swaps (7)	Late 1970s	1982-83	224.0	675.0	Commercial and investment banks

(e): BIS estimate.   n.a.: not available.

1. On US exchanges only.
2. Netherlands.
3. United States and elsewhere.
4. Source: Federal Reserve Bank of New York: Summary of Results of US Futures Foreign Exchange Market Turnover Survey in March 1986. Sales of foreign currency options over the counter reported by 123 banking institutions and 13 non-bank financial institutions. Over-the-counter purchases were equal to $5.2 billion.
5. Source: Bank of England, Quarterly Bulletin (february 1987).
6. Swaps arranged during 1986, in billions of US dollars.
7. Value of notional principal amounts of interest rate and currency swaps reported by domestic US banks (world-wide consolidated) in billions of US dollars. Positions may be double-counted. (Source: US Call Report).

Table 2

INTERNATIONAL CREDIT AND CAPITAL MARKETS

Instrument	Date of first appearance	Date of market maturity	New facilities arranged or securities issued during 1987 (in billions of dollars)	Amounts outstanding at end-1987 (in billions of dollars)	Intermediaries (arrangers)
Syndicated Euro-credits	Late 1960s	mid-1970s	87.9 (1)	250-300 (e)	Commercial banks (as lenders)
Euro-notes/Euro-commercial paper (2)	Late 1970s	1982-83	70.2 (1)	52.7 (3)	Investment and commercial banks
Fixed-rate bonds (4)	Late 1960s	mid-1980s	120.3 (1)	686.0 (e)	Investment and commercial banks
Floating-rate notes	1970s, but revised in early 1980s	1982-83	12.0 (1)	156.0 (e)	Commercial banks (investment banks)
Equity-related bonds (5) and Euro-equity	Early/mid-1960s or early/mid-1980s	1986	43.3	119.0 (e)	Investment and commercial banks
Securitised loans (pass-through mortgage-backed securities in the United States)	1970s	mid-1970s	148.6 (a)	641.2 (6)	Specialised institutions
Private securitised debt (collateralised mortgage obligations in the United States)	1986	Still developing	n.a.	20.0 (e)	Investment and commercial banks (insurance companies)

(e): BIS estimate.   n.a.: not available.   (a): first three quarters at annual rate.

1. Source: Bank of England.
2. Total fixed-rate international bonds (Euro-bonds plus foreign bonds), including partly paid issues as well as zero-coupon and dual-currency bonds but excluding equity-related bonds.
3. Underwritten and non-underwritten promissory notes issued in the international markets, including medium-term notes.
4. Convertible bonds and bonds with equity warrants.
5. Source: Federal Reserve Bulletin. End of third quarter 1987.
6. Source: Euroclear.

Source: Unless otherwise stated, various BIS publications.

Chapter III

NEW FINANCIAL INSTRUMENTS: CHARACTERISTICS, INFORMATION NEEDS AND ACCOUNTING IMPLICATIONS

SUMMARY

by
Pieter Wessel
Adviser, Ministry of Justice
(Netherlands)

The most important conclusion one could arrive at after having heard the speeches by the various experts in the field of new financial instruments is that in fact there is nothing particularly new and that the issue is not connected with financial institutions only. Engaging in economic activities has always been closely connected with risk-taking. A manufacturing company normally has to invest in plant, machinery, stocks, etc. This constitutes a risk because it is by no means certain that customers will buy the company's products. Where prices of, say, raw materials fluctuate considerably, it has always been quite common for enterprises to hedge against that special type of risk by entering into forward contracts if possible, the risk being completely eliminated as soon as the open position, the exposure, is reduced to nil.

Recent macro-economic developments, especially in the financial sector, have created new risks for enterprises or increased existing risks. The reason for this was the high volatility of both interest and foreign exchange rates. For many enterprises it was no longer good business practice "to suffer the slings and arrows of outrageous fortune". Therefore, management looked for ways and means to have the enterprise relieved of that additional burden. Moreover, the development of new financial instruments gave users the possibility of access to financial markets that previously were not available to them, thus resulting in lower financing costs.

Gradually, quite an arsenal of financial instruments has been built up by intermediaries responding to customers' needs. Where such intermediaries did not react swiftly or flexibly enough or were too expensive, a tendency to disintermediation sometimes occurred; the bigger corporations became active on the financial markets themselves where this was technically possible. The banks and other financial intermediaries became functionally the place where the various risks the enterprises wished to divest themselves of are pooled.

The emergence of new financial instruments led to greater efficiency, stability and fairness in the financial markets, but it cannot be denied that they also caused new problems in these areas, such as mispricing owing to lack of proper understanding of the nature of various new instruments or pressure from increased competition.

It was pointed out that new financial instruments are often combinations of elements of already existing ones, and that in order to understand them well one should unbundle their component parts and risk elements. In the beginning there was considerable secrecy regarding the particularities of many of the various new financial instruments, but gradually a more open attitude started to prevail. The sophisticated user can now choose between tailor-made combinations of old and new products, although the majority will use the standard versions available.

The new financial instruments, of which there are now some five hundred species, can be categorised as:

-- First tier instruments, such as futures, options and swaps; and

-- Second tier instruments -- the more innovative versions -- which are developments of first tier instruments, transfers of structures used in one market to another market, or refinements of traditional instruments, such as forward contracts and transferable loan facilities, to meet specific market needs.

Gradually over this decade, the volume of the new financial instruments grew to such proportions that supervisory authorities and organisations of dealers felt compelled to react by means of new regulatory activities in areas such as market operation, management and control structures, and accounting and disclosure aspects. With regard to these regulatory activities, a number of steps have been taken in some countries, particularly in France, whereas efforts are under way in the United Kingdom and the United States. However, scientifically structured economic research, education and training are perhaps issues even more important than standard-setting.

With regard to accounting for new financial instruments, as unbundled, it was pointed out that the following fundamental principles should be applied to the component parts:

-- Substance over form (unbundling as mentioned);

-- Matching or accrual, to be applied to the income and expenses, as otherwise results could be manipulated;

-- Prudence, i.e. a neutral, down-to-earth approach;

-- Consistency.

In the field of accounting, the following problem areas were identified:

-- Individual or collective valuation of (groups of) financial instruments and other related assets and liabilities;

-- Netting of gains and losses;

-- Distinction between realised and unrealised as applied to gains and also with respect to losses;

-- Distinction between hedging and trading operations, if indeed necessary.

With respect to valuation, the prevailing trend appears to be the mark-to-market approach (current values). In the end this could also affect the approach to the valuation of other balance sheet items, such as long-term loans and tangible fixed assets, and the delimitation of the profit concept. Others have pointed out that in a thin market, it is sometimes difficult to judge the reliability of the market price, while estimates arrived at by means of models will often be coloured by sentiment. "Current value accounting should not be allowed to add respectability to imprudence."

It was repeatedly stressed that narrative disclosure on the impact of new financial instruments, supplemented to some extent by quantitative information, would facilitate the assessment of the risks incurred.

It should be realised, however, that this approach too has its limitations. The narrative must be relevant and on the other hand, enterprises will often be hesitant to disclose too much about the risks they run -- which after all, if properly managed, contribute to their profits.

Perhaps, as it was pointed out, a period of experimentation is required to establish the appropriate form, and improved disclosure on the new financial instruments will go hand in hand with improved disclosure on the traditional on-balance-sheet instruments.

In the future, it may well be that the income statement (as one of the truly future-oriented financial statements) of non-banks as well as banks will be completely risk-oriented, i.e. source-oriented in the very sense of the word. The most comprehensive catalogue of risks identified during this part of the Symposium includes:

-- Pure operating risk connected with the enterprise's business purpose;

-- Interest rate risk;

-- Foreign exchange risk;

-- Liquidity risk;

-- Credit risk;

-- Cross-border risk;

-- Legal risk and tax implications risk.

Such financial statements would constitute a giant step forward to the purely economically oriented financial statements, to the liberation of reporting from its legal, historical handcuffs -- a decisive step forward "devoutly to be wished" for the benefit of all parties having a legitimate interest in financial statements, such as investors, employees, creditors, governments, etc.

1. FUTURES AND OPTIONS

by
Gérard de la Martinière
Chairman, Chambre de compensation des instruments financiers de Paris
(France)

This paper describes briefly the irruption of futures and options into
the French financial landscape, and the implications thereof.

Financial futures were recently introduced in France in a standardized
and tradable form. Futures had long been traded on the commodities exchange,
but the new market in financial futures, modelled on the markets in the United
States and the United Kingdom, was launched by the French financial pro-
fessions (banks, stockbrokers, money-brokers, insurers, etc.). These new
financial instruments comprise:

-- Futures contracts based on a notional government bond [introduced in
   the financial futures market, the Marché à terme des instruments
   financiers (MATIF) on 20th February 1986];

-- Share options [introduced in the traded share options market, the
   Marché des options négociables de Paris (MONEP) on 10th September
   1987];

-- Futures options (introduced in the MATIF on 14th January 1988).

These new financial instruments have developed very rapidly. Although
France was the first country to launch them in continental Europe, it did so
much later than the United Kingdom and the United States; however, it is
making great efforts to catch up, as the following description of the new instruments shows:

1. For the ten categories of share options, approximately 10 000 blocks
   have been traded a day, and 140 000 positions taken;

2. The future on a notional government bond with a 10 per cent coupon is
   an instrument for managing the risk attached to long-term interest
   rates. Contracts are deliverable at maturity at a price set with
   reference to underlying and similar government bonds that have
   actually been issued. In 1986 1.6 million contracts were traded
   (outstripping all other new products in the world that year) and in
   1987 12 million contracts were traded again (more than any other product in the world that year in terms of growth in activity, achieving
   third position for long bond contracts, behind the Chicago Treasury
   Bond and the Tokyo Japanese Governmental Bond). These futures contracts were used extensively to hedge or manage bond risks when world
   interest rates came under heavy pressure during the period August-
   November 1987, and it was acknowledged at the time that they had
   performed very satisfactorily. A hundred thousand contracts, worth
   FF 50 billion, or four times the value of the total bond market, were
   traded every day during this period. Up to 200 000 positions were
   taken, worth FF 100 billion, which was equivalent on average to a

third of the value of the positions on the Chicago Treasury Bond. The market has calmed down in 1988, but 50 000 contracts, worth FF 25 billion, are still being traded every day;

3. The options are based on the notional government bond future contract. They include a right to buy or sell a notional government bond future at a prearranged price. Positions are hedged by means of futures and options, with the deposit calculated on the basis of what the market value of the portfolio would be if it were liquidated instantaneously. Market makers are required to post their prices and to deliver at the prices posted. Options have clearly been a success, with 15 000 contracts a day and 170 000 positions taken.

These developments have been accompanied, or even anticipated, by over-the-counter trading in:

-- Notional government bond contracts: Continuous trading has been regularised since February 1988 by the introduction of a provision whereby transactions taking place outside normal trading hours must be registered;

-- Options: Over-the-counter trading in options started in April 1986; it expanded considerably during the Autumn of 1987, but there were considerable risks owing to the fact that contracts were not registered or offset;

-- Contracts based on the Paris Interbank Offered Rate (PIBOR): Interbank dealing in these contracts was launched at the end of 1987, moving to the official market in September 1988.

Extensive use is made of these tradable instruments by: members (major bank and financial institutions) acting on their own behalf, who account for approximately one third of transactions; non-member financial intermediaries and their clients, accounting for between one quarter and one half of transactions; collective investment funds [Organismes de placement collectif en valeurs mobilières -- (OPCVM)], accounting for between one eighth and one quarter; and non-financial companies (up to 15 per cent). The volume of transactions by non-residents is increasing steadily, and now accounts for about one tenth of total transactions.

Tax and accounting regulations have adapted remarkably quickly to these new instruments. Work on drawing up new accounting standards for futures began in March 1986. The opinion of the Conseil national de la comptabilité (CNC) was delivered on 9th July 1986 and adopted as a banking rule in September 1986. The CNC also handed down an opinion on options on 10th July 1987.

The solutions adopted were simple but audacious -- simple because they laid down the basic rule that transactions should be valued at market prices, but made a narrowly defined exception for hedging, which is the basic purpose of financial futures; audacious because they laid down that valuation at market prices should be applied as a general principle. An effort was also made to bring tax and accounting rules closer into line with one another. The first Tax Act on 31st December 1985 was passed before the accounting standards came into force, and was ill-adapted to the new instruments. The new Tax Act of 17th May 1985 therefore stipulated that transactions should be valued at market prices, and made some provision for hedges in tax law (the possibility of carry-overs and symmetrical positions).

Notwithstanding the substantial progress that has been made, much still remains to be done. Commercial law needs to be amended to take account of the new instruments, and work should continue to close existing gaps in accounting law and tax law. Lastly, efforts to achieve international harmonization should be continued.

Apart from the field of accounting, it is also necessary to improve information about the new financial instruments, but without focusing too closely on one particular area, and to improve assessment of risk exposure (position limits, danger thresholds, crisis-scenarios, etc.). Lastly, internal auditing and external auditing need to be improved.

2. INTEREST RATE AND CURRENCY SWAPS

by
Malcolm Walley
Barclays de Zoete Wedd Ltd;
Board Member of the International Swap Dealers Association

A. Introduction

"In 1987 the swap industry has come of age". These were the words of Patrick de Saint-Aignan of Morgan Stanley and retiring Chairman of the International Swap Dealers Association (ISDA) at its annual conference in February 1988. In support of his assertion he cited several pieces of evidence:

-- Commodity pricing at levels that may not cover all costs or provide an adequate return;

-- Standardization of documentation;

-- De-emphasis of the commodity end of the business in favour of value-added, customised transactions;

-- Diversification of dealers into related products;

-- Fewer new market entrants and gradual concentration of business.

In this report I shall discuss the characteristics and accounting implications of swaps -- a product which has exhibited a phenomenal growth in market volume since the first well-publicised transactions in the early 1980s.

I shall begin with a brief historical review of the development of the product and its market, and a definition of the structure and mechanics of both interest rate and currency swaps, together with the rationale for their use by the principal participants -- users and intermediaries. I shall then discuss the accounting problems that such transactions present. Finally, after a brief examination of the accounting/statutory framework, I shall propose accounting procedures and policies which will ensure that financial accounts appropriately reflect their economic substance.

B. Historical review

The year 1973 saw the real beginning of the present environment of high volatility in exchange rates and interest rates. One key influence was the profound change of the Bretton Woods Agreement in that year with the introduction of floating exchange rates. Other factors adding volatility to the financial markets were the quadrupling of oil prices in the Winter of 1973/74, the arrival of double-figure inflation, deficit financing and unemployment.

These were followed in the early 1980s by the ascendancy of debt securitisation over syndicated lending, which developed out of the Latin-American debt crisis and the consequent pressure on banks' capital ratios.

Thus the stage was set for the arrival of the swap transaction, as a tool to hedge interest rate and currency exposure and to enable borrower arbitrage between capital markets, providing lower borrowing costs and access to currencies not previously available.

The first major and well-publicised swap transaction was the now-legendary currency swap between the World Bank and IBM in August 1981. Since then, the growth in the technical development and market volume of swaps has been truly exponential!

For an indication of the size and composition of the swap market today, please refer to the Annex, which contains statistical data collected by the International Swap Dealers Association in their recent survey covering member activity in the first six months of 1987.

However, as is usual in such areas of rapid financial product innovation and market expansion, the legal, accounting, taxation and regulatory implications have been slow to be assessed, and with even less alacrity have they been addressed.

This is not to say that there has not been progress in each of these areas, but rather to note the relative inertia of the professionals concerned.

Before going on to discuss the one particular aspect to be dealt with in this report -- the accounting implications of swaps -- it is first necessary to define the product clearly. While there exist in practice many variations on the scenarios presented, all have the basic characteristics described.

C. What is an interest rate swap?

An interest rate swap is a financial transaction in which two parties agree to exchange streams of payments over a predetermined period of time. These payments represent interest payments calculated by reference to an agreed underlying amount of principal stated in a common currency, although at no time is this amount actually exchanged between the counterparties.

Such a transaction will usually involve the exchange of interest streams calculated on a fixed- and floating-rate basis; less frequently, it involves the exchange of floating-rate interest calculated with reference to one basis rate with floating-rate interest calculated on another basis (the so-called "Basis-Rate Swap").

Interest rate swaps may be used to hedge interest rate mismatches which, for example, arise where the assets of a company yield a fixed-rate income stream while its cost of servicing liabilities is based upon floating rates, or vice versa.

More importantly, they are used to enable the borrower to reduce his costs where he is able to borrow more cheaply in one form (i.e. fixed or floating) and can transfer the comparative price advantage to the desired form.

Conversely, an investor might use an interest rate swap to convert the income stream on an asset and at the same time effectively increase the yield on that asset.

Example of an interest rate swap

Let us now consider a simple example of an interest rate swap. Suppose there are two companies of different credit standing, AAA plc and BBB plc. Let us now suppose that each has access to borrowings at the following rates:

	AAA plc	BBB plc
Fixed-rate funds	8.5 %	9.75 %
Floating-rate funds	LIBOR+0.25 %	LIBOR+0.75 %

Hence company AAA plc has an advantage over BBB plc in that it has the ability to raise finance on both a fixed- and floating-rate basis more cheaply. However, you will note that its advantage in raising fixed-rate funds is 1.25 per cent, yet only 0.5 per cent as regards floating-rate funds. Now let us assume that AAA plc wishes to raise floating-rate funding and BBB plc requires fixed-rate funding. A swap opportunity exists which will enable both companies to reduce their effective costs of borrowing.

Diagrammatically, this can be represented as follows:

Figure 1

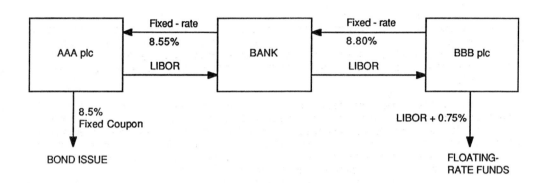

Thus each company has reduced its cost of borrowings:

AAA plc	With swap	Without swap	Gain
Fixed-rate borrowing	8.50 %		
SWAP: Pays Receives fixed	LIBOR (8.55) %		
Net cost of funding	LIBOR-0.05 %	LIBOR+0.25 %	0.30 %

BBB plc	With swap	Without swap	Gain
Floating-rate borrowing	LIBOR+0.75 %		
SWAP: Pays fixed Receives LIBOR	8.80 % (LIBOR)		
Net cost of funding	9.55 %	9.75 %	0.20 %

This is merely an example of the basic economic law of comparative advantage. Both companies have reduced their cost of funding and in addition the bank has made a margin of 0.25 per cent in the process. Everybody gains!

It will be noted that the example introduces a third party: the financial intermediary. This is a subject to which I shall return later.

D. What is a currency swap?

Currency swaps evolved out of back-to-back and parallel loans, which had become popular with international groups of companies in the late 1960s and early 1970s as a means of financing their overseas operations. Currency swaps were developed to overcome the problems associated with the right of set-off and the complicated legal documentation associated with back-to-back and parallel loans.

They differ from interest rate swaps in two key respects. First, the reciprocal payments between the two counterparties to a currency swap are denominated in two currencies, whereas in an interest rate swap they are denominated in only one. Secondly, in an interest rate swap there is no exchange of principal -- indeed there is no need. In a currency swap, however, there is an exchange, precisely because the principal is denominated in two currencies. Foreign exchange rates therefore become part of the equation, determining the amounts in each currency to be exchanged and on which the periodic interest will be calculated.

It is this exchange of principal that provides the swap's currency-hedging element. At the start of a currency swap the principal amount of one currency is exchanged for the currency equivalent of the other, calculated at the spot foreign exchange rate. At maturity, the exact amounts exchanged at the outset are re-exchanged, even though the spot value of the two currencies will have changed.

In practice, the initial exchange of principal is optional, but a notional exchange does take place to set the spot foreign currency exchange rate. At maturity, however, an exchange of principal (or compensation to create the same effect) is vital. Without it, one party would make a profit, the other a loss, representing the spot foreign exchange rate's change over time.

The effect of such a transaction is similar to a conventional spot-against-forward foreign exchange deal, except that the interest rate differential implied by the forward premium is accounted for by the periodic exchanges of swap interest payments rather than in the form of a lump sum at maturity.

The most common currency swap is the currency coupon or "Circus" swap, which combines the exchange of fixed- and floating-rate interest payments with an exchange of currencies.

Thus currency swaps enable a company to change the currencies in which they make or receive interest payments. This means that they can effectively restructure the currency composition of their assets and liabilities at will in order to hedge against foreign currency exchange rate movements.

As with interest rate swaps, the benefit may be a cost saving (in terms of reduced cost of funding of the borrower's original debts) or access may be gained to borrowings in currencies not previously available.

To see the currency swap in action, imagine the scenario illustrated in Figures 2 to 4. The German company and United States corporation both wish to provide an intercompany loan to their subsidiaries for five years. The German company wishes to lend its US subsidiary dollars. The US corporation wishes to lend its German subsidiary Deutschmarks.

Several possibilities arise. One option, if either parent company has available the necessary foreign currency required by its subsidiary, would be to on-lend it directly.

Another possibility would be for the parent companies to sell their domestic currencies (taken from an existing surplus or raised under a new borrowing) on the spot foreign exchange market for the currency they require to on-lend.

Both these approaches, however, may result in the parent companies incurring foreign currency exposure when the respective loans are repaid.

One way to eliminate any currency exposure that arises is for the two companies to enter into a five-year currency swap with a bank, structured as follows:

i) Initial exchange of principal

The German company will give its Deutschmark principal to the bank, which will pass it on to the US corporation in return for dollars which are paid to the German company. The exchange takes place at the prevailing spot rate of DM 2 = $1. The German company then on-lends the dollars to its US subsidiary, and the US corporation lends on its Deutschmarks to its German subsidiary. (See Figure 2.)

ii) Periodic payments

During the life of the swap, the German company and the US corporation will make periodic interest payments through the financial intermediary to each other, calculated on the currency amounts they received (or notionally received) under the initial exchange. These periodic payments will typically be serviced by the interest received from their subsidiaries on the intercompany loans. (See Figure 3.)

iii) Re-exchange of principal

In five years, the German company and the US corporation agree to re-exchange currencies at the spot rate of exchange agreed at the outset regardless of what is now the prevailing exchange rate. (See Figure 4.)

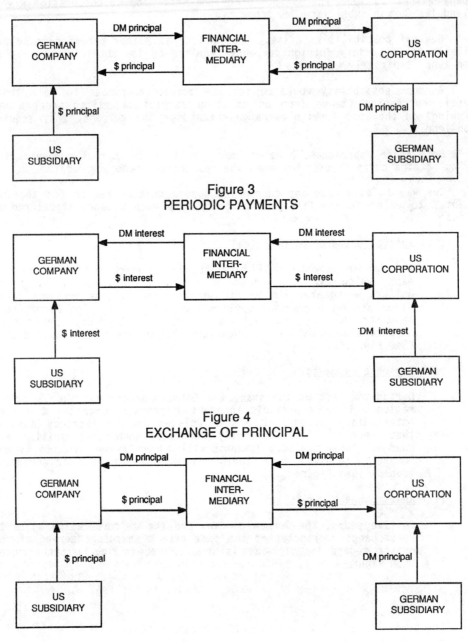

Figure 2
INITIAL EXCHANGE OF PRINCIPAL

Figure 3
PERIODIC PAYMENTS

Figure 4
EXCHANGE OF PRINCIPAL

* DM = Deutschmarks
* $ = US Dollars

E. Beneficial features

There are a number of principal features in the swap which provide benefit to the user and underline the rationale of the product. These may be summarised as:

Capital markets arbitrage

A swap can enable two companies to access capital markets more efficiently-based on the relative strengths of the two companies' borrowing powers. As a result of this feature, both companies are able to obtain a lower cost of funding.

Portfolio Management

A swap gives users the ability to change from one type of debt to another (i.e. changing its interest rate nature and/or its currency denomination). This flexibility provides a number of benefits to the user:

-- The reduction or elimination of interest rate risk;

-- Reduction or elimination of exchange rate exposure;

-- Interest rate management in accordance with the user's perception of future interest rates;

-- Asset/liability management for financial institutions.

Avoidance of prohibitive regulatory controls

A swap may be used to circumvent regulatory controls that prohibit a user from directly accessing a particular capital market. An example of this is use of basis-rate swaps by European banks that find the regulatory disclosure requirements in the US commercial paper market prohibitive. They are able to obtain simulated commercial paper funding through a basis-rate swap.

Accounting implications

Because swaps are off-balance-sheet, they do not affect the type of debt reported in the company's financial statement. Thus a company that converts its floating-rate debt to fixed rate will still report the floating-rate debt. This can be important to a highly geared company that may have a desire in the future to raise long-term funds without fully absorbing its long-term credit facilities.

The limitations of forward foreign exchange markets

This specifically relates to the benefit of currency swaps:

-- The market in exotic currency foreign exchange deals is relatively illiquid;

-- Forward foreign currency exchange rates in most currencies are not actively traded beyond two years;

-- A series of spot/forward transactions may not be desirable due to:

  a) Their inability to match specific cash flows; and

  b) The additional costs arising from the dealers' bid/offer spread.

F. The role of financial intermediaries

Let us now return to the subject of financial intermediaries. We shall consider their role and why it is necessary.

Firstly, it is unlikely that the company will be able to find a counterparty with a requirement exactly equal and opposite to its own. This could be because the requirements of one party are very large (in terms of principal), or unusual in terms of the period to be covered, the timing of cash flows required or the currencies involved. Secondly, even if such a sophisticated barter economy did exist, it is unlikely that corporate counterparties would even wish to get together to transact a swap. This is because of the reciprocal obligations which arise under a swap transaction whereby one party accepts risk based on the other's ability to meet its payment obligations. By dealing with a bank or financial intermediary, the company may obtain an element of credit insulation in that the creditworthiness of the counterparty is:

  a) Generally more easy to assess than that of unrated companies; and

  b) Probably of a higher standing.

Other reasons for companies preferring to deal with a financial institution are access and liquidity both at the time of arrangement and in the event of unwinding, taxation, and the preservation of confidentiality.

A bank may act as:

  i) An agent, identifying counterparties and arranging a swap between them in return for a fee receivable from each;

  ii) A principal, by: a) entering into swaps as an end-user in order to hedge its own interest rate and currency exposures (structural swaps); b) standing between two parties as a matched intermediary; c) as a swap trader by hedging open positions either on a swap-by-swap basis using appropriate treasury instruments ("warehousing") until a matching swap is located, or by managing a swap portfolio whereby hedging action is taken against the exposures of the portfolio as a whole.

Now acquainted with the basic mechanics of swap transactions and the underlying rationale of users and intermediaries, we shall consider their accounting implications.

G. Accounting and disclosure problems

What are the accounting problems that swap transactions present? We should seek to answer the following questions.

Balance sheet treatment

To what extent should amounts arising in respect of swap transactions be recorded on or off the balance sheet? If assets and liabilities are to be shown on the balance sheet, what value should be attributed to them? Further, to what extent may they be offset?

Profit-and-loss treatment

What sort of revenues and expenses arise out of swap transactions? How should they be recognised in the profit-and-loss account? In particular, how should irregular payments of interest and fees be dealt with?

Disclosure

What additional information should financial statements contain in respect of swap transactions? Should information about credit risk, interest rate exposure, market values, etc. be disclosed? If so, how does one measure and record such factors?

Before attempting to provide solutions to these questions, let us briefly consider what guidance is presently available to us -- the so-called "accounting framework".

H. The accounting framework

Unfortunately there are as yet no specific rules, regulations, standards or guidelines governing the accounting for interest rate and currency swaps -- certainly not in the United Kingdom or the United States. There does exist, however, a number of authoritative sources of a more general nature or on related topics which may provide some assistance.

These include Statements of Standard Accounting Practice (SSAPs) in the United Kingdom. For example, SSAP 2 sets out the fundamental accounting concepts underlying the preparation of accounts. SSAP 20 on foreign currency translation and SSAP 18, Accounting for Contingencies, are other examples. In the United States there is a Financial Accounting Standard 52 (FAS 52), again on foreign currency translation; FAS 91 which deals with, inter alia, the recognition of fees by banks; and the recently issued proposed FAS on disclosures about financial instruments.

In the absence of any specific rules, it is necessary to fall back upon fundamental accounting principles. These may be summarised as:

1. Prudence -- in the recognition of profits and revenues;

2. Accruals (or "matching") of income and expense;

3. Consistency in accounting for like items and over time;

4. Going concern -- accounts should be prepared on the assumption that the entity will continue in activity for the foreseeable future;

5. In recent years another possible concept has become widely accepted: "substance over form", i.e. the accounts should reflect the economic substance of the transaction and not just its legal form.

Given this accounting framework, let us now derive some basic rules for accounting for swaps.

I. Accounting for swap transactions

Because of their differing roles in a swap transaction, it is necessary to consider the accounting treatment for corporate users and financial intermediaries separately. It will, however, become apparent that some of the rules are common to both.

Corporate Users

Balance sheet treatment

The notional principals upon which the cash flows in a swap are based are not shown on the balance sheet. This is so because in an interest rate swap there is no actual exchange of principal and therefore no asset or liability arising. Similarly, in a currency swap, the obligation of each party to pay one currency at maturity is contingent on the receipt of the second currency.

The balance sheet should, however, record the interest accrued to the reporting date. This will generally be shown as a net receivable or payable, following the legal form of swap agreement. Netting will normally be carried out on a swap-by-swap basis. In instances where the swap has been transacted under a master agreement such as ISDA Standard documentation whereby each swap transaction between two parties is deemed to form part of one overall agreement, netting of accrued swap payments may be carried out on a counterparty basis. (It should be noted that the effectiveness of such master agreements has not yet been fully tested in the courts.)

Profit-and-loss treatment

The interest payable and receivable under the swap transaction should be recognised under the accruals basis. Further, the two amounts should be offset in the profit-and-loss account. The resulting payable or receivable should then be added to or deducted from the accrued interest calculated on the asset or liability upon which the swap was based. For example, if a company has entered into a swap to hedge a bond issue, the net interest on the swap should be offset against the interest charge on the bond so as to disclose the net overall cost of the bond borrowings.

The simple accruals method will have to be modified where payments are irregular, such as where there are up-front or "balloon" payments which would distort the profit-and-loss account impact of a swap transaction were they to be recorded on an arising basis. In such cases it is necessary to calculate the overall income or expense and to spread the resulting profit or loss over the life of the transaction. This spreading is ideally calculated on an actuarial basis, so as to arrive at a constant yield over the life of the swap. In practice, a straight-line apportionment may suffice.

The treatment of fees is less straightforward. A company may incur brokerage and/or arrangement fees which are paid up-front at the inception of a swap transaction. The normal approach is to write off such expenses as incurred. Where, however, the fee is built into the swap payments, it is more common to recognise it as part of the overall accrual of income or expense on the swap. More complicated is the situation where a fee is paid at the outset which comprises both arrangement fee and a yield adjustment for off-market interest rates. In such cases a company should follow the profit-and-loss treatment of irregular swap payments which I have described.

One further problem regarding profit-and-loss recognition arises in respect of currency swaps. Take the case of the company which effectively hedged, by means of a currency swap, the foreign exchange exposure of an asset or liability denominated in a currency other than its reporting currency. The translation gain or loss that arises as a result of the restatement of the asset or liability at current exchange rates should not be recognised in the profit-and-loss account. This is because a gain or loss will be exactly offset by an equal and opposite amount upon the re-exchange of currencies at the maturity of the swap. It should therefore be carried in a suspense account in the balance sheet, to be reversed when the swap matures.

Financial intermediaries

In an earlier section I described the possible roles of financial intermediaries in a swap transaction. Let us now consider the accounting implications for such entities.

Again, all swaps are off-balance-sheet transactions. This basic rule holds true for all entities, whatever their interest in the swap. What other items arising as a result of swap transactions should appear on the balance sheet, then? The answer to this depends on the basis of income recognition that a bank adopts. For this reason we should immediately examine the profit-and-loss account aspects.

First, where a bank acts as a broker to two counterparties and receives a fee for bringing them together, it has no legal or economic interest in the swap beyond that point. Such fees should therefore be recognised in the profit-and-loss account as soon as all the related services have been discharged.

Where a bank instead acts as a principal between two matched swaps on equal and opposite terms, it would generally make a turn between the periodic payments on them. This margin remunerates the bank for a) its services in arranging the transaction; b) accepting the credit risk of each party; and c) the administration of the two transactions over their lives. In practice

95

it is often impossible to identify any of these elements separately. In such cases it is therefore usual for a bank to accrue the payments and receipts evenly over the period of the swap. Alternatively, the bank could make a subjective judgment as to the portion of the spread that is attributable to the arrangement of the transactions, and recognise this element in the profit-and-loss account immediately. FAS 91, which deals with the accounting for fees, argues for spreading them over the life of the transaction.

We noted earlier that a financial intermediary may take a third role in the swap market -- that is, as a trader by running unmatched or mismatched swap positions and by hedging its exposures either on a "warehouse" or "portfolio" basis. In these circumstances it is generally accepted that the profits should be calculated by marking to market and thereby recognising both realised and unrealised profits. This applies to both the swap transactions themselves and any related hedging instruments.

The advantages of this approach are:

-- It is a simple method of computing profitability;

-- It properly records the profits and losses earned by a trader in addition to those merely realised;

-- It is consistent with the view that profits and losses arising in respect of marketable instruments should be recognised whether realised or not, merely by virtue of their realisability -- either by disposal in the secondary market or by executing the appropriate hedging action;

-- It avoids the distortions caused by hedge accounting;

-- It more accurately records the impact of interest rate risk on the profits of the bank;

-- Where a fully hedged portfolio exists, the mark-to-market approach effectively achieves the spreading of "locked-in" profits over the life of the transactions within it.

How then does one arrive at market values for swap transactions? One possibility is to use prices quoted by dealers. This may be practicable for a company with only a few simple generic swaps. However, for a large trader with many swaps of unusual construction and/or in exotic currency denominations with various quality counterparties, reference to market prices will either not be possible or of dubious reliability.

A second method is to adopt the "cost to cover" principle, whereby the swap is valued at the cost of putting into place a perfect hedge. Again, for complex swaps the theoretical hedge may not be achievable in practice.

The most common method used to revalue swaps is by calculating the net present value of all future cash flows by the application of discount factors. Discount factors can be derived from widely quoted market rates using the zero-coupon curve. Each leg of each swap transaction, together with related hedge instruments, should be discounted separately to arrive at the overall portfolio valuation. Changes in the valuation are immediately recognised as profits or losses.

The credit risk inherent in all swaps of positive value ("in-the-money swaps") can be dealt with either by making round-sum provisions or by incorporating the credit factor into the discount rates used.

The net value of a swap portfolio should be recorded as an asset in the balance sheet, and increases or decreases in its value recorded in the profit-and-loss account as trading income.

Finally, a bank may enter into a swap as a hedge against its own interest rate or currency exposure. In this case, the net profit or loss on the swap should be recognised in accordance with the accounting treatment for the asset or liability being hedged. If the latter is accounted for on an accruals basis, that basis should be used for the swap also. If the accounting basis is mark-to-market, the swap should also be revalued as described above.

J. Disclosure requirements

Finally, let us consider the disclosure requirements of swaps. In the United Kingdom there are no specific rules to be followed. Companies are, however, required by statute to disclose the details of their borrowings. Where a swap has been used to alter their effective terms, the details of the swap should be disclosed by way of note. Banks give little information as to either the volume or risks of their swap business, other than to mention its existence in the contingent liabilities note.

In the United States the Financial Accounting Standards Board has sought to address the need to disclose information about financial instruments in the accounts of all companies in its Exposure Draft published in December 1987. It is intended to issue an accounting standard that will require extensive disclosures by all entities for all financial instruments. Such disclosures should include information about:

-- Credit risk -- maximum credit risk, reasonably possible and probable credit risks, and concentrations of risk in individual counterparties or groups of counterparties engaged in similar activities in the same region;

-- Future cash receipts and payments -- amounts contracted to be received or paid within one year, one year through five years, and after five years, and amounts denominated in foreign currencies if significant;

-- Interest rates -- amounts of interest-bearing financial instruments contracted to reprice or mature within one year, after one year through five years, and after five years, as well as their effective interest rates, and amounts denominated in foreign currencies if significant;

-- Market values -- determined by quoted market prices or estimated, unless the entity is unable to determine or estimate the market value.

While there is quite clearly a need to address the relative scarcity of information currently found in financial reports, the FASB has in my opinion taken the proverbial "sledge-hammer to crack the nut". It remains to be seen how the professionals concerned with the preparation of accounts respond to the challenge laid before them and whether the far-reaching proposals in the United States will be replicated by the accounting standards authorities of other countries.

INTERNATIONAL SWAP DEALERS ASSOCIATION SWAPS MARKET SURVEY --
SUMMARY OF FINDINGS

Report Date: February 1988

Survey Period: 1st January 1987 to 30th June 1987

A. General

-- Total interest rate swaps transacted were $182 billion covering 13
   currencies, of which $139 billion or 76 per cent were US dollar-
   denominated;

-- Total currency swaps transacted were $44 billion, of which
   $39 billion had dollars as one currency (90 per cent);

-- 68 per cent of all swaps were between a financial intermediary and
   an end-user.

   32 per cent were therefore inter-dealer swaps (an increase of
   16 percentage points since 1985);

-- The average size of dollar interest rate swaps was $23.3 million,
   whereas the average size of currency swaps was larger.

B. Interest rate swaps

   -- Analysis by currency

   Dollar   76.4 %
   Australian dollar   2.1 %
   Deutschmark   5.5 %
   Pound sterling   5.1 %   It is believed that the
   Japanese yen   7.6 %   pound sterling percentage
   Other   3.3 %   share is understated due
                       _____   to a less-than-proportion-
                                      ate response rate.
                       100 %

-- 97 per cent of all interest rate swaps are fixed against floating;

-- Their average maturity is 4 to 5 years, although dollar interest
   rate swaps have a shorter maturity of 1 to 2 years.

-- <u>Analysis by end-user</u>

Corporate	23 %
Financial	68 %
Government	9 %
	___
	100 %

-- <u>Analysis by country</u>

United States	32 %
Canada	3 %
Europe	33 %
Asia	25 %
Australia/New Zealand	4 %
Other	3 %
	___
	100 %

C. <u>Currency swaps</u>

-- <u>Analysis by interest basis</u>

Fixed/Floating	68 %
Fixed/Fixed	21 %
Floating/Floating	11 %

-- Average Maturity = 4 to 5 years

-- <u>Analysis of End-Users</u>

Corporate	23 %
Financial	55 %
Government	22 %
	___
	100 %

<u>Geographic Analysis</u>

United States	12 %
Canada	3 %
Europe	53 %
Asia	21 %
Australia/New Zealand	9 %
Other	2 %
	___
	100 %

3. NEW FINANCIAL INSTRUMENTS: SECOND TIER INNOVATION

by
Michael Fowle
Senior Banking Partner, Peat Marwick McLintock

Introduction

The past decade has seen what is usually described as a "financial revolution" -- a period during which there has been an explosion in the number of different types of financial instruments available and a broadening in their nature and use.

Initially, financial instruments were developed both to provide a means of raising finance and as vehicles for investment. Since the early 1970s, following the abandonment of the Bretton Woods Agreement and the resulting freely floating exchange rates and gyrating interest rates, financial instruments have been developed for a completely new purpose -- "the management of market risk".

This change in rationale was responsible for the initial revolutionary innovations in the financial markets, those which can be termed as "first tier innovations" -- a category that would include futures, options and swaps.

These have been followed by a bewildering array of new instruments with names such as TIGRs, LYONs and FOX, to mention just three examples from what some call the "financial market menagerie". These instruments can be referred to as the "second tier" of financial innovation.

The pace of new product development has been phenomenal and the new breed of investment bankers -- "the financial engineer" -- is responsible. The task of keeping up with the latest in new financial instruments is now virtually impossible. However, "second tier innovations" do not break new ground in concept or technique.

Most of the new instruments fall into one of three categories.

Categories of second tier innovation

1. Instruments resulting from further development of first tier financial innovations to overcome market-perceived shortcomings

The best examples of instruments in this category are the proliferating currency option-based products currently on offer.

Currency options initially met with resistance from corporate treasurers. The main reason was that the cost of obtaining the insurance against exchange rate risk was felt to be too high. Corporate treasurers also disliked the idea of having to pay a premium, let alone an up-front premium. The "financial engineers" found a solution -- in fact they came up with nearly twenty, with names like SCOUT and FOX.

The instruments in this category tend not to be entirely new but involve a combination of other instruments. In the case of the option-based products, they are designed to overcome the perceived drawbacks of the currency option, such as the high cost and up-front premium, while largely retaining the profit potential of a conventional option.

Other examples of instruments in this category include:

-- <u>Interest rate option products</u> such as caps, floors, collars, etc.; and

-- The numerous variations of <u>interest rate and currency swaps</u>, such as sawtooth swaps, roller-coaster swaps, and blended interest rate swaps -- to mention a few with imaginative names.

2. <u>Instruments resulting when a structure or technique developed in one area of the financial market is transferred in order to improve a product in another area</u>

Probably the best illustration of this type of instrument is the asset swap.

An asset swap uses the cash flow exchange technique perfected with currency and interest rate swaps for liabilities to alter cash flows related to assets, enabling the "repackaging" of securities in issue into more marketable or attractive forms.

The simplest form of an asset swap is the transformation of a fixed-rate security into one with a floating rate, through the investor entering into an appropriate fixed/floating interest rate swap in order to exchange the interest income cash flows.

Investment banks have developed the idea further. They now market securities that are repackaged using the asset swap technique -- so-called "synthetic securities".

Other examples in this category include:

-- The use of the <u>mortgage-backed securities</u> structure to issue securities backed by:

a) Credit card receivables -- called "CARDs" (Certificates of Amortized Revolving Debts); or

b) Automobile loans -- called "CARs" (Certificates of Automobile Receivables); and

-- The transfer of the use of commercial paper for short-term funding from the United States (where it has been in existence since the last century) to other domestic markets. The United Kingdom now has Sterling Commercial Paper ("SCP"), and the international markets have Euro-commercial Paper ("ECP").

3. Instruments resulting from the refinement of traditional instruments
   to meet specific emerging market needs

Financial instruments in this category include:

-- Transferable loan facilities ("TLFs"), created to make loans more
   easily transferable, readily marketable and, therefore, more competitive against securities. The three most common kinds used are:

   i) Transferable loan instruments ("TLI");

   ii) Transferable loan certificates ("TLC"); and

   iii) Transferable participation certificates ("TPC");

-- The several innovatively structured Euro-bond issues, such as heaven
   and hell bonds, drop lock bonds, double drop lock bonds, LYONs
   ("Liquid Yield Option Notes"), etc.

   "Financial engineering" is a rapidly growing activity. New instruments
are developed each day, further improving upon existing instruments. The
possibilities are numerous given that many of the instruments are treated like
children's building blocks and used to construct seemingly complex instruments
from combinations of simpler instruments.

Accounting

   It is naïve to expect that a standard accounting treatment should exist
for every given financial product or even for classes of products. No standard method could deal satisfactorily with the wide variety of instruments
appearing on the scene.

   How then should accounting cope with the challenge of new instruments?

   First, we should examine each new product. Is it truly a new product
or is it an old product repackaged?

   Then, we should look for guidance from the three well-established
accounting concepts:

1. First, there is the matching of income and expense, often called the
   "accruals concept". If matching is not applied, accounting results
   are probably meaningless, certainly misleading, and unquestionably
   easy to manipulate. To include income without matching expense or
   vice versa fails to capture true profit. But we must not be
   simplistic. What is the product's income? And what is its expense
   in any given period?

2. The second concept is prudence. Prudence is fundamental when
   measuring income, expense and valuation of any financial instrument,
   asset or obligation;

3. Finally, consistency. Financial accounting treatment needs to be
   comparable for similar instruments.

Next, a careful analysis of the product should be undertaken. Then, the fundamental accounting principles mentioned above should be applied to the individual components of the transaction, taking into account the methods of applying these principles to the crucial issues, such as:

-- Recognition of fees;

-- Hedging and trading; and

-- Valuation.

Valuation

Of the above points, valuation is the key matter that warrants separate consideration since it raises two important issues.

First, what is market value?

The markets for many of the new instruments may not be that deep and it is therefore necessary to treat quoted prices with some care. Even more care is needed when valuations are made on the basis of mathematical but subjective formulae. True market prices are not always what they should be as determined by mathematical models. Often they are more influenced by market sentiment than by theoretical pricing.

Second, how realisable are valuation gains?

Relatively little thought has been given to this issue, probably because the recognition of realisable gains has been felt to be acceptable both in terms of materiality and market liquidity. But it is an area that will need to be watched. Current value accounting must not add respectability to imprudence.

Conclusion

I have provided a brief guide to "second tier" instruments, and have suggested an approach to dealing with the apparent accounting problems they raise. The key to the accounting issues is to understand the underlying commercial reality and how best to apply the fundamental accounting concepts to that reality.

4. INFORMATION NEEDS OF USERS

THE APPROACH TAKEN BY THE COMMISSION BANCAIRE IN MONITORING
THE USE OF NEW FINANCIAL INSTRUMENTS BY FRENCH BANKS

Claude Vulliez
Head of Service for Research, Accounting and Computer Projects,
Commission bancaire
(France)

The risks inherent in the use of new financial instruments are not new in nature, since the concept of risk is inseparable from banking activity. What is new is the way in which these risks become apparent -- or rather, may not become apparent -- to bankers and to the non-bank authorities responsible for monitoring banking operations.

The fact is that these risks are off-balance-sheet risks; recorded in nominal terms, they do not directly express the real amount at stake or the margin sought. Furthermore, it is difficult to take the time factor into account.

Faced with this situation, the French authorities responsible for supervising and monitoring the banking profession have tried both to encourage credit institutions to organise effective internal monitoring of the risks they undertake and to lay down standards for assessing and classifying transactions involving new financial instruments.

Certain new financial instruments have been covered for a number of years now by French accounting and regulatory provisions (NIFs, RUFs, etc.); these off-balance-sheet commitments were recorded under risk/asset and risk allocation ratios. Other instruments such as futures, interest rate swaps and options were not adequately integrated into our monitoring system.

As early as September 1985, Mr. Camdessus, then Governor of the Banque de France, together with his opposite numbers in the Group of Ten, stressed in a letter to the banking profession the importance of monitoring closely developments with respect to these new transactions. In March 1987, the Banque de France and the Commission bancaire published a White Paper on new financial instruments and bank risk; four fundamental points made there are worth restating:

-- The authorities stress the need for comprehensive assessment of the market risks incurred by a bank through all its transactions, whether on or off-balance-sheet.

This approach requires the drawing up of a maturity structure, currency by currency, based on the date of renewal of the debit and credit terms for all transactions, with off-balance-sheet transactions being recorded as lending and borrowing transactions. The rate risk can thus be measured;

-- The authorities insist on the basic principles governing correct utilisation of the new instruments: prior knowledge of market risks, analysis of the final profitability of transactions, and implementation of a permanent, real-time, internal surveillance system;

-- The authorities clearly express their desire for close collaboration with the banking profession. The first stage in this collaboration was marked by the joint preparation, in June 1987, of a questionnaire on the surveillance system in operation in banks; a summary of the replies has been distributed.

As regards accounting standardization, on 24th November 1986, the Comité de la réglementation bancaire adopted Regulation No. 86-23 on the accounting treatment of transactions on the Paris financial futures market (MATIF) and on organised foreign markets operating under similar conditions; this Regulation also covered transactions by mutual agreement outside the organised markets. Regulation No. 86-23 was in line with the recommendations on the accounting treatment of MATIF transactions in the standard issued by the Conseil national de la comptabilité on 9th July 1986 for non-bank enterprises.

The rapid development of interest rate options and the increasing number of over-the-counter transactions involving both conditional contracts and firm transactions, have led the Comité de la réglementation bancaire to reinforce and refine the regulations previously laid down.

At the same time, the traditional financial market has undergone rapid growth, sustained by modernisation measures such as the offering of government debt issue for sale by tender, the creation of treasury securities specialists and of market makers, and the establishment of continuous trading in the most prestigious shares listed.

Together, these measures have promoted the development of market activities in the form of transactions and arbitrage between the different financial instruments.

The activities all require strict reporting, monitoring and surveillance rules: they involve substantial leverage, are handled with on highly volatile markets and increase or reduce exposure to interest and exchange rate risk. Lastly, they involve a large number of rapid decisions which need to be made on the basis of comprehensive, high-performance monitoring systems.

At its meeting of 22nd February 1988, therefore, the Comité de la réglementation bancaire adopted three regulations in line with the monitoring and supervisory authorities' concern to oversee the conditions under which these activities are carried out, reported and monitored by French banks.

The first of these regulations, No. 88-02, restates and adds to Regulation No. 86-23 on financial futures. Notably, it includes the particular case of interest rate options in the accounting system which had previously been adopted for traditional forward transactions in financial instruments. It also lays down the accounting treatment for transactions outside the organised markets, distinguishing between over-the-counter contracts with sufficient liquidity to permit interconnection with markets that have a clearing house and over-the-counter transactions realised without reference to the organised markets. In the first case, where the liquidity of the financial instruments market is guaranteed by the presence of market stabilizing bodies, the reporting of gains on non-unwound contracts is authorised.

Regulation No. 88-03 is broadly in line with the Opinion of the Conseil national de la comptabilité of 10th July 1987 on the same subject.

Lastly, Regulation No. 88-02 requires the publication by all the banks with commitments on the financial futures markets of all significant information concerning transactions not unwound at the balance sheet date; this is based on the provisions of the EC Directive of 8th December 1986 on the annual and consolidated accounts of banks and other financial institutions.

As the French banking sector now has accounting provisions covering all types of interest rate futures, it is in a position to supply the Commission bancaire with all relevant information; studies currently under way are aimed at further improving the system for assessing foreign exchange risk.

Regulation No. 88-03 authorises credit institutions to identify and evaluate, according to specific rules, the transactions they conduct on the financial securities market with the aim of realising very short-term gains. Immediate recognition in the profit-and-loss account of gains and losses on transactions, which has been accepted for several years by international and US/UK accounting standards for trading activities, has proved indispensable if financial statements are to be produced which accurately reflect economic reality in securities dealing.

Regulation No. 88-04 requires the institutions concerned to establish, by the end of the third quarter of this year, strict monitoring and surveillance regulations for financial futures and to forward to the Commission bancaire all significant information relating to results and to open positions.

NEW FINANCIAL INSTRUMENTS: INFORMATION NEEDS OF USERS

by
Gerald A. Edwards, Jr.
Supervisory Financial Analyst, Federal Reserve System
(United States)

I. INTRODUCTION

Before discussing the information needs of users, I will briefly provide background information on some of the Federal Reserve's activities relating to financial instrument accounting issues, specifically: a) the role of the Federal Reserve in establishing regulatory reporting requirements for banks and bank holding companies; b) some of the information on off-balance-sheet activities required in regulatory reports; c) the inter-agency framework for resolving accounting and reporting issues relating to new financial instruments; and d) interaction between the Federal Reserve and standard-setting bodies in this area.

II. OVERVIEW OF FEDERAL RESERVE EFFORTS TO ENCOURAGE APPROPRIATE REPORTING STANDARDS FOR NEW FINANCIAL INSTRUMENTS

In the United States, federal bank supervisory authority is vested in three banking agencies. The Federal Reserve, as the central bank of the United States, supervises bank holding companies and state-chartered banks that are members of the Federal Reserve System. Two other federal banking agencies also supervise banks. The Office of the Comptroller of the Currency supervises national banks, and the Federal Deposit Insurance Corporation supervises the state-chartered banks it insures that are not members of the Federal Reserve System.

These three agencies co-ordinate the development of supervisory policies and regulatory reporting guidelines pertaining to banks through the Federal Financial Institutions Examination Council -- an organisation that I shall refer to hereafter as the Examination Council.

The Examination Council requires federally insured banks to file, on a quarterly basis, consolidated Reports of Condition and Income, which are referred to as "Call Reports". It prescribes the reporting guidelines that banks must follow for the Call Reports.

The Federal Reserve also requires bank holding companies to file quarterly financial reports, referred to as "Y-9 Reports". Both Call and Y-9 Reports are fixed-format reports presenting balance sheets, income statements and other financial data. These reports provide information for the research, examination, and off-site monitoring activities of the federal supervisory agencies. They are also generally made available to the public, as are financial ratio "performance reports" based on the reported data. Thus, these reports fulfil an important disclosure function as well.

I should point out that the Federal Reserve requires that the Y-9 Reports be prepared in conformity with US generally accepted accounting principles. Call Reports, prepared in accordance with specific instructions provided by the federal banking agencies through the Examination Council, for the most part also follow generally accepted accounting principles.

The federal banking agencies have long recognised the need for banks to provide more information on their off-balance-sheet activities and maintain adequate internal controls for these types of transactions. Since 1979, they have required Call Reports to contain information on banks' standby letters of credit and, since 1984, certain information (generally contractual amounts) on other selected off-balance-sheet financial instruments.

Those subject to reporting standards are:

1. Commitments to extend credit through loans and leases (unused portions);

2. Futures and forward contracts not used in foreign exchange (par value of purchase/sale contracts);

3. When-issued securities transactions;

4. Standby contracts and other option arrangements;

5. Commitments to purchase and sell foreign currencies and dollar exchange;

6. Standby letters of credit and foreign office guarantees;

7. Commercial and similar letters of credit;

8. Participations in acceptances conveyed and acquired by the reporting bank;

9. Securities borrowed and lent; and

10. Information on any significant commitments and contingencies not mentioned above.

In addition, the total notional principal amounts of interest rate swaps are presented in the Call Reports.

The Federal Reserve requires similar disclosures in the consolidated Y-9 Reports filed by bank holding companies with assets of $150 million or more.

For Call Report purposes, if any risk is retained by the selling bank, a sale of assets with recourse will generally be recorded as borrowings on the balance sheet. Since Y-9 Reports are prepared in conformity with US generally accepted accounting principles, any assets sold with recourse that meet these accounting criteria will be removed from the Y-9 balance sheets of bank holding companies. However, the amounts of these transactions and their impact on consolidated earnings and capital must be reported in memorandum items in the Y-9 Reports.

The disclosures listed above provide consistent information about off-balance-sheet activities of banking organisations in the absence of established accounting and disclosure standards in this area. This information is primarily intended for use as a "scaler" -- that is, as a broad indicator of the extent to which a banking organisation is involved with these transactions and a rough approximation of the changes in that involvement over time. Furthermore, this information is helpful in focusing supervisory attention on those institutions that are heavily involved or experiencing growth in certain off-balance-sheet areas and targeting particular areas for review during upcoming supervisory examinations.

However, since the information disclosed does not indicate the volume of the financial instruments that are used for hedging purposes or that have been offset by other on- or off-balance-sheet instruments, these disclosures by themselves cannot provide the supervisor or other users with information concerning the impact of such instruments on the risk profile of a banking organisation. Examinations of banks and inspections of bank holding companies, which utilise detailed information from bank management information systems, are the primary source of information of that kind for the Federal Reserve and other bank supervisory agencies.

A consistent accounting and disclosure framework does not exist at the present time for off-balance-sheet financial instruments in the United States and other countries. Furthermore, for new financial instruments, appropriate accounting treatment and disclosure guidelines are often difficult to determine from existing accounting standards. As a result, differences -- and, sometimes, wide variances -- arise in what constitutes acceptable accounting practice for these instruments. The Federal Reserve and the other federal banking agencies meet periodically to discuss emerging accounting issues and to determine whether regulatory guidance is needed until accounting standards are issued by the Financial Accounting Standards Board (FASB). These meetings will typically be conducted under the auspices of the Examination Council's Reports Task Force and its accounting subcommittee. If regulatory guidance is deemed necessary, it will generally be issued as an amendment to the Call Report instructions or a supervisory policy statement.

The Federal Reserve and the other agencies also maintain close contact with the FASB, the American Institute of CPAs (AICPA) and its Banking Committee, and accounting officials in the banking industry in order to identify emerging accounting issues associated with new financial instruments and to encourage the development of appropriate accounting guidance and standards for these transactions. For example, members of the Federal Reserve staff participated in the FASB advisory group on financial instrument disclosures. In addition, the Federal Reserve and the other banking agencies frequently provide comments on major accounting proposals of the FASB and AICPA.

The Federal Reserve is also involved in an international effort to refine and further improve the supervisory assessment of the risks associated with off-balance-sheet activities. This has resulted in the risk-based capital framework, which has been jointly proposed by the bank supervisory agencies of a number of countries. Using this framework, information on the off-balance-sheet risks of banking organisations will be reflected explicitly in the capital ratios used by the supervisory agencies in their assessment of capital adequacy.

III. NEW (OFF-BALANCE-SHEET) FINANCIAL INSTRUMENTS:
USER INFORMATION NEEDS

Clearly, there are a number of different types of users of information about financial instruments. Major groups include regulators and supervisors; other governmental agencies; financial analysts and rating agencies; employees and their unions; financial services firms, including banks; depositors; creditors; investors; suppliers; competitors; and many others. Regardless of the differing objectives of these groups, they share an important need for information that will help them to understand the financial condition and performance of the reporting entity, the prospects for its future performance, and the major aspects of its risk profile that affect, and perhaps threaten, its condition and performance.

Supervisory authorities, like the Federal Reserve, have access to the detailed information on these financial instruments contained in bank management information systems, through their examinations of banks and inspections of bank holding companies. For this reason, supervisory examinations are their primary source of information on the impact of these activities on banking organisations. Other users, however, must generally depend on information presented in the annual reports to shareholders and in the Call and Y-9 Reports.

Financial statements that do not provide information on significant positions in off-balance-sheet financial instruments will not present a true and fair view of the financial condition and performance of the reporting entity. Off-balance-sheet activities that are used for hedging purposes should, in theory, reduce the overall risk of the reporting entity, and therefore information regarding these hedge transactions should be reflected in financial statements so that users can be apprised of risk-reduction efforts. Likewise, off-balance-sheet financial instruments that are not being used for hedging purposes may increase -- sometimes dramatically -- the overall risk of the reporting entity. In such cases, users clearly need to be apprised of the impact of these transactions on the risk profile of the reporting entity.

While it seems clear that disclosures about off-balance-sheet financial instruments are needed, the kind of information that should be disclosed may not be readily apparent for a number of reasons. For one, the risks associated with these instruments are complex in nature, and their interaction with the risk profile of the reporting entity is also very complex. Second, a detailed quantitative data approach to disclosure which is focused on the presentation of point-in-time information may not adequately describe the risks. Third, the significance of the impact of the off-balance-sheet activity needs to be assessed before determining the amount of quantitative data that needs to be disclosed. Finally, the information needs of users may differ as to the extent of disclosure required.

An organisation should be responsive to the reasonable information needs of the users of its financial statements, and design its disclosures to meet those needs. Generally, users need two types of disclosures relating to off-balance-sheet financial instruments: 1) narrative or qualitative disclosures about the major attributes of the management control environment of the reporting entity and its use of financial instruments; and 2) supplemental quantitative information for significant or potentially significant exposure. The disclosure of quantitative data alone may not provide the appropriate level of user understanding. Care should be taken to explain any quantitative data provided, so that users will not misinterpret this information and draw wrong conclusions.

It is my opinion that the most important information regarding financial instruments that a reporting entity can provide to users is primarily qualitative in nature. Users of financial statements need narrative disclosures that will inform them of the major types of risks associated with the reporting entity's on-balance-sheet activities and off-balance-sheet financial instruments. The disclosures should include a description of the major classes of the reporting entity's financial instruments. This should be followed by a thorough discussion of the major elements of the control system that enable it to monitor and manage these risks to the benefit of the reporting entity.

For example, the narrative disclosure should explain the credit, liquidity, interest rate, foreign exchange 'and market value risks to which the organisation is exposed, and how it evaluates these risks. It could then describe the major types of off-balance-sheet commitments involved, interest rate and foreign exchange instruments and other activities, and the risks associated with these transactions. The narrative disclosure should indicate the extent to which these instruments are used for hedging purposes. In addition, the following should be addressed: a) board of director approval of major off-balance-sheet activities; b) the frequency with which these positions are monitored, reviewed and revalued by senior management or senior committees of the board; c) the use of limits and other controls to manage risk; and d) the frequency of review of these activities by internal and external auditors.

Users also have a need for information about the major aspects of the accounting policies adopted. For example, management's discussion should distinguish between the accounting treatment used for hedging and non-hedging transactions and the related income recognition practices. Particular mention should be made about the use of mark-to-market accounting for certain financial instruments, the general principles determining market values, and the accounting treatment followed when terminations of hedge instruments occur. The manner in which the company records in the financial statements and the risks associated with these exposures -- either through provisions or by other means -- should also be discussed. In addition, the company's consolidation policy should be addressed if it materially affects the presentation of information about on- and off-balance-sheet exposures.

The disclosures that I have mentioned will greatly assist the user of financial statements in understanding the off-balance-sheet activities and the way in which management monitors and controls the associated risks. Most of the largest banks in the United States provide disclosure of the types of risks, financial instruments and control policies in the "management discussion and analysis" sections of their annual reports. Accounting policies for these instruments are usually addressed in the notes to the financial statements.

However, management should also provide quantitative information to supplement the narrative discussion of accounting, controls and risks if it can be determined that the benefits to users of financial statements exceed the costs associated with such disclosure. Quantitative information can help users to understand the size of the off-balance-sheet exposures relative to those recorded on the balance sheet. If presented in a reasonably consistent manner, it may also help users to compare one company's exposures with those of other organisations.

The determination of the nature and amount of quantitative information to be provided to users should begin with an assessment of the materiality of the off-balance-sheet activity -- that is, the significance of its impact or potential impact on the reporting entity. Users should not be bombarded with extensive quantitative information about financial instruments that is not expected to have a material impact on the financial condition and performance of the company. On the other hand, for companies having significant positions in off-balance-sheet instruments, disclosure of extensive quantitative information may be necessary for the reader to understand the manner in which these activities will affect the company.

The type of quantitative information users will benefit most from is supplemental objective information that is consistent with the way the organisation manages and controls such activities. For example, in the case of financial instruments used for hedging purposes, quantitative information could be provided on a) the par value or notional principal amounts of major classes of hedging instruments; b) the impact of hedging activities on earnings during the accounting period; c) the deferred gains and losses recorded on the balance sheet; and d) the related average deferral period. To enhance the usefulness of this type of disclosure, management should relate this quantitative information to the positions on the balance sheet that are being hedged.

In the case of credit risk, information could be presented on a) the cost to close out positions; b) the amount of instruments with counterparties that are experiencing difficulties; c) the volume of defaults or terminations that have occurred and the related earnings impact; d) the amount for which the organisation is at risk as a result of asset sales with recourse; and e) significant concentrations of credit risk.

With regard to interest rate risk, users would generally benefit from information on a) the impact of financial instruments -- both the hedging instruments previously discussed and non-hedges -- on the net interest earnings during the most recent accounting period; and b) the impact of these instruments on the interest rate sensitivity "gaps" of the reporting entity. To assist the user in understanding the narrative disclosures on the management of liquidity risks, supplemental disclosure could include a) contingent commitments and liquidity-related guarantees provided to customers; and b) the expected maturity structure or weighted average maturities of major classes of financial instruments.

Also, for those off-balance-sheet instruments that management may reasonably be expected to sell and for which reliable market values exist, disclosure of this expectation and market value information would be beneficial to users. However, let me emphasize again that quantitative information should be supplemental to the narrative information on policies, risks and controls that is provided by management, and would generally be provided only if off-balance-sheet exposures are significant.

IV. CONCLUSION

Users of financial statements clearly need better information on the off-balance-sheet activities of banks and non-bank companies. They will benefit greatly from narrative disclosures that address these financial instruments and their use by the organisation, discuss their risks, describe major accounting policies, and set forth the major attributes of management's internal control and risk management systems relating to off-balance-sheet positions.

For organisations with significant off-balance-sheet exposures, disclosure of quantitative data should be provided to supplement this information and to meet specific user information needs. However, care should be taken to ensure that these disclosures are meaningful and not misleading to users.

Although this discussion has focused primarily on the information needs of financial statement users that are not supervisory authorities, the latter group uses information that is similar, albeit in much more detail.

In conclusion, I look forward to the development of consistent accounting and disclosure frameworks for financial instruments by national standard-setting bodies that will improve the information available to users and enhance the international comparability of financial reports.

WHAT SHAREHOLDERS NEED TO KNOW ABOUT THE NEW FINANCIAL INSTRUMENTS

by
Patrick Mordacq
Secretary-General, Commission des opérations de Bourse
(France)

Since the early 70s, economic agents have tried to protect themselves from the growing volatility of exchange and interest rates characteristic of the international economic environment.

Initially inspired by US commodity futures markets, forward financial instruments have grown in sophistication and proliferated in all financial markets.

In France, the use of these instruments has increased very quickly in recent years, along with financial deregulation and easier access to international finance.

The way they work is highly complex and involves major and rapid leverages -- and sometimes, substantial risk transfers.

For the Commission des opérations de Bourse and for the bodies regulating stock exchanges and financial markets in other countries, the use of these instruments is pertinent to their responsibilities for overseeing the smooth operation of the markets as well as for protecting savings and providing information to investors.

They have also aroused the concern of other authorities charged with formulating methodology and accounting rules, either for specific economic activities -- as in the case of the Comité de la réglementation bancaire and the Commission bancaire -- or generally, as in the case of the Conseil national de la comptabilité, whose views and recommendations serve as a basis for the standardization of accounting rules in our country.

Faced with the development of the new financial instruments, the French authorities have, generally speaking, collaborated with the financial market-place in formulating rules and improving the quality of published information. My present concern, however, is more specifically the regulatory authority responsible for protecting savings and ensuring that proper information is furnished to shareholders.

1. Ensuring provision of reliable, useful, high-quality information on the new financial instruments

On 3rd February 1988, the Commission des opérations de Bourse published a recommendation concerning the information to be supplied by companies on the use of the new financial instruments. This recommendation was drafted in consultation with the other competent authorities, accountants and representatives of quoted companies.

However, as this is a subject that has recently drawn widespread comments from the French financial market, it seems useful to consider the general context of this discussion before turning to the recommendation itself.

1.1. The general response to the new financial instruments in France

Two reviewing committees have recently been set up in France. Their work, backed up by very wide consultations in the financial market and among companies, has made a major contribution to establishing a generally accepted French school of thought on the new financial instruments.

To develop a code of ethics among financial professionals, the Chairman of the Commission des opérations de Bourse asked Mr. Brac de la Perrière to head a committee enabling financial specialists and market regulating authorities to consider the question jointly.

This Committee, whose report was made public in March 1988, suggested rules for the conduct of financial intermediaries, their staff and discretionary portfolio management operations. The Committee identified the principles that should govern such conduct, i.e. the primacy of clients' interests and the integrity of the market. Taking into account the advances in market operations stemming from the speed with which transactions are performed and the methodology of negotiations, the Committee laid down new and very precise rules for the recording of orders, the timing of which must immediately be noted when they are received and at each stage of execution. Finally, the Committee laid down criteria to assure the independence of discretionary portfolio management operations.

In line with its conclusions, the Commission des opérations de Bourse will ensure that the actions of professional market authorities and firms at least conform to the minimum level required to give investors adequate security in the new market environment.

In December 1987, Mr. Balladur, Minister for Economic Affairs, Finance and Privatisation, asked another leading market personality, Mr. Deguen, to head a review committee on the new financial instruments and futures markets.

The Committee, whose conclusions have been published in April 1988, stressed that the financial crisis of October 1987 should on no account inhibit the use of the new financial instruments and that the creation of these markets meet a clear need. The Committee considered that these instruments would not only be very useful to enterprises but also improve stock exchange operation and liquidity. The Deguen Committee produced four series of proposals:

-- The first proposals relate to the new products to be created: the futures and share-index related options markets. The Committee stresses that the launching of these markets must be contingent on previous improvement of the liquidity of the underlying securities market, in particular by the emergence of a market making function;

-- The second proposals concern the conditions governing the access to secondary markets of enterprises and mutual funds (or unit investment trusts) (Organismes de placement collectif en valeurs mobilières -- OPCVM). In the case of enterprises, the Committee makes access to these markets subject to previous authorisation by the Board of Directors and provides for the auditors to comment on such interventions in their general report. With regard to investment trusts, the Committee suggests that the rules governing their intervention in futures markets should be revised to some extent to increase the transparency of the portfolios under their management;

-- A third series of observations concerns market security and, more particularly, the organisation of clearing arrangements. In more general terms, it is desirable that recently established bodies be fully aware of the interconnection between the cash market and the market for derivative products, so that the regulatory framework and equipment vital to the operation of each segment develop harmoniously in accordance with the needs of the market as a whole;

-- The fourth series of proposals concerns auditing and the accounting rules applicable to derivative market operations. On this last point, the Committee has approved the position expressed by a working group set up at its request by the Commission des opérations de Bourse. This working group concluded that enterprises should be induced to improve their risk management by introducing rigorous internal monitoring, backed up by financial vetting of their commitments.

The conclusions reached by the Committee draw on examples from abroad. For instance, the Committee followed the recommendation issued by the Commission des opérations de Bourse on 3rd February 1988 in advocating the publishing of annotated tables in line with the Exposure Draft No. 54 published in the United States on 31st December 1987, "Disclosures about Financial Instruments". The Committee similarly supported the desirability of consolidated information (i.e. of inducing companies publishing consolidated accounts to supply comprehensive information on new financial instruments and to include any subsidiaries not fully integrated) while FAS 94 in the United States requires, since 1st January 1988, that subsidiaries engaged in financial activities be fully integrated into the consolidated accounts of groups with a different main line of business.

These two examples, chosen because they relate to published texts, bear witness to the declared international desire for the provision of high-grade information at company group level.

1.2. The phased introduction of rules and regulations

On 9th July 1986, the Conseil national de la comptabilité (CNC) issued a standard on the accounting procedure to be applied to financial instrument transactions in the futures market and followed this up on 10th July 1987 with a second standard on the accounting procedure for interest rate options. These standards reflecting the consensual CNC view are interim stages in a process which should be continued despite the legal obstacles and the difficulties arising from the diverse and complex nature of the new financial instruments.

The Comité de réglementation bancaire, whose jurisdiction encompasses credit institutions and security firms, has also issued accounting standards with the chief purpose of facilitating its own monitoring role. These rules relate to an economic sector where the use of the new financial instruments is especially important.

The Commission des opérations de Bourse has established that what shareholders and the public require from annual reports and accounts is information satisfactorily explaining the policy pursued by companies in the use of the new financial instruments and the effect this has on income. It has therefore issued a recommendation dated 3rd February 1988 on the information to be provided by quoted companies, irrespective of their business.

Before that date, the published information about the new financial instruments was inadequate. This recommendation, published at the point when annual reports were just being compiled, marks a fresh and probably unprecedented step. Aware of the problems liable to beset quoted companies in making high-grade information publicly available and easily verifiable by the auditors, the Commission des opérations de Bourse, while primarily concerned with public access to information, considered it necessary as an initial measure to recommend methods of internal analysis and data processing to companies quoted on the stock exchange.

The Commission suggested the preparation of tables and a questionnaire, which could be adapted to suit the character of each enterprise and would be useful not only internally but also to auditors and authorities such as the Commission des opérations de Bourse for quoted companies and the Commission bancaire for credit institutions. Company executives would be provided with a tabulated summary showing the accounting methods used, the risks incurred and the essence of the information to be conveyed to the public.

This is the basis on which quoted companies should work to supply the public with information along the main lines also suggested by the Commission in its recommendation of 3rd February.

2. Improved information to the public should extend to the new financial instruments

The vigorous -- and of course desirable -- development of the new financial instruments presents the Commission des opérations de Bourse and the regulating authorities of other countries with a difficult problem. As is confirmed by the questions frequently appearing in the press, the investors' legitimate need for information calls for a clear and public explanation of the use of instruments. The confidence of investors in the markets and in the use which companies make of these techniques should not be shaken by a lack of information or by its inadequacy or obscurity, as it is a fact that these financial instruments can actually reduce the number and scale of the risks incurred.

2.1. Progress on the road to acceptance by companies

While this attitude has always been accepted in principle, several different objections have been advanced, and we should consider whether they are legitimate. The first objection is the difficulty of providing the public with clear relevant information and the dangers of misunderstanding that arise when, say, information is given on the gross volume of the positions taken by a company at the end of the accounting period by the use of the new financial instruments.

This argument seems to me the most difficult to accept, if only because it is invariably used to rationalise any hesitancy about providing more financial information. I am quite ready to admit, however, that the task is also difficult.

The second argument concerns the insufficient homogeneity of the published information, especially at international level, and it is quite true that at a time when accounting standards have not yet been established for a number of products and when countries have made varying progress towards formulating rules, the financial analyst, not to mention the individual investor, may well be puzzled by the diversity of accounting techniques applied to operations using these instruments. Perhaps the desire of the regulating authorities that the public be properly informed will stimulate an acceleration of national or international standardization in this field.

A third argument often put forward concerns competition. I can well understand that certain businesses, in the banking sector especially, are hesitant about disclosing information which they believe may harm the confidentiality normally considered vital in a sharply competitive environment. However, when we see the largest banks in some countries all producing profits for 1987 which show virtually identical rates of growth over the previous year, we may view with some doubt the information to be gleaned from the detailed accounts of these credit institutions, particularly where the use of the new financial instruments is concerned. Faced with the silence of their competitors in what has now become a world market, we can understand the unwillingness of some credit institutions to provide details about their strategy, and here the objective of defending themselves against their competitors must be interpreted as carrying greater weight than their wish to keep their shareholders informed.

In this situation the Commission des opérations de Bourse has endeavoured to assume an empirical attitude in its recommendation. It cannot, however, exempt certain types of enterprise from a requirement which encompasses all quoted companies. It also hopes that international co-operation between the bodies responsible for regulating stock exchange operations will lead to the development of uniform practices, at least among those countries that are anxious to see the expansion of their financial market.

2.2 The recommendation of 3rd February 1988 by the Commission des opérations de bourse

The Commission des opérations de Bourse wanted tangible improvement in the information supplied to the public with effect from the 1987 financial year. It was the Commission's particular wish that annual reports and accounts make clear the reasons for, and the results of, interventions on the new financial instrument markets.

The information supplied must cover the accounting methods used and the follow-up of the positions taken, and must enable the extent and changes of the risks incurred to be measured.

Where a quoted company conducts activities via the new financial instruments and does so through subsidiaries, the information must be included in the consolidated accounts; even when the subsidiaries in which the company has a majority shareholding are included only by the equity method as their accounts are compiled according to the rules relating specifically to, say, insurance companies or credit institutions. The purpose of this consolidated presentation of information is to ensure that, at group level, information that might otherwise be presented in an excessively globalised and impenetrable form can be meaningful and useful.

The information called for by the Commission des opérations de Bourse is now being provided by companies either in their annual reports or in the prospectus submitted for approval to the Commission des opérations de Bourse on the occasion of public issues. The first signs are encouraging and bear witness to a desire for market consensus as regards provision of quality information. In particular, the explanatory comments accompanying the figures mostly provide a true picture of how the new financial instruments are actually being used. The point must be made, however, that some companies, especially in the banking sector, have displayed a certain reluctance to provide information. This reaction was understandable in initial applications of the recommendation. But this reluctance has been considerably dissipated since very large industrial and banking groups have published significant information about the new financial instruments.

2.3 A gradual improvement in the quality of published information is required

In its recommendation, the Commission des opérations de Bourse expressed the wish that companies become aware as quickly as possible of the need to provide information about the new financial instruments. The information required for the 1987 financial year came within the scope of existing processing systems. Obviously, the development of these processing systems will necessarily modify the content of the information published henceforth. Companies are gradually acquiring rigorous internal monitoring procedures together with more efficient processing systems better at analysing the risks inherent in the new financial instruments.

With the same aim in view, the Comité de réglementation bancaire has instructed credit institutions to install systems for the measurement, monitoring and management of risks together with internal vetting procedures.

All these similarly oriented measures will enable quoted companies to improve the quality of the information supplied to the public. Beyond the crude data on positions and results, this information must reveal companies' overall sensitivity to exchange and interest rate fluctuations.

In future, this component must be included in the information on the new financial instruments, and the details given must reflect the total extent of interest or exchange rate risks.

2.4 International co-operation is needed between stock exchange regulating bodies to achieve progress in providing the public with homogeneous information about the new financial instruments

Unlike the central banks with their long-standing close links symbolised by the Cooke Committee, it is only recently that stock exchange regulating bodies have adopted the custom of multilateral meetings. One particular difficulty explains this relative delay, and that is the fact that the established public bodies vary according to country, and the balance between self-regulating authorities and public control bodies is not the same everywhere. Despite this, very tangible progress has now been made towards co-operation in this area.

In 1986 the Wilton Park Group was formed on United Kingdom initiative for co-operation in conducting enquiries.

The IOSCO (International Organisation of Securities Commissions) has recently set up a Technical Committee comprising the representatives of twelve countries (1). This Committee has itself created a number of working groups, one of which is specialising in the problems of harmonizing accounting standards.

With its aim of reciprocal recognition of the prospectuses published when issues take place on several financial markets, this working group is naturally interested in efforts to harmonize standards relating to the new financial instruments. The Commission des opérations de Bourse will suggest how work should proceed in this direction.

To return briefly to the central concern of the Commission des opérations de Bourse in particular and of financial market regulating bodies in general, the disclosure of clear information equally available to every shareholder is necessarily one of the basic objectives of an enterprise opting to raise funds through the stock-market.

The use of the new financial instruments is central to the strategy of enterprises in the financial and banking sector. It may also play an important part in the financial policy of any quoted company. The observations recently published by Mr. Jacques-Henri David (2), Chief Executive of Saint-Gobain, clearly stress the importance of this financial element in overall company strategy and underscore the "productivity potential inherent in the explosive growth of financial thinking".

The various professionals whose business is to translate economic realities into accounting terms have to focus their attention on the presentation of accounts and explain their significance to the public -- in other words -- to be effective intermediaries between the company and the shareholder. The direct or indirect contribution made by individuals investing in companies is essential to the enhancement, maintenance or mere preservation (according to one's personal optimism) of economic prosperity. It follows that the education of the shareholder in company financial strategy, and more particularly in its potential risk and security components, must be a priority objective for accountants, auditors and financial analysts.

NOTES AND REFERENCES

1.   Australia, Canada (the provinces of Quebec and Ontario), the United States, France, Italy, Japan, the Netherlands, Hong Kong, Germany, the United Kingdom, Switzerland and Sweden.

2.   Jacques-Henri David, "Entreprise et innovation financière", in Commentaire No. 41, pp. 255-259.

INFORMATION NEEDS OF TAX AUTHORITIES

by
Tytti Tunturi
Senior Governmental Secretary, Ministry of Finance
(Finland)

I. INTRODUCTION

A tax system should be equitable, which is to say that all taxpayers -- individuals and corporations -- should contribute their "fair share" to society. Moreover, efficient means are needed to guarantee that the tax system is equitable in practice as well as in theory. To this end tax authorities need information concerning taxpayers, information without which equitable results are impossible.

The new financial instruments present tax authorities with additional needs for special information. This is mainly due to the fact that developments in the field of financial instruments have been so rapid that legislators in many countries have difficulties keeping in step. They will have to adapt the legal terminology relating to financial instruments for use in the present-day world of increasingly liberalised capital markets. This need for change seems to concern legislation in both accounting and taxation.

II. SPECIAL INFORMATION NEEDS IN CONNECTION WITH THE TAXATION OF NEW FINANCIAL INSTRUMENTS

New financial instruments often contain elements that are incompatible with traditional taxation terminology. While in the past, tax authorities had no difficulty identifying a certain income item as, say, interest or capital gain, considerable difficulties arise in connection with new financial instruments.

A number of questions ought to be answered:

1. When is a gain or loss to be recognised?

2. How should purchasing costs and other expenses be allocated to different parts of the financial instrument?

3. What is the nature of the income?

4. What is the character of the income?

5. What is the source of the income?

In addition, there are several questions to be answered concerning use of different currencies:

1. What is the translation method to be used?

2. What is the exchange rate to be used in translation?

3. Should the foreign currency transaction and the underlying transaction be integrated or separated?

4. Should a hedging transaction be integrated with or separated from its underlying transaction?

Timing of recognition

It is necessary for tax authorities to decide when a gain or loss is to be recognised, i.e. recorded in the relevant accounts as a gain or loss and/or taken into account as such for tax purposes. The essential problem is whether such a gain or loss should be recognised before it is realised, or not until it is realised.

In connection with recognition there may be an additional problem in determining the base value for the calculation of a gain or loss.

Allocation of expenses

There may be difficulties in allocating the purchasing costs and other expenses to different parts of the financial instrument.

Nature of income

It is usually essential to know whether income should be considered as interest or non-interest income, as taxation of interest may differ from that of other kinds of income.

The nature of the income received in connection with new financial instruments is especially important from the point of view of international taxation, i.e. when two or more countries are involved. In tax treaties, states agree on how to divide the right to tax certain incomes. Different kinds of income are accorded differentiated treatment. The question here usually is whether the income is to be considered as interest or non-interest income.

Character of income

The question may arise whether the income is to be treated as ordinary income or as capital gains. Where special rules apply to the taxation of capital gains, they usually are more favourable from the taxpayer's point of view than the tax rules governing ordinary income. Correspondingly, a capital loss is usually accorded less favourable tax treatment than an ordinary loss. Consistency in this connection is important, that is, where a gain is treated as a capital gain, a loss should correspondingly be treated as a capital loss, and where a gain is treated as ordinary income, a loss should be treated as an ordinary loss.

Source of income

It may also be important to know whether the income is to be treated as received from domestic sources or from foreign sources. In the former case there will be no foreign tax credit granted for any foreign tax paid on that income.

Additional questions regarding the use of different currencies

A. Translation method

The methods generally used in translating accounts kept in a foreign currency are:

1. The "specific transactions" method;

2. The "profit and loss" method; and

3. The "net worth", "net investment" or "balance sheet" method.

The amount of taxable income may vary depending on the translation method used. Some countries accept the use of any of these three providing that the method adopted is used in a consistent manner. On the other hand, some countries accept only one or two of the methods for taxation purposes.

The United States adopted the "profit and loss" method in the Tax Reform Act of 1986 (Subpart J, Taxation of Foreign Currency Gains and Losses). The method was adopted by the Financial Accounting Standards Board in 1981 (FAS 52), following business community demands for a translation method that would not make an annual impact on the income statement. Prior to the Tax Reform Act of 1986 all of the translation methods mentioned above were acceptable.

The "profit and loss" method has the effect of deferring the recognition of exchange gains and losses attributable to assets and liabilities until they are actually realised. In other words, fluctuations in the value of assets and liabilities induced by exchange rates are not reported in the income statement. This is in contrast with the "net worth" method, which leads to the inclusion of currency fluctuations in the value of assets and liabilities in taxable income. The "specific transactions" method had the same effect, but the method was rarely used because of the difficulties of separate accounting where numerous transactions were involved.

Although flexibility is a value in itself in connection with taxation, some guidelines on the application of different translation methods may be useful. Co-operation on these questions between accounting bodies and tax authorities would be of great value.

B. Types of exchange rates

In translating foreign currency transactions into domestic currency, one needs to know the exchange rate to be applied. The main types of exchange rates used are:

1. The "historic" rate;

2. The "closing" rate; and

3. An average rate.

The "historic" rate method (sometimes known as the "temporal" method) translates transactions at the exchange rate current at the time the transactions are carried out. The historic rate is usually used when the "specific transactions" method is applied. The "closing" rate method translates financial statements utilising the rate prevailing at the end of the year or at balance sheet date. An alternative to the closing rate is an over-the-year average rate. The use of a closing rate or an average rate is characteristic of both the "profit and loss" method and the "net worth" method.

C. Connection between foreign currency and underlying transactions

In many countries it is still an unresolved question whether a foreign currency denominated transaction should be treated as an integrated transaction or as two separate transactions -- the currency transaction on the one hand and the underlying transaction on the other hand. The "integration" approach is difficult to apply when an exchange gain or loss arises in a tax year other than the gain or loss of the underlying transaction. According to the "separate transactions" approach, the gain or loss of the underlying transaction is separated from the exchange gain or loss and the nature, character, source and timing of the amounts are determined separately for tax purposes.

In the United States the Tax Reform Act of 1986 (Sec. 988) in many cases requires that a foreign currency gain or loss should be quantified and treated separately from any underlying transaction. However, the Conference Report (No. 313, 99th Cong. 2nd Sess.) indicates that the "separate transactions doctrine" is modified in such a way that if there is no net gain or loss from the transaction taken as a whole, then any currency gain or loss realised will not be recognised. Foreign currency gains or losses will generally be treated as ordinary income. The source of exchange gains and losses will usually be deemed to be the country of residence of the taxpayer.

D. Hedging transactions

As in other transactions, parties involved with new financial instruments may hedge foreign currency risks. The question here is whether the hedging transaction and the underlying transaction are treated as integrated or separate. By treating them separately, the nature, character, source and timing of the gain or loss could be treated in different ways.

Under the US Tax Reform Act of 1986, certain hedging transactions (Sec. 988) are to be integrated with the asset or liability hedged, and thus treated as a single transaction. The regulations will not, however, require complete integration if the hedge is considered to be of an "exposure in a particular currency" type, but they will require consistent treatment. The other type mentioned in the Senate Report (No. 841, 99th Cong., 2nd Sess.) is the full "integrated economic package" hedge, which is to be treated as dollar borrowings with dollar interest payments since the taxpayer has assured himself of a cash flow that will not vary with exchange rates.

An attempt to provide conformity in the treatment of hedging between accounting rules and tax rules would be highly desirable.

III. PRACTICAL EXAMPLES

1. Debt with equity warrants

The term "debt with equity warrants" describes a financial instrument through which a debt is issued with warrants to subscribe for equity. These warrants may allow the purchase of shares in the original issuer (or its parent company), or a third party. This financial instrument consists of two parts:

1. The debt itself; and

2. The separately tradable warrant or warrants.

The interest rate is usually below the market rate, as the investor anticipates a profit on the exercise of the warrant or warrants received.

A number of questions arise regarding the taxation of debts with equity warrants, which ought to be answered:

1. How should the purchasing costs be allocated between the debt and the warrants?

2. How should the increase in the market value of the debt be treated for taxation purposes? Should it be treated (strictly or to some extent) as interest, since the interest rate was below the market rate at the time of issue, or should the market value increase be treated (strictly or to some extent) as a capital gain?

3. When should an increase in the market value of the warrant be recognised?

4. If the warrant is used, does it mean that at that time an increase in the value of the warrant had been realised?

5. When is the share, which is subscribed by the warrant, considered to be received?

6. If the warrant expires without value, can the investor deduct the entire loss, or part of it, in his taxation form?

2. Currency swaps

A currency swap involves two parties to a contract agreeing to exchange assets or liabilities in different currencies, including the related interest payments. The methods of calculating the interest must be identical, e.g. fixed interest swapped for fixed interest, floating for floating.

Currency swaps typically involve exchange rate risks where interest payments are to be made in foreign currencies or where repayment is made in a third currency, which is translated into the local currency at the rate prevailing at the expiration of the contract. Currency swaps do not normally involve interest rate risks.

Here again, the following questions should be answered:

1. When should an exchange gain or loss be recognised?

2. Should the foreign currency transaction and the underlying transaction be integrated or separated?

3. What is the nature of the exchange gain or loss?

4. What is the character of the exchange gain or loss?

5. What is the source of the exchange gain or loss?

6. What is the translation method to be used?

7. What is the exchange rate to be used in translation?

IV. CONCLUSION

As taxation is often based on accounting legislation and practice, it would be desirable to adapt accounting terminology and methods for use in the present-day world with its increasingly liberalised capital markets. This would enable legislators to make clearer tax laws. It would also be of great value if different accounting bodies could issue guidelines on the complicated accounting issues involved. Clearer tax laws and a better knowledge of these accounting issues will greatly assist tax authorities in their efforts to implement an equitable tax system.

INFORMATION NEEDS ON NEW FINANCIAL INSTRUMENTS: THE POINT OF VIEW OF FINANCIAL ANALYSTS

by
David C. Damant
Managing Director, Paribas Asset Management (United Kingdom);
International Co-ordinating Committee of Financial Analysts Associations

Users of accounts -- in spite of their diversity -- have needs that are much more alike than is often thought. External to the company and having no access to private information, these users need to make decisions based (in part) upon the information provided in the company reports. The decisions in question concern the buying and selling of shares, the prospects for jobs, the granting of credit lines, etc., and are essentially concerned with the future -- the user's aim is to estimate future cash flows, their size, timing and certainty. The information contained in annual accounts and in the historical figures given should assist users in making forecasts.

That fact is not very widely recognised, since much more emphasis (e.g. in press reporting) is placed on the yearly earnings per share figure. However, the concerns set out above are clearly reflected in projects undertaken by a number of accounting bodies, most notably the Financial Accounting Standards Board in the United States and the International Accounting Standards Committee at the international level, to analyse the framework within which accounts should be prepared. And the principles involved apply as much to accounting for new financial instruments as to the more traditional items.

However, there is one exception to the unity of approach mentioned above. In the case of banks, which are of course important users of the new financial instruments, the published figures are scrutinised by supervisory authorities -- whether central banks or some other governmental organisation. This authority's main concern is something quite different from that of a normal user: quite simply, the maintenance of a reliable and secure banking system. It is obvious that there may be a conflict of aims. For example, a user wishing to make forecasts wants the information to be recorded neutrally, without secret reserves, and such a user would not be very impressed with the concept of prudence. On the other hand, a supervisory authority may prefer a prudential approach; the figures may not reflect exactly what is going on; a conservative margin of error is acceptable. It is therefore important that discussions concerning accounting problems for banks, including those relating to new financial instruments, take place in a very clear context: either that of supervision or that of the external user. If this point is not clear, there may be confusion in the debate.

This consideration about supervisory authorities applies only to banks and certain other financial companies; in the case of an ordinary industrial or commercial company, the needs of the external user are obviously the most important.

I do not have a great deal of experience with the requirements of the supervisory authorities of banks, although my first reaction would be that, where possible, they should be the same as those of an external user. If they are not, the user should be aware of any changes imposed for supervisory reasons. The rest of my comments deal with the question of accounting for new financial instruments from the point of view of the external user.

There are two possible approaches. The first is to establish general principles. Analysis of the purposes of accounts cannot, of course, produce theorems that will solve all accounting problems. However, a framework of ideas can be useful and an attempt could be made to define assets and liabilities in a conceptual way. The question can then be asked, does a certain financial instrument fit the definition of a liability? When should it be recognised? How should it be measured? This is the approach adopted in the United Kingdom in its recent Exposure Draft on the subject. The approach has the advantage of very general application. Also, by delineating principles, it is easier to choose from among competing interests and to explain to parties who do not favour a certain accounting proposal why it is required.

On the international level this approach is the more difficult of the two, since the principles that need to be established must themselves be international. The International Accounting Standards Committee has recently produced a framework for the preparation and presentation of financial statements, and reactions from all interested parties are eagerly awaited. This is of course a matter of much more general importance than the particular issue of accounting for new financial instruments.

The second possibility is the purely practical approach, which offers the advantage of relevance as well as practicality. A number of solutions of this type have been proposed -- for example, by the Financial Accounting Standards Board in the United States. The approach is valuable but the disadvantage is that with so many new instruments on the market, the procedural problems of discussion and implementation are considerable. And in tackling so many problems at once -- as would be necessary on practical grounds -- some useful individual treatments may be lost. Comparability is not the point. Obviously, each financial instrument should be accounted for in the same way by all companies; however, it is not necessarily correct that different financial instruments should be treated in the same way.

A final point that arises in accounting both for the new instruments and generally is the question of disclosure versus accounting treatment. In my view the matter is fairly straightforward. As far as the capital markets are concerned, disclosures of the facts about a financial instrument are adequate. The market will make its own assessment of the impact of the disclosed facts on the company and the share price. Capital will be efficiently priced, although only to the extent that the disclosure is complete and understandable. However, one must in these circumstances take account of other users. The trade creditors, for example, need a reliable balance sheet with an accurate presentation of information regarding assets and liabilities. Some complex item buried in a note may be discovered by a full-time analyst but missed by a trade creditor. It does not seem too much to ask that the information in question be correctly incorporated in the accounts.

THE TRADE UNION VIEWPOINT

by
Ingrid Scheibe-Lange
Trade Union Advisory Committee to the OECD (TUAC)

1. General remarks

The importance of the new financial instruments is growing. In particular, off-balance-sheet transactions are increasingly common in banks as well as in major non-banks. The necessity for new rules is evident, rules ensuring that:

-- All transactions are properly recorded;

-- All facts relevant in the use of these new financial instruments are disclosed in the accounts and the notes thereto;

-- Internal management rules are developed to control these instruments;

-- The regulatory bodies include these instruments in their rules, e.g. with regard to capital-ratio requirements, risk limitation and general supervision of financing activities.

Accounts should disclose information on all financial instruments, whether or not they are recognised in the balance sheet itself. Otherwise, a user of the accounts will be unable to assess the financial position of the enterprise, the risks involved, the level of income, the level of activities or the general financing policy. These aspects are important for employees and their trade unions, with regard to both micro-economic and macro-economic questions.

To date, the national and international disclosure requirements concerning off-balance-sheet transactions of banks and non-banks simply have been insufficient. The most interesting proposal being discussed at the present time is the 1987 FASB Exposure Draft "Disclosures about Financial Instruments". The proposed special disclosure requirements, if generally applied, would be a sound step forward.

2. Necessary disclosure requirements

Accounts should disclose the amounts of all types of commitments, contingent liabilities and other outstanding transactions -- receivables as well as payables -- existing at the balance sheet date. They should describe the different types of transactions, disclose and describe the different risks involved, and also disclose the full amount of activities by type during the period and the risks related thereto, even if these transactions are already settled without any loss at the end of the reporting period, in order to indicate management policy with regard to new financial instruments. Information should also be provided on realised and unrealised gains and losses incurred through using such instruments and the related amounts recognised in the accounts.

A. Off-balance-sheet transactions as at year-end

The information should be provided by type of transaction, including traditional commitments and contingent liabilities as well as new financial instruments, indicating the outstanding amounts and the risks involved. The commitments should include at least those that are irrevocable, e.g. commitments to extend credit that cannot be withdrawn at the enterprise's discretion without the risk of incurring significant penalty, expense or problems with its customers. In the case of banks, additional disclosure of revocable credit lines and similar commitments would also be desirable.

Off-balance-sheet items concerning group enterprises (to the extent that they are not consolidated), affiliated enterprises and other related parties should each be disclosed separately.

The risks involved should be described by type -- e.g. financing/liquidity risk, credit risk, interest rate risk, exchange rate risk and other market value risks -- and amounts. A good example of how to indicate risk amounts is the FASB proposal to disclose the maximum credit risk, the reasonably possible credit loss and the probable credit loss.

Another important item for disclosure is the concentration of credit risk by individual counterparties, by groups of counterparties (e.g. industries, regions) and by currencies.

The FASB proposal gives further good examples of how to disclose information on the contractual timing and amounts of prospective cash flows and of interest rate groups for different classes of financial instruments. Such information should also be given by main currencies.

An important question that needs to be answered in disclosure is whether the transactions are hedges or dealing/speculative transactions.

Unrealised losses taken to income as well as the related provisions in the balance sheet concerning off-balance-sheet transactions should be disclosed separately. The same applies to gains and losses realised in later periods when such transactions are settled.

These items of information should be disclosed, as a matter of principle, with regard to all financial instruments, on-balance-sheet as well as off-balance-sheet items, if applicable. Some items are already disclosed with regard to on-balance-sheet items, e.g. information by maturity date, by consumer groups and, in some countries, by interest rate groups. In such cases it may be easier to develop similar disclosure standards for off-balance-sheet items. Nevertheless, steps should also be taken to fill the remaining gaps and develop new types of disclosure standards.

B. Off-balance-sheet transactions during the period

Information similar to that described in the context of year-end data is necessary on the amounts of such transactions during the year, in order to indicate the level of activities by type of financial instruments and risk involved. Depending on the type of activity, the amounts should usually be the maximum and average levels and, in some cases, period-related amounts. The enterprise's policy should be described; in particular, which financial instruments are used for what purposes, and to what extent? This information should be provided by type of counterparty, indicating risk concentration. If only outstanding items as at year-end are disclosed, the information could easily be misleading with regard to the full level of activity, since several types of new financial instruments may be short-time transactions and the outstanding items at a single date could be much lower or higher than they would normally be.

3. Recognition of unrealised gains?

In principle, unrealised gains should be disclosed in notes but not recognised in financial accounts. A gain not yet realised may not be realisable. Financial accounts are primarily a means of providing reliable information to users who are not members of the enterprise's management. Reliability means *inter alia* that as little discretion as possible should be allowed in the preparation of the accounts. Furthermore, the earned income must exceed the distribution of profits; unrealised gains should never be distributed. These are the main reasons why the valuation principle "the lower of historical cost or market value" is preferable to mark-to-market techniques. The latter may be more useful when applied for other purposes, e.g. for management's own information as a measure of its performance. Mark-to-market techniques may also provide valuable information for other user groups, e.g. workers' representatives, supervisory and regulatory bodies, and even the public, if such data are disclosed separately in addition to financial accounts prepared under the prudence principle.

This means that in financial accounts, all investments should be valued with historical cost or the lower of cost or market; it also means that positive foreign currency translation differences should not be taken to income, but rather attributed to undistributable reserves. If these principles are applied, the question whether certain trading transactions or certain hedges may be valued by the mark-to-market technique no longer arises.

The question that does remain is whether, in cases of direct matching, unrealised losses may be set off against the corresponding unrealised gains. If at all, this should only be allowed when transactions are expressly designed for and identified as hedging. But even in such rare cases it would be preferable to disclose both losses and gains and to indicate that they concern such hedging transactions. And in no case should the hedging transactions as such be netted off and remain undisclosed, since this would not allow a true and fair view of the level of activity of the enterprise.

4. Final remarks

Financial instruments, whether on- or off-balance-sheet, should be disclosed by type, and the amounts involved and the related risks should be indicated and described. This applies to banks and non-banks alike, to enterprises as a whole and to individual entities. A special problem is caused by the fact that group accounts sometimes do not include subsidiaries with different activities. For example, industrial or trading groups sometimes exclude banking subsidiaries for the reason that the activities are too different; sometimes they even create special forms of financing subsidiaries, the so-called dependent non-subsidiary companies, for the purpose of not consolidating the financing activities carried out through these entities. Such practices need to be prevented.

Considering that non-banks, in particular big multinational enterprises, are increasingly engaged in financing activities, a final question arises whether non-banks carrying out a substantial volume of financial transactions should apply the same rules as banks: rules for accounting and disclosure, rules for internal controlling procedures, perhaps even rules to be supervised by regulatory bodies.

5. ACCOUNTING IMPLICATIONS OF NEW FINANCIAL INSTRUMENTS

by
Hans Havermann
Chairman of the Board of Directors, KPMG — Deutsche Treuhand AG
(Germany)

I. INTRODUCTION

The development of new business activities has resulted in a proliferation of diverse and complex new financial instruments. The treatment of such instruments in financial statements has been a source of uncertainty and some controversy. Clearly, standards must be developed on the basis of general accounting principles, taking into consideration the objectives of the financial statements as well as the principal characteristics of the innovations. The accounting treatment must fairly reflect the instruments themselves.

However, as the development of the new instruments has been extremely rapid in terms of both form and volume, establishing standards will be far from easy.

II. BASIC ACCOUNTING PRINCIPLES

Normally the only transactions accounted for are those in the balance sheet, for which at least one of the parties to the contract has fulfilled his obligations. The fulfilment of the contract leads to movements in assets and/or liabilities.

In the case of transactions outstanding on both sides, a balance of opposing rights and obligations exists. Movements in assets can only have taken place to the extent that compensation has been paid at the outset of the contract. Therefore these rights and obligations are not recorded in the balance sheet ("off-balance-sheet transaction"), but they are recorded in memorandum accounts.

In accordance with the prudence concept, only unrealised losses from outstanding transactions are anticipated and accounted for by means of a provision. On the other hand, in some countries no account is taken of unrealised profits, in accordance with the realisation principle. With regard to the valuation of unrealised profits and losses, there are considerable national differences in accounting treatment.

A strict application of the principle of individual valuation can lead to the link between two opposing transactions not being reflected in the accounts, even though it exists in commercial terms. If the principle is applied, unrealised losses should not be netted against unrealised profits, but should be recorded on an individual basis by means of a provision.

Often the real commercial result is not reflected in the accounts. Especially in relation to foreign currency items, the netting of related transactions forming one combined valuation has become general practice. Consequently, unrealised losses are netted against unrealised profits. In these cases, a transaction not accounted for has an influence on the valuation of particular assets or liabilities in the balance sheet.

Items of income and expense such as interest receivable/payable are allocated to the respective accounting periods according to the accruals concept.

In some countries, commitments are disclosed in the notes. It is of considerable importance that this disclosure makes a clear distinction between potential liabilities and potential obligations to granting credit. The potential credit obligation may in turn involve a potential loss, which should be provided for.

III. ACCOUNTING FOR NEW FINANCIAL INSTRUMENTS

1. SWAPS

Swaps involve the following risks:

-- A credit risk exists only to the extent that the bank has made payments in advance due to timing differences of interest payment dates;

-- Exchange rate risk exists for currency and cross-currency swaps in the form of interest and capital repayments if the bank receives payments in foreign currencies.

Exchange rate risks may be eliminated through combining foreign currency items of equal and opposite amounts;

-- Interest rate risks exists only for interest rate swaps and cross-currency swaps, in which the interest margin for the bank may be reduced by a change in the floating interest rate.

The interest rate risk may similarly be eliminated by entering into interest-related transactions of equal and opposite amounts.

Although the exchange rate risk and the interest rate risk are initially eliminated by entering into relevant transactions, the risk still remains that the contractual partner will default and that a replacement contract can only be agreed on less favourable terms.

A. Interest rate swap

The accounting treatment normally distinguishes between:

1. "Matched swaps" -- the bank is an "intermediary", i.e. a party in two equal and opposite contracts.

   Positive and negative results are set off against each other so that potential losses do not arise.

   Matched swaps remain unrecorded in the balance sheet. Interest income and expense are accounted for in the profit-and-loss account according to the accruals concept, independently of the payment dates;

2. "Hedged swaps" involve combined valuation for:

   -- Individual interest-related securities that are linked with individual swaps (micro-hedge);

   -- The total of similar interest-related items that can be identified with individual or several unmatched swaps (macro-hedge).

   Only in exceptional cases will it be possible to identify a link between a swap transaction and a particular hedging position (micro-hedge). However, in those cases, swaps and the related hedged asset should be combined in a single valuation since they do not involve any exposure to interest rate risk.

   In other cases, only the total amounts of swaps and hedged assets (e.g. securities) can be set off against each other. If they are exactly equal (and opposite), interest rate risk will be eliminated;

3. "Unhedged swaps", which is to say swaps that cannot be viewed in the same category as other interest-related items.

   For unhedged swaps (particularly trading positions), there exists an interest rate risk which arises out of the fact that the differing bases for calculating interest rate income and interest expenses may reduce the margin or even cause a loss (the bank's exposure to interest rate risk).

Accounting for interest rate swaps

Normally, interest rate risks are not provided for, since the interest income or expense relates strictly to well-defined time periods. The allocation of interest payments to accounting periods should be calculated using the relevant basis (LIBOR ± X%) for the particular period.

a) Profit-and-loss account

Interest rate swaps are intended to exchange one method of calculating interest expense for another (e.g. fixed for floating), and thus ensure against interest rate risk. Therefore, in the case of matched and hedged swaps, the accrued net payments should be treated as a correction to the primary interest expense arising from refinancing in the profit-and-loss account:

Bank	Industrial Concern
Net interest claim:	Net interest obligation:
-- Set off against primary interest expense arising from refinancing (fixed rate).	-- Addition to the (floating-rate) interest expense arising from loans received.

Profits and losses from dealing positions, on the other hand, should be accounted for separately from interest.

b) Balance sheet

In principle, outstanding transactions are not recorded in the balance sheet (off-balance-sheet operation). However, unrealised losses should normally be provided for.

In connection with interest rate swaps, the following questions are currently under discussion:

-- Could the interest transactions result in losses, which should be provided for in the balance sheet? If so:

    -- Should each individual swap transaction be revalued separately at the balance sheet date (individual valuation)? or

    -- Should the total of all unhedged swap contracts be revalued by netting off unrealised losses with unrealised profits so that only the remaining balance is to be provided for (combined valuation)? and

    -- Under what conditions could swap transactions and opposite transactions qualify as a hedge (micro-hedge) which would not result in any potential losses and therefore require no provision?

The principle that would normally be adopted for the valuation of outstanding transactions in relation to potential losses is that consideration to be given and consideration in return should be netted off against each other. This point leads to the following conclusions.

Analysis of swap transactions in isolation (individual valuation)

a) Receiver of fixed rate (industrial concern)

At the outset of the contract, if LIBOR remains constant there will be a net payment obligation over the duration of the contract. If it is appropriate to treat this net payment obligation as a future loss, a provision should be created for the difference between payments and receipts over the whole period.

If LIBOR should fall, the provision should be increased; if LIBOR should rise, the provision (in part) should be released. However, since the future net payments are only concerned with interest which should be allocated to accounting periods according to the accruals concept, a provision for future interest expenses would be inappropriate.

b) Grantor of fixed rate (bank)

If LIBOR should rise to the extent that a net payment obligation would result, a provision should be created for the remaining period in question, if it is appropriate to treat the net payment obligation as a future loss. As mentioned in the preceding paragraph, however, there should not be a provision for interest expense relating to future periods.

On the other hand, at least in the case of trading positions, a significant number of banks apply the mark-to-market technique, whereby the swap is revalued by means of a comparison of current market rates as at the balance sheet date with the interest rates as stated by the swap contract. This mark-to-market technique is based on the theory of opportunity cost.

In some countries unrealised losses are set off against unrealised profits in all swaps held, which are not designed for hedging purposes, and only the balance is provided for, whereas in other countries unrealised losses are provided for taking no account of unrealised profits.

The treatment of swap transactions as trading positions is currently the subject of a fierce debate, at least in Germany. As with revaluation of foreign exchange transactions, there is a tendency to move away from the individual valuation in favour of the combined valuation, thereby netting off unrealised profits and unrealised losses and only providing for the balance.

Hedging positions

Swaps transacted for the (demonstrable) purpose of eliminating the risk of other positions (e.g. securities), and in which the period of the transaction, the volume transacted and the method for calculating the interest are similar, lead to an overall reduction of risk. At the balance sheet date an individual valuation of the hedged asset may lead to a reduction in value, which would be compensated by a corresponding increase in value of the swap contract. The accounts can present a true and fair view of the commercial reality only if the provision takes into account any related off-balance-sheet transactions.

The conditions for the micro-hedge are, however, rarely satisfied. Consequently, banks frequently practise the following:

-- All unmatched swaps are revalued on an individual valuation basis using the mark-to-market technique;

-- The resulting unrealised profits of individual swaps are netted off against unrealised losses of other swaps;

-- A provision is created for any excess of losses.

Conclusions -- interest rate swaps

If the mark-to-market technique is applied, swaps are revalued at the balance sheet date, as if they were marketable securities whose market value constantly varies in relation to the change in the interest rate level. If on this basis a provision for future losses (where appropriate after setting off unrealised profits) is created in commercial terms, a future profit forgone would be accounted for as expense. Thus owners' equity would be understated.

The creation of a provision for future losses from interest rate swaps (except in the case of swaps for dealing purposes) is inappropriate and should be avoided according to general accounting principles, for the following reasons:

1. If the purpose of the swap for both parties is interest although no capital amounts are exchanged, then the accrued interest payments should be considered as time-apportioned income/expense items for which potential losses should not be anticipated in the form of a provision;

2. If, on the other hand, a provision were to be created on the assumption that LIBOR will not change, the relevant accounting periods would be charged with costs which would not conform to commercial reality;

3. The size of the provision for both parties must be set according to the current relevant interest rate level -- thus the provision needs to be altered at each balance sheet date;

4. The adjustment to the provision could lead to an accounting presentation that is no longer consistent with the objective of the transaction or the commercial reality (industrial concern: fixed-rate interest expenses; bank concern: floating-rate interest expense, LIBOR);

5. From the bank's point of view it is not threatened potential losses but potential reductions in the future interest margin (profits

forgone) that are a part of the general commercial risk and, according to general accounting principles, need not be provided for.

Local legislation, however, may require or allow charges against income for general banking risks or other unforeseeable risks. Where these charges result in overstatements of liabilities or undisclosed accruals, they present the opportunity to distort reported earnings and owners' equity. If such items are not disclosed, financial statements cannot present reliable information about the financial position and results of operations (IASC E29, paragraph 32).

Interest rate swaps held for dealing purposes do not serve the objective of exchanging a floating rate for a fixed rate. Therefore a method for calculation for future losses from these transactions similar to the valuation of securities (mark-to-market technique) can be applied.

The question whether this valuation method is appropriate for accounting purposes and unrealised losses should thereby be netted off against unrealised profits is currently the subject of fierce debate.

B. Currency swap

A currency swap involves two parties to a contract agreeing to exchange assets/liabilities in different currencies; included in the swap are the related interest payments, for which the methods of calculating the interests are identical (fixed exchanged with fixed, floating exchanged with floating).

The exchange of the capital amounts takes place subject to the proviso that they are to be re-exchanged at the end of the contract using the same exchange rate.

Through such swaps, the parties to a contract can reduce their exposure to foreign currency risk while at the same time deriving maximum benefit from the credit rating in each party's local market.

Currency swap trading by banks is similar to interest rate swap trading.

The distinction between matched swaps, hedged swaps and unhedged swaps mentioned in section III.1.A. also applies in the case of currency swaps. Swaps of different currencies should not be combined into one valuation unit.

An exchange rate risk exists for interest payments to be made in foreign currencies. The exchange rate risk associated with the capital repayments is eliminated if the repayment is performed in the bank's local currency. If, however, the repayment is performed in a third currency, an exchange rate risk arises from the exchange of the third currency into the local currency applying the current rate at the end of the contract.

Accounting for currency swaps

The capital amounts are accounted for using the exchange rate to be applied on repayment. If there is an exchange rate risk pertaining to the value of the amount to be received, a provision should be created for a potential loss, in the case where there has been a corresponding change in the exchange rate up to the balance sheet date.

For matched swaps in the same currency, a revaluation at each balance sheet date ceases to be necessary, since unrealised profits and losses arising from a swap transaction and the opposite transaction balance each other. Unmatched swaps should be distinguished into hedged positions and unhedged positions. For hedged swaps, valuations should be on either an individual basis or a combined basis; in the latter case, unrealised losses are netted off against unrealised profits. Unhedged positions are valued individually.

The calculation of unrealised losses or profits is normally based on the value of the payments as at the balance sheet date (mark-to-market technique). This calculation recognises changes in interest rates as well as changes in exchange rates.

Conclusions -- currency swaps

The revaluation of currency swaps using the mark-to-market technique leads to an anticipation of losses when the interest rate has risen -- even when the exchange rate remains constant -- with the result that agreed fixed rates cause potential profits to be forgone.

Since interest rate changes are not provided for, it would appear necessary as part of the revaluation procedures to make the distinction between exchange rate and interest rate changes. The exchange rate risk should be accounted for as part of the valuation of the global exchange rate exposure.

C. Cross-currency swaps

In cross-currency swaps, parties to the contract agree to exchange liabilities in different currencies and different interest methods (e.g. Deutschmarks at a floating rate in return for dollars at a fixed rate).

Cross-currency swaps have the characteristics of both interest rate swaps and currency swaps.

Accounting for cross-currency swaps

A distinction is made between matched and unmatched swaps: the latter, depending on whether they have been hedged or not, are either combined in value with an opposing item or revalued at the current market value on an individual basis (mark-to-market technique). Any unrealised losses resulting from the revaluation of the payments are normally provided for.

Since the market value is influenced by both interest rate and exchange rate fluctuations, this revaluation may lead to a provision in the case where the exchange rate has not changed but the interest rate has risen, and the value of the fixed interest payments is thereby reduced.

Conclusions -- cross-currency swaps

Unhedged swap transactions should be considered as part of the bank's foreign currency activities; for each currency, unhedged transactions as well as any unhedged portion of hedged transactions require a provision.

Normally, no provision should be created in respect of interest rate risks. Consequently, the interest component should not be included in the calculation of the provision for unrealised losses.

D. Summary -- swaps

In banking, swaps held for dealing purposes are treated as marketable assets which possess a corresponding market value. This value depends on how the interest rate and exchange rate have developed in relation to the rates contractually agreed.

The revaluation of swap contracts for purposes of establishing a provision in the balance sheet includes any opportunity costs involved. This means that the provision also comprises profits forgone.

This accounting practice, which is currently adopted by a significant number of banks, does not comply with the prudence concept (that is, only to account for potential losses resulting from outstanding transactions), since unrealised losses and unrealised profits are set off against each other and no distinction is made between losses and profits forgone. On the other hand, this accounting practice may be more appropriate for swaps held for dealing purposes.

Where the mark-to-market technique is applied to hedged as well as trading positions, it will lead to the creation of a provision for interest rate risks including expenses -- which, according to the accruals concept, should be allocated to future periods. A uniform practice has not yet been established since the "correct treatment" is still under discussion.

2. OPTIONS

A. Characteristics

An option is a contract conveying the right, but not the obligation, to buy (call) or sell (put) a specified financial instrument (the underlying) at a fixed price (the strike price) before or at a certain date. The parties to the option contract are the option-seller (writer or seller) and the option-purchaser (buyer or holder). The buyer pays a premium to the writer for the commitment that the option-writer will sell or purchase a specified amount of the underlying instrument on demand. If the option can be exercised at any time between the date of writing and the expiration date, it is called an American option. A European-type option can be exercised only at maturity date.

Underlying financial instruments are:

-- Foreign currencies;

-- Interest rates;

-- Precious metals;

-- Other specified assets.

Options may be traded on organised markets or bilaterally. On organised markets, dealing is standardized in terms of:

-- Currencies;

-- Amounts;

-- Maturities.

Items of bilateral transactions ("over the counter") are individually negotiated. Since options fall into two categories and there are two positions for each option, four different situations are relevant for accounting treatment:

a) Buyer or holder of a call option;

b) Writer or seller of a call option;

c) Buyer or holder of a put option;

d) Writer or seller of a put option.

In terms of the position of the buyer of an option (call or put), there is no risk in excess of the premium paid.

The buyer has a choice:

-- Exercise the option right;

-- Resell the option; or

-- Let the option expire at maturity date.

The writer is incurring a potential commitment to deliver (in cases of calls) or to purchase (in cases of puts) the underlying object at a fixed price (take-up price).

Options involve the following risks:

-- If the underlying object of the option is denominated in a foreign currency, an exchange rate risk exists, which can be limited or eliminated by entering into opposing transactions;

-- If the underlying object of the option is sensitive to interest rate changes (e.g. long-term fixed-rate bonds) there exists a risk regarding a changing market value of the option.

B. Accounting for options

Options are to be accounted for as outstanding transactions; the right to purchase (or sell) as well as the potential commitment is not entered into the balance sheet accounts. The commitment, however, is to be recorded in the "off-balance-sheet accounts" (memorandum accounts). Disclosure should be made of these commitments in the notes to the financial statements.

Accounting for purchases of call options

The premium settled should be recorded as an asset in the balance sheet (in an option premium suspense account). At the balance sheet date, there are various accounting methods that can be adopted. The general rule is that calls are revalued at the balance sheet date on the basis of the current market price; any difference between the cost and the revalued premium is recognised in the profit-and-loss account as an unrealised gain or loss. In some countries, unrealised gains must be disregarded, according to the concept of prudence.

Accounting for sales of call options

The premium received for sales of a call option should be deferred until the option is unwound through exercising the option right or through expiry. For this reason a provision corresponding to the amount received is appropriate.

The calculation of unrealised gains or losses is as follows: if the current market price of the option exceeds the premium received, the difference is credited to a provision in addition to the premium received.

In the case of delivery, no additional loss would occur because the changes in the market price of the underlying asset are equal to the changes in the market price of the call option.

Accounting for purchases of put options

The accounting is the same as for purchases of call options.

Accounting for sales of put options

The accounting is the same as for sales of call options.

Accounting for hedges

The criteria for hedged transactions are:

-- Purchasing positions can only be regarded as a hedge;

-- The item hedged exposes the bank to one of the following specific risks:

i) Foreign currency risk (hedged by a foreign currency option);

ii) Interest rate risk (hedged by an interest rate option);

-- At the date of the signature of the contract, the purpose of the transaction must be clearly documented as a hedge of specified assets or liabilities;

-- There should be a high degree of correlation between the price of the option contract and the price of the hedged item.

In addition, for anticipative hedges the characteristics of the proposed transaction must be clearly defined and the underlying commitment must be reasonably firm.

If options have been used for hedging purposes, then the recognition of the profit or loss on the option should occur over the same period as the recognition of the income or expense produced by the hedged transaction. Where the hedged items are valued at market price, the mark-to-market principle must be applied for valuation of the option.

For hedging purposes, the purchase of a call option can be regarded as matching a writer's position of a call if the underlying object and maturity match each other. The same rule is applicable for the purchase and writer position of a put option.

3. FINANCIAL FUTURES (AS EXEMPLIFIED BY INTEREST RATE FUTURES)

A. Characteristics

Interest rate futures are standardized contracts for the future supply or receipt of particular fixed interest rate notes with extremely short durations (90-day US Treasury Bills, Certificates of Deposit, three-month Eurodollar Deposits) at a price fixed in advance. The underlying notes are subject to fluctuations in value caused by interest rate changes during the contract. Interest rate futures can be acquired from the futures exchange on providing a deposit (the so-called initial margin -- between 1 per cent and 5 per cent of the contract value). An increase in value of the interest rate future caused by a drop in the related interest rate is to the benefit of the purchaser. Because the deposit is small, considerable profits may be made relative to the capital invested as a result of only small falls in the interest rate.

If, however, the market value of the future should fall due to rises in the interest rate, the drop in value of the contract is charged in full against the deposit and leads to a payment call to the extent that the new market value falls below the minimum account balance (generally the initial margin).

Financial futures are not designed for the physical completion of the contract. This would be impossible, for example, in the case of stock index futures. The only purpose is to achieve a profit on settlement. In addition to speculation purposes, however, financial institutions may enter into interest rate futures to limit their exposure to interest rate risks.

Futures involve the following risks:

-- According to whether the object of the futures contract is related to interest rates or foreign currencies, the market value risk contains an interest rate risk or an exchange rate risk. These risks can be partly eliminated by entering into opposing transactions;

-- The commitment to give a stated deposit. A reduction in the contract's market value will lead to a call for additional payment (liquidity risk).

B. Accounting for financial futures

Futures are outstanding transactions which in principle remain unaccounted for, i.e. off-balance-sheet items. In accordance with general accounting principles, only potential losses should be recorded in the form of a provision. Increases in value are not accounted for. The initial margin is a deposit.

Hedging

In the case of transactions undertaken for the purpose of risk reduction, a rise in the floating interest rate will result in a potential profit on settlement of the contract, which is reflected in increased refinancing costs. Similarly, if the floating interest rate were to fall, the reduction in refinancing costs would be balanced by a potential loss on settlement of the contract.

In accordance with general accounting principles, an unrealised profit at the balance sheet date arising from an interest rate futures contract which is characterised by increased refinancing costs should not be accounted for.

Since there is a general obligation to provide immediately (i.e. the next day) for losses in the margin account, there are normally no contingent liabilities at the balance sheet date.

On the other hand, unrealised losses from interest rate futures contracts, which are balanced by increased margins from the loan contract, should be provided for. There is therefore a strong argument in favour of recording the value and the payment terms of the interest rate transactions in the balance sheet in a manner similar to the valuation of exchange rate transactions, since in these cases the financial institution is not exposed to any interest rate risk. For this reason FAS 80 states that expense/income from interest rate futures contracts that can be viewed as risk-reducing transactions can be deferred and set off against income/costs from the opposing transaction. Certain conditions (hedge criteria) must be satisfied in order to follow this treatment; these are detailed in FAS 80.

A similar method employed for the valuation of exchange rate transactions is permitted in Germany. In contrast to forward foreign exchange rate transactions, interest rate futures contracts can be settled at any time.

In addition, there is a higher correlation in the United States between the underlying position (for which the interest is based on US Treasury Bills) and the standardized futures. The settlement dates and amounts are also standardized, so that in comparison to Europe there is a higher probability that the unrealised profits and losses from underlying positions and the corresponding futures contract existing as at the balance sheet date will indeed balance each other in the future.

Individual valuation

On an individual basis, no credit should be taken as at the balance sheet date for unrealised profits, in accordance with the prudence and realisation concepts. It is also not permitted to set them off against unrealised losses from other future contracts that have not been entered into for risk-reducing purposes (individual valuation principle).

In the United States, however, FAS 80 requires that every increase in value on the Chicago Futures Exchange may be paid out and hence treated as a realised profit, even if the contract has not yet been settled.

4. FORWARD RATE AGREEMENTS (FRAs)

A. Characteristics

In a forward rate agreement, two parties agree on the interest rate to be paid on a notional deposit/credit of specified maturity at a specific future date ("settlement date").

Example:

At 1st July 1987 a bank notices an "unmatched" position in its debt capital for a future period, 1st October until 1st January, of $1 million. At 1st July the bank and the third party (also a bank) agree on the interest rate (6 per cent) to be paid on the $1 million (notional deposit/credit) for the period beginning 1st October and ending 1st January. The contract period for FRAs is quoted as "three against six months" (3/6-month FRA), meaning the interest rate for a three-month period ending in six months' time.

At 1st October the interest rate (e.g. LIBOR) has risen to 7 per cent. The bank receives the difference between the current market rate and the interest rate agreed on the $1 million deposit for three months (i.e. 1 per cent). The amount settled in cash is treated as a reduction of the interest rate to be paid on a three-month borrowing period.

If the market rate at 1st October were 5 per cent, the bank would have to pay the difference in addition to the interest rate expense on the effective borrowing.

FRAs offer a means of managing interest rate risks that does not inflate the balance sheet.

Changes in interest rates may lead to an obligation to make a payment which will increase the interest cost and reduce the margin. The risk can be eliminated to the extent that it is possible to set off the risks attached to interest-related items against one another.

B. Accounting for FRAs

FRAs can be used as a perfect hedge or for speculative purposes.

a) FRAs for hedging purposes

Where the FRA qualifies as a hedge, no interest rate risk exists for the three-month period agreed. The FRA should be recorded in a memorandum account. On settlement date (1st October) the settlement amount is deferred and released to the profit-and-loss account over the fixed-rate period.

Accounting treatment for an FRA qualifying as a hedge should follow the accounting method applied to the items hedged. Where the items hedged by an FRA are marked to market, the FRA should be accounted for using the mark-to-market technique. Where the FRA is linked with a short-term commercial paper, the gain or loss should be deferred and released over the period between the settlement date and the maturity date.

b) FRAs for speculative purposes

Where the FRA is to be accounted for as a speculative position at each balance sheet date (before settlement date), the estimated settlement amount (using forward LIBOR quotation) is to be seen as an unrealised gain or loss.

In this case the only purpose of the FRA is the settlement of the difference between the interest rate agreed at the deal date and the interest rate at the settlement date (as is the case with futures).

The settlement amount (normally cash) cannot be viewed as income or loss arising from the difference between two interest rates. For that reason the expected settlement amount cannot be treated as a correction to future interest rate expense/income.

Applying the concept of prudence, unrealised losses on FRAs (from LIBOR falling below the interest rate contractually agreed) should be accounted for, while unrealised gains should be disregarded. Applying the matching principle, however, banks usually account for unrealised gains.

Unrealised losses (i.e. expected settlement amounts) should be accounted for in the balance sheet as a provision for contingent liabilities.

Regarding the calculation of unrealised gains/losses, the generally accepted practice is to account for speculative FRAs using the mark-to-market technique. At the balance sheet date the interest rate agreed is compared with the rate at which an equal and opposite FRA could be purchased for closing out the contract.

5. FACILITIES (AS EXEMPLIFIED BY NOTE ISSUANCE FACILITIES)

Facilities are mediumto long-term financial guarantees for liquidity granted by the bank in return for a commission by issuing a series of short-term notes. Should the notes not be taken up, the bank as underwriter is required to purchase the notes or to grant credit. The weaker the credit solvency of the customer, the higher the probability of this obligation crystallising and therefore the greater the exposure to credit risk.

In practice, facilities differ considerably in form; nevertheless, they always involve the potential commitment to make a payment to a customer up to a specified amount.

Accounting treatment

The underwriting commitment does not appear in the balance sheet.

The proposed International Accounting Standard (in IASC's E29: "Disclosures in the Financial Statements of Banks") states: "The commitments of a bank are frequently significant in amount and are normally substantially larger than those in other commercial enterprises. Hence, the users of the financial statements of banks need to know about irrevocable commitments because of the demands they may put on a bank's liquidity and solvency".

The EC Fourth Directive requires from non-bank companies the disclosure in the notes to financial statements of commitments not appearing in the balance sheet. As required by the IASC's proposed E29 (paragraph 42), banks should disclose:

1. The nature and extent of the commitments to extend credit that are irrevocable because they cannot be withdrawn at the discretion of the bank without the risk of incurring significant penalty or expense;

2. The amounts of commitments arising from off-balance-sheet items.

The underwriter's commitment to purchase at a fixed price the notes that a customer is unable to sell may also lead to a credit risk or to an unrealised loss because of the lower market price of the notes.

IV. FINAL REMARKS

In the accounting treatment of new financial instruments, two main problem areas can be identified:

1. How to allocate any profit or loss arising from an instrument between the respective accounting periods;

2. The extent of any explanatory information which should be provided concerning the bank's activities in the field of new financial instruments in the notes to the financial statements.

The allocation of profits or losses arising from new financial instruments depends not only on whether the instruments are used for managing interest rate and currency rate risks or for dealing purposes but also on the general objectives of financial statements. Regarding the profit-and-loss account, two objectives predominate. One is to present the bank's performance in such a way as to show the profits and losses occurring from all transactions undertaken within the accounting period whether they are realised as at the balance sheet date or not. The second is to present a profit distributable to shareholders in accordance with the concept of prudence.

Since new financial instruments are outstanding transactions, rights and obligations arising from these contracts are normally not recorded in the balance sheet. They should, however, be recorded in memorandum accounts.

Potential contingent losses arising from outstanding contracts should be recognised by means of a provision where losses are likely to occur. This rule applies to all types of business in accordance with IAS 10, "Contingencies and Events Occurring After the Balance Sheet Date".

The most appropriate method of accounting for contingencies of new financial instruments has not yet been established. Where outstanding contracts are revalued as at each balance sheet date and contingent losses are calculated by comparison with contractual conditions agreed (mark-to-market technique), not only losses but also profits forgone are accounted for. This may be appropriate where the objective of the financial statements (particularly the profit-and-loss account) is to show the bank's performance. Where the objective, however, is to show the profit distributable to shareholders in accordance with the concept of prudence, the appropriateness of the mark-to-market technique is debatable -- and, in fact, currently under discussion.

In practice, different accounting methods are applied. In view of the fact that new financial instruments and the risks related thereto are of substantial importance to them, banks should explain the accounting treatment for each type of new financial instrument in the notes to their financial statements.

In addition, specified information on commitments and off-balance-sheet items is required by the EC Directive of December 1986 on the annual and consolidated accounts of banks, as well as by the IASC's Exposure Draft No 29.

Article 41 (2) h) of the EC Directive requires:

"a statement of the types of unmatured forward transactions outstanding at the balance sheet date indicating, in particular, for each type of transaction, whether they are to a material extent for the purpose of hedging the effects of fluctuations in interest rates, exchange rates and market prices, and whether they are made to a material extent for dealing purposes".

Financial institutions should, in addition, disclose any contingent liabilities and irrevocable commitments which could give rise to a risk.

6. INTERACTION BETWEEN STANDARD-SETTING BODIES, OFFICIAL SUPERVISORS AND AUDITORS

by
Peter Chapman
Deloitte, Haskins & Sells

A. Background

The joint task force established by the International Auditing Practices Committee (of IFAC) and the Basle Committee published, in December 1987, an Exposure Draft: "The Relationship between Bank Supervisors and External Auditors". The first paragraph of the preface to that document includes the following: "The growing complexity of banking makes it necessary that there be greater mutual understanding, and where appropriate, more communication between bank supervisors and external auditors". That is a view I thoroughly support.

External auditors are being brought into the ambit of prudential supervision in an increasing number of countries, and this reinforces the need for mutual understanding between all parties.

B. Objectives and concerns

Official supervisors

Objectives:

-- Protection of depositors;

-- Integrity of banking systems.

Concerns:

-- Solvency/liquidity of the banking system and individual banks;

-- Integrity of banks' systems;

-- Integrity of banks' management;

-- Concentrations of risk (whether country risk, investment risk, exchange rate risk, etc.);

-- Integrity of prudential information.

Auditors

Objectives:

-- Statement of opinion on the fair presentation of the state of affairs of the bank and its income for the period (subject to scope).

Concerns:

-- Integrity of accounting systems;

-- Integrity of management;

-- Solvency/liquidity (going concern concept);

-- Presentation of financial statements.

Standard-setting bodies

Objectives:

-- Narrowing the differences in financial accounting and reporting treatments;

-- Codifying best practice.

Concerns:

-- Presentation of financial statements/information.

Below, the Venn diagram approach maps the overlapping concerns of the three parties.

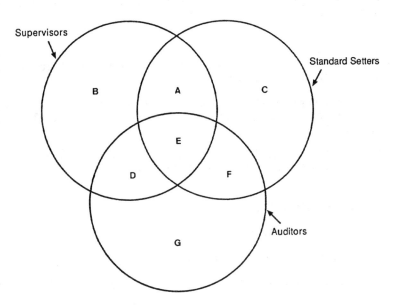

1.   The concerns of the standard-setters must always be concerns of the auditors by virtue of their impact on financial statements -- i.e. A and C are non-existent (or empty sets);

151

2.   Similarly, the concerns of auditors must always be the concerns of supervisors. The supervisors do not want misleading financial information in circulation, i.e. F and G are non-existent.

Therefore, the remaining concerns relate to B, D, E, or

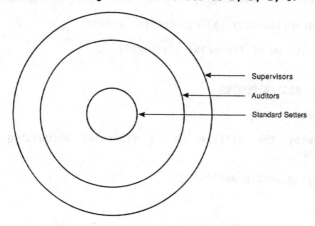

C. Interaction

The standard-setters tend to be drawn, by and large, from the professional bodies of accountants and auditors. Therefore, the relationship or interaction between these two elements of the equation is to some extent automatic.

Looking instead at the interaction between the supervisors and these other two elements it can be seen that they really reflect the differing levels of the supervisors' concerns:

-- With standard-setting bodies -- discussions centre on accounting policies or auditing standards as they apply nationally across the industry;

-- With individual auditors -- discussions will revolve around the circumstances of a particular banking client.

The need for interaction

Benefits to the supervisors:

-- Better understanding of the nature of an audit;

-- Ability to influence standard-setting in auditing and accounting;

-- Encouragement of uniformity of accounting treatments (e.g. financial instruments);

-- Use of additional resources to undertake work of a prudential nature.

Benefits to auditors and standard-setters:

-- Better understanding of the problems facing the industry;

-- Better perception of the supervisors' views on major issues (e.g. LDC debt provisions);

-- Audit opinions not misunderstood or misused by supervisors;

-- Understanding the auditor's position in disputes with client management.

The prime responsibility of the auditor is to his client. No action should therefore be taken without the client's consent, except in the most exceptional circumstances. In the United Kingdom guidance has been given on this subject.

D. Conclusion

The development of the relationship between supervisors and the accounting and auditing profession can only benefit both parties in the longer run. The added responsibilities will perhaps weigh more heavily on the shoulders of the auditors, particularly where they are being brought into the prudential supervision system, but this is a challenge the profession must rise to meet in order to demonstrate that it can play its part "on the cutting edge".

Chapter IV

NATIONAL AND INTERNATIONAL APPROACHES TO ACCOUNTING AND REPORTING FOR NEW FINANCIAL INSTRUMENTS

SUMMARY

by
Arthur J. McHugh
Senior Director, Corporate Law,
National Companies and Securities Commission
(Australia)

Mention was made of a Platonic island on which we might erect an ideal society, and of the analogous opportunity for accountants round the world to create uniform standards to deal with the "new" financial instruments. From the papers delivered at this Symposium, we can see that occupation of the island has already commenced. Prompt action will be required in order to ensure harmony.

There are many interesting themes in the papers in Chapter IV, but I shall only mention a few. A preparatory point is the question of whether all of the new financial instruments we have heard described are truly off-balance-sheet items. Does this assessment remain constant from the time of the initial contract to the date of completion? It is interesting to note that at least one major Canadian bank apparently records acceptances as giving rise to both a liability and an offsetting asset of the same amount. It is also interesting to see that gains and losses determined from some off-balance-sheet activities are recognised in income either as they accrue or over the term of the activity. How do we reconcile this with fundamental concepts such as revenue being an increase in an asset or a decrease in a liability?

Mr. Mosso stated that the FASB hopes to analyse the new financial instruments in terms of standard building blocks termed "fundamental financial instruments". These might comprise guarantees, options, forward contracts, etc. Complex instruments may be reduced to these elements. If the accounting rules for the elements are specified, the composite can be dealt with in this way. There is some support for this approach. We heard Mr. Renshall describe the activities of bankers, etc. as financial engineering and the products as tailor-made combinations of certain basic elements. This conceptual approach should be applauded because it offers the possibility of not having to devise a separate treatment for each new variant. There seems to be a fair measure of similarity developing in how banks account for the new instruments -- in particular, the deferral and recognition of gains/losses in the case of hedging activities. This contrasts with the mark-to-market approach for "trading positions". As I understand it, there is a degree of arbitrariness in determining the character of the activity -- hedge or trading. We should seek objective rather than subjective classifications where possible, particularly when this leads to different fundamental approaches. Even when the distinction is readily apparent, it is troubling conceptually to have different treatment, especially as national treatment is not uniform. For example, in Japan there is no distinction between accounting for hedges and speculative/trading activity.

A further theme is the need to develop supervisory systems for banks, both within the institutions and by the regulatory authorities. Because some jurisdictions have a variety of regulated non-banks with similar financial risk elements in their business, there may be a need for our banking colleagues to lead us through the conceptual underpinnings of the final, rather crude-looking capital adequacy adjustments. I refer to the regulatory approach to brokers in both the stock and futures exchanges and to other dealers in financial products. The numbers and the risk categories may differ for non-banks but the methodology should be transferable. Similarly, whereas the theme of the Symposium is accounting for the new financial instruments, it is necessary to be certain that the appropriate audit procedures are widely disseminated and standardized.

There is an implication from this regulatory activity that increased capital will be required by banks to support their continued creation of off-balance-sheet instruments. This will in turn lead to higher costs to the end-users, typically non-banks which, may cause a lessening of demand for the financial instruments. Nevertheless, unless the market is saturated, the volume may continue to grow.

Mr. Renshall also referred to off-balance-sheet activity pursued by means of the so-called "controlled non-subsidiary". This is a problem shared by all jurisdictions with a non-judgmental legal criterion for specifying the set of companies or other entities to be consolidated. In my opinion, some early attention to this problem is merited by these jurisdictions. However, the holding company subsidiary relationship in company law has wider ramifications than in the purely accounting context, e.g. company purchase of its own capital, etc. Thus, any review and adoption of a more subjective criterion needs to address these questions unless there is to be a special-purpose test limited to the consolidation of accounts. The Australian accounting profession has reacted in a similar fashion to the UK Exposure Draft ED42.

However, in the example given by Mr. Renshall, I found it intriguing that in identifying the substance of a transaction the test was to be whether the transaction has increased or decreased the enterprises' assets or liabilities. If we couple this with the commonly accepted notion that a guarantee does not set up a liability (or asset), it is difficult to see how that particular difficulty of controlled non-subsidiaries will be solved. Unlike the United Kingdom with its ability to reconcile these proposals with the UK Companies Act 1985, Australia would, I believe, require legislative amendment.

Mr. Cooke mentioned that many banking supervisory authorities view the information given in published accounts of banks as generally insufficient for shareholders and depositors. They would welcome discussions with the accounting profession on these issues. We should all take note of this warning and invitation.

It was evident that the banking regulators have (wisely) retreated from the attempt to provide measurement rules for the treatment of the new instruments covering income recognition, the creation of provisions and the recognition of assets and liabilities. However, we should presume that this forbearance will be of indefinite duration. The clock is running against us.

Mr. Cooke also referred to the importance of management systems. We in Australia have had a recent celebrated case of a middle-ranking industrial company which lost its way in this field. Apart from a considerable actual loss, there has been damage to the credibility of the auditors, the directors and other parties who might have suspected a problem. The beneficial outcome has been that directors of all companies are now aware of the risks and the need to install appropriate reporting systems.

The final issue addressed in Mr. Cooke's paper is possibly the most interesting -- namely, the proper forum and parties for the development of accounting standards. I think one could deduce that he would not be unsympathetic to a larger role for the IASC. We cannot long delay a decision on the question of international harmonization.

1. NATIONAL APPROACHES

CANADA

NATIONAL/INTERNATIONAL APPROACHES TO ACCOUNTING AND REPORTING FOR NEW FINANCIAL INSTRUMENTS

by
David Robertson
Tax and Accounting Policy and Research Division,
Office of the Superintendent of Financial Institutions
(Canada)

Introduction

Off-balance-sheet business is not new to Canadian banks. For many years they have reported various commitments and contingent liabilities, including guarantees and letters of credit.

To set the scene, Table 1 shows the extent of the participation of Canada's largest banks in off-balance-sheet activities. The table highlights the growth of various new financial instruments between 1986 and 1987. This growth has been especially strong in the swap and futures markets because of the recent volatility in interest rates and foreign exchange. These products generate fee and trading income for the banks and are also used to reduce their exposure to movements in rates.

This paper presents the approach being taken in Canada, and more specifically by Canadian banks, to the disclosure and accounting treatment of new financial instruments. The paper discusses:

1. Requirements that have been established by the national standard-setting bodies;

2. Accounting treatment that is being used in practice; and

3. Disclosure provided by the major banks in Canada through their financial statements and annual reports to their shareholders.

1. Requirements of national standard-setting bodies

As in so many other countries, the development in Canada of accounting standards and guidelines for new financial instruments is lagging behind the growth in their use.

Accounting standards in Canada are developed by the Accounting Standards·Committee of the Canadian Institute of Chartered Accountants (CICA) and are promulgated in the CICA Handbook. Federally chartered financial institutions are required to follow these standards except where specifically prescribed otherwise by the Office of the Superintendent of Financial Institutions. To date, neither body has issued guidelines for off-balance-sheet transactions, but these organisations are actively involved in addressing the topic of new financial instruments.

Table 1

GROWTH IN OFF-BALANCE-SHEET ACTIVITY IN CANADA
(in millions C$)

Instrument	1987	1986	% increase
Guarantees and letters of credit	26 486	26 499	0.0
Acceptances (1)	26 549	24 903	6.6
Commitments to extend credit	228 219	222 076	2.8
Issuance facilities (NIF/RUF)	7 366	6 230	18.2
Foreign exchange forward contracts	468 268	353 396	32.5
Foreign currency and interest rate swaps	97 972	57 856	69.3
Foreign currency and interest rate futures	24 796	14 165	75.1
Future rate agreements	41 857	20 012	109.2
Foreign currency and interest rate options	5 603	4 240	32.0

1.   Acceptances are on-balance-sheet transactions in Canada.

In February 1987, the Accounting Standards Steering Committee of the CICA established a task force on financial institutions. The membership of the task force comprises individuals from public practice as well as from the various sectors of the financial services industry. Representatives from the Office of the Superintendent of Financial Institutions also participate as observers at the task force meetings. A primary purpose of the task force is to enhance the ability of the standard-setting process to respond on a timely basis to the need for guidance on emerging accounting and financial reporting issues in the financial services industry.

At one of its early meetings, the task force identified off-balance-sheet activities of financial institutions as a topic on which accounting guidance should be developed as a matter of high priority. Accordingly, the task force is currently preparing an Issues Paper on the accounting measurement and disclosure of off-balance-sheet activities of financial institutions. This paper will identify and analyse each of the major accounting measurement and disclosure issues relating to off-balance-sheet transactions, and examine how an appropriate framework within which to address these transactions might be developed. For the purpose of examining the relevant accounting issues, it is proposed to categorize transactions according to the nature of the primary risk being transferred: credit risk products, price risk products and liquidity risk products.

It is intended that the completed Issues Paper will be made available for public discussion and comment later this year. This may then lead to the development of accounting standards or guidelines for inclusion in the CICA Handbook.

As a regulatory body, the Superintendent's Office is concerned that off-balance-sheet transactions be disclosed and that their relative risks be assessed. The Office therefore strongly supports the CICA's efforts to develop a generalised framework that will guide the development of appropriate accounting practice not only for today's financial instruments, but also for those that will undoubtedly evolve in the future.

A representative of the Office is also a member of the Committee on Banking Regulations and Supervisory Practices of the Bank for International Settlements (BIS). On 17th March 1986 the Committee issued new guidelines for disclosure on the regulation of banks' off-balance-sheet risks. The Committee suggested that off-balance-sheet risks should not be analysed separately from on-balance-sheet risks but form an integral part of the banks' risk profile. The Committee concluded that "the particular perspective of supervisory authorities, in relation to off-balance-sheet risk, is to seek to ensure that banks are adopting appropriate procedures to measure and control the risks" by:

-- Keeping abreast of new developments by engaging in dialogue with banks and other interested parties;

-- Reviewing prudential reporting systems to ensure that all major off-balance-sheet activities are adequately captured in supervisory returns; and

-- Reviewing supervisory policies to ensure that they take full account of developments in off-balance-sheet business.

In this regard, the Superintendent's Office is working closely with the Canadian Bankers' Association. This Association, representing Canadian banks, has made proposals to the Superintendent on how banks should account for the new instruments and how risks should be measured.

In addition, since September 1986 off-balance-sheet reports have been submitted quarterly to the Superintendent's Office by a number of "test" banks. This reporting format will eventually be modified to reflect the reporting needs of any new risk asset weighted system of capital adequacy measurement.

The Office of the Superintendent is also concerned that financial institutions establish appropriate internal procedures for controlling these new instruments. During annual bank inspections, information is obtained that enables the Office to assess these practices.

Also with regard to supervisory policies, the Committee on Banking Regulations and Supervisory Practices issued a consultative paper in December 1987 called "Proposals for International Convergence of Capital Measurement and Capital Standards". This paper advocates that off-balance-sheet activity be included in the assessment of bank capital adequacy where the instrument or technique represents a credit risk to the bank. Canada has participated in and supports the efforts of the BIS in this regard.

2. Accounting treatment

Given the lack of formal guidance by the standard-setting bodies, the Canadian banks have developed their own practices for these instruments. These practices are consistent with those followed by other large international banks.

The Annex describes the accounting treatment used in Canada for those new financial instruments identified in the OECD background report. The treatment reported is based on a review of the practices of the six largest banks in Canada. These banks account for 96 per cent of Canada's total domestic banking assets.

The accounting principles relating to recognition of income from off-balance-sheet instruments can be briefly summarised as follows:

-- Gains and losses as a result of activities undertaken to hedge assets and liabilities are deferred and recognised in income over the remaining life of the hedged item;

-- Trading positions are revalued to prevailing market rates and the resulting gains and losses from trading activities are recognised in income as they accrue;

-- Fees for acting as an intermediary are accrued over the life of the instrument in other income.

3. Annual report disclosure

The OECD background report notes three kinds of problems of financial disclosure in annual reports. These are:

-- Information on accounting principles used;

-- Disclosure of the level of off-balance-sheet commitments; and

-- Disclosure of the risks incurred.

The following is a review of the disclosure provided by the six largest Canadian banks in their 1987 annual reports. It is divided into three parts corresponding to these three "problem" areas. The analysis includes information provided in the notes to the financial statements and in management's discussion and analysis of the financial results.

Information on the accounting principles used

Most major Canadian banks disclose the accounting principles they follow for specific new financial instruments in Note 1 to their financial statements. This note presents a summary of significant or prescribed accounting policies and practices. The disclosure of accounting principles used for new financial instruments for the six major Canadian banks is summarised in Table 2.

Table 2

INFORMATION ON ACCOUNTING PRINCIPLES FOR NEW FINANCIAL INSTRUMENTS
PROVIDED IN NOTE 1 TO FINANCIAL STATEMENTS

Instrument	A	B	C	D	E	F
Acceptances	x	x			x	x
Financial futures and future rate agreements	x	x	x		x	
Cross currency and interest rate swaps	x	x	x		x	(1)
Foreign currency options	x	(2)	(3)		x	
Translation of foreign currencies	x	x	x	x	x	x

1.   Reference to treatment of swapped deposits is made under translation of foreign currencies.

2.   Prescribed accounting policies describe treatment of foreign exchange trading positions.

3.   Summary of significant accounting policies describes treatment of foreign exchange and precious metals trading.

The following excerpts from Note 1 to the financial statements of a Canadian bank illustrate the type of information disclosed on the accounting principles relating to the new financial instruments. This example is typical of the kind of disclosure of accounting principles provided by the major Canadian banks.

"Acceptances

The potential liability of the Bank under acceptances is reported as a liability in the Consolidated statement of assets and liabilities. The Bank's recourse against the customer in the event of a call on any of these commitments is reported as an offsetting asset of the same amount.

Financial futures and future rate agreements

Financial futures and future rate agreements are used to protect the Bank against the risk of adverse interest rate fluctuations and may also be part of trading activities.

The principal amounts outstanding under financial futures and future rate agreements represent future commitments and are not included in the Consolidated statement of assets and liabilities. Gains and losses on any of these instruments which are designated as hedges of assets and liabilities are deferred and recognized in income over the remaining life of the hedged item. Where these instruments are used in trading activities, any gains or losses are recognized in income as they accrue.

Cross currency and interest rate swaps

The Bank enters into cross currency and interest rate swaps either to earn fee income as an intermediary between counterparties or to manage its own funding requirements and foreign currency exposure. The fees for acting as an intermediary are accrued over the life of the swap in other income; for non-intermediary swaps the associated income or expense is accrued over the life of the swap as an adjustment to interest income or expense as appropriate.

Foreign currency options

The Bank enters into foreign currency options either to earn option premiums as a writer or to manage its own foreign currency exposure as a purchaser. Any gain or loss resulting from marking these options to market is recognized in other income. The amount of the option premium represents the maximum gain for written options and the maximum loss for purchased options. The difference between the spot and the strike price represents the maximum loss for written options and the maximum gain for purchased options.

Translation of foreign currencies

Foreign currency assets and liabilities, other than investments in foreign currency securities and fixed assets that were purchased with Canadian dollars and carried at historical cost, are translated into Canadian dollars at prevailing year-end rates. Foreign currency income and expenses are translated into Canadian dollars at the average exchange rates prevailing throughout the year.

Unrealized translation gains and losses related to the Bank's net investment position in foreign operations, net of any offsetting gains or losses arising from economic hedges of these positions and applicable income taxes, are included in retained earnings.

Unrealized and realized gains and losses on instruments designated as hedges are deferred and amortized over the remaining life of the hedged item. All other unrealized translation gains and losses and all realized gains and losses are included in other income in the Consolidated Statement of Income."

In summary, Canadian banks are generally providing adequate information on the accounting methods used to record off-balance-sheet transactions that have a significant impact on financial statements and thereby are meeting the requirements of the section on disclosure of information in the OECD Guidelines for Multinational Enterprises. However, where and how this information is provided is not standardized. From the viewpoint of ease of access for readers of the financial statements, more specific guidance is desirable.

Disclosure of banks' off-balance-sheet commitments

Banks in Canada are required to disclose commitments and contingent liabilities in the notes to their financial statements. With respect to new financial instruments, the note generally takes this form:

"In the normal course of business the Bank undertakes various other commitments and has contingent liabilities which are not reflected in the financial statements. These include commitments to extend credit, foreign exchange forward contracts, interest rate futures, forward rate agreements, interest rate and cross-currency swaps and foreign currency options written. In management's view, any losses that may result from these transactions would not be material."

The note is accompanied by specific details on contingent liabilities for letters of credit and guarantees.

Five of the six major banks provide a table of significant off-balance-sheet commitments. Four of them provide this in the body of their annual report; one provides it in the note to the financial statements on commitments and contingent liabilities. The following is an extract from the annual report of one of the banks. It is fairly typical of the disclosure given by all.

"Because of the contingent nature of some of these transactions and the fact that no principal sums are at risk in others the ultimate degree of risk often is significantly less than the notional principal amount disclosed in the accompanying table.

MAJOR OFF-BALANCE-SHEET COMMITMENTS
(in millions of dollars)

	1986	1987
Contingent liabilities and commitments		
Guarantees (including standby letters of credit)	xx	xx
Letters of credit	xx	xx
Commitments to extend credit	xx	xx
Note issuance and revolving underwriting facilities	xx	xx
Foreign exchange and interest rate related transactions		
Foreign exchange spot and forward contracts	xx	xx
Foreign currency and interest rate futures	xx	xx
Future rate agreements	xx	xx
Foreign currency and interest rate options	xx	xx
Foreign currency and interest rate swap	xx	xx "

Combining the disclosure of the off-balance-sheet commitments under commitments and contingent liabilities with the detail in the table shows that Canadian banks are providing most of the information required by the Council of the European Communities in its Directive of December 1986 on the annual and consolidated accounts of banks.

However, the fact that not all the banks provide this disclosure and that there is no consistency in presentation among those that do indicates a need for standards in this area.

Disclosure of the risks incurred

The concern is with regard to four specific kinds of risk: credit risk, financing and liquidity risk, interest rate and foreign exchange exposure, and management and internal control exposure. These are defined as follows:

-- Credit risk relates to the situation where a contractor fails to honour a commitment at maturity date;

-- Financing and liquidity risk (market risk) corresponds to the risk that a bank will be called upon to provide funds at a time when it cannot easily do so, either because the individual bank is unable to fund itself at market rates or because of the general conditions in the interbank market;

-- Interest rate and foreign exchange exposure is the risk that interest rates or exchange rates may change after the date of the bank's commitment;

-- Management control exposure is the risk that transactions may take place before limits and proper internal controls are in force.

Table 3 summarises the types of disclosures contained in the annual reports of the major Canadian banks. These are usually narrative presentations, sometimes accompanied by tabular disclosures. With one exception, the information is provided as part of the financial or operational review, not as part of the financial statements.

Five of the six banks discuss credit risk generally in the context of loan loss provisioning. They discuss in varying degrees of detail liquidity and interest rate risk. Only one bank specifically mentions management control or operations risk:

"Both the clerical process and electronic data processing within the Bank are subject to tight operations controls, which are continuously subject to independent review by the Corporate Audit Department. The levels of errors and defalcations continues to be low."

The format and content of these presentations vary considerably from bank to bank. For example, in the bodies of their annual reports, five of the big six Canadian banks provide information on interest rate risk (one of these banks includes this under its discussion of market risk). Two of the banks provide tables of their interest rate sensitivity position (similar to what is suggested in the OECD background report). One provides a table of interest rate sensitivity asset-liability mismatches. The other two provide only a narrative commentary.

Table 3

DISCUSSION OF RISKS ASSOCIATED WITH NEW FINANCIAL INSTRUMENTS
PROVIDED IN ANNUAL REPORTS

Type of risk	A	B	C	D	E	F
Interest rate sensitivity analysis table	x		(1)		x	
Interest rate sensitivity	x	x	x		x	
Liquidity		x	x	x	x	x
Foreign exchange			x			
Credit					x	
Market					(2)	
Operations				x		
Portfolio management					(3)	

1. Interest rate sensitivity asset-liability mismatches.

2. Acknowledges the volatility of interest rates, foreign exchange rates and market conditions generally.

3. Risk Asset Monitoring System tracks the status of commitments, guarantees, letters of credit and other off-balance-sheet items.

One of the banks includes its discussion of risk in the notes to the statements under commitments and contingent liabilities. The following is an extract from that note:

"The commitments and contingent liabilities reported below reflect various degrees and types of risks, including credit, interest rate, foreign exchange rate and liquidity risk. The amounts reported represent financial commitments to perform, but do not necessarily reflect the economic risks associated with the commitments.

Many commitments to extend credit do not ultimately involve any outlay of funds to customers and therefore have neither liquidity nor credit risk. Foreign exchange and interest rate contracts, since they generally consist of offsetting commitments, involve limited foreign exchange and interest rate risk to the Bank. Credit risk is the exposure to loss in event of non-performance by the other party to a transaction and is a function of the ability of the counterparty to honour its obligations to the Bank. For all types of foreign exchange and interest rate contracts, only exposure created by movements unfavourable to a customer's foreign exchange or interest rate position creates a potential for credit risk. Hence, only half the contract amounts outstanding will generally be a source of any credit risk at a particular time, and then only for an amount equal to changes in foreign exchange or interest rates. The Bank controls all credit risks through credit approvals, limits and monitoring procedures.

Certain foreign exchange and interest rate contracts are entered into by the Bank to reduce the exposure of certain assets and liabilities on the balance sheet to foreign exchange or interest rate risk."

This same bank also includes in the body of its annual report a discussion of portfolio, interest rate and liquidity risk and an interest rate sensitivity analysis table.

Clearly, disclosure of risk is a critical element to the accounting and reporting of new financial instruments. The banks are taking the lead in disclosing and discussing it in their annual statements. The Canadian Institute of Chartered Accountants is considering using risk as a basis for establishing accounting standards and guidelines in this area. Risk weighting of these instruments is also being discussed in great detail by the Office of the Superintendent of Financial Institutions in Canada and internationally by the BIS for the implementation of capital adequacy measurements.

General Conclusion

Canada's national approach to the disclosure and accounting treatment of new financial instruments is not unlike that used by many other countries today. The national standard-setting bodies have yet to pronounce in this area, but they are researching it actively and are closely following developments in other countries and within the international organisations.

Our major banks, however, are following accounting practices that are consistent with those of their international counterparts and with those outlined in the OECD background report. They are also providing disclosure of these accounting practices on the level of off-balance-sheet commitments and of the risks incurred. But the disclosure varies in extent (from non-existent to quite extensive) and location (in statements or in annual reports).

In Canada, as in other countries, there is a need for greater consistency so that the information can be put to better use both by the investment community and the regulators.

ACCOUNTING TREATMENT OF NEW FINANCIAL INSTRUMENTS -- THE CANADIAN APPROACH

This Annex outlines the accounting treatment for new financial instruments that is used in Canada. It follows the format of the OECD background report.

1. Contingent liabilities

Banks' main contingent liabilities are guarantees and other direct credit substitutes; acceptances and endorsements; documentary letters of credit; and warranties.

A guarantee is an undertaking by a bank to stand behind an obligation of a client and to carry out this obligation should the client fail to do so. These are not reported on the balance sheet by Canadian banks but are disclosed by way of note to the financial statements.

Similar treatment is given documentary letters of credit. Because no amount becomes payable unless the beneficiary presents the documents stipulated in the letter of credit, commercial letters of credit are treated as contingent liabilities and included as part of this note to the financial statements.

Unlike many other countries, the potential liability under acceptances is reported in Canada as a liability on the balance sheet. This is because the holder of acceptance will seek payment at maturity from the bank, not from the drawer of the draft. The equal and offsetting claim against customers in the event of a call on these commitments is reported as an asset.

2. Commitments

This category, as defined in the OECD background report, comprises all the irrevocable facilities and arrangements. More specifically, it includes non-utilised confirmed credits (and the issuance facilities of debt securities), and forward sales and purchases of assets.

Credit commitments, an expression of willingness by a bank to extend credit up to a specific amount for an agreed purpose for a specified time period, are not reported on the balance sheet. When commitments are drawn, the bank records the asset (loan, security, acceptance, etc.) in the appropriate balance sheet category.

Note issuance facilities (NIFs) are arrangements whereby a customer issues short-term notes supported by an undertaking by a bank that if the customer is unable to issue the notes at a predetermined price, the bank will buy them at that price. The underwriting commitment remains off-balance-sheet unless the bank purchases notes or extends credit in some other form in accordance with the NIF. Holders of notes issued under NIFs show them as assets on their balance sheets.

Repurchase agreements involve the sale of a loan, security or fixed asset with a simultaneous commitment whereby the seller, after a stated period of time and for a purchase price agreed upon at the time of sale, will repurchase the asset from the original buyer. The accounting for repurchase agreements by securities dealers in Canada considers the transactions as financing in nature. In a financing arrangement, ownership of the underlying securities remains effectively with the vendor/borrower, the "sale" of the securities is recognised by recording a liability, and the related asset account remains undisturbed. The Canadian Bankers' Association proposes that a similar treatment be used by banks. The proposal is under consideration by the Office of the Superintendent of Financial Institutions.

3. Foreign exchange, interest rate and other market-rate-related transactions

These commitments correspond to agreements relating primarily to foreign exchange, interest and other market rates, such as stock indices, which are generally binding on both parties, but in some cases exercisable at one party's discretion. Apart from traditional forward foreign exchange transactions, no exchange of principal is generally involved.

These instruments are used by the banks in trading activities or as hedges. The accounting principles used by Canadian banks can be summarised as follows:

-- Hedges: gains and losses as a result of activities undertaken to hedge assets and liabilities are deferred and recognised in income over the remaining life of the hedged item;

-- Trading activities: trading positions are revalued to prevailing market rates and the resulting gains and losses are recognised in income as they accrue; and

-- Fee income: fees for acting as an intermediary are accrued over the life of the instrument in other income.

To date neither the CICA nor the Office of the Superintendent of Financial Institutions have issued accounting guidelines on these transactions. The accounting described in the following paragraphs reflects what is generally used by the Canadian banks.

a) Forward foreign exchange transactions

A forward foreign exchange contract represents commitments to purchase or sell foreign currencies for delivery at a specified date in the future at a predetermined exchange rate.

Exchange adjustments on forward exchange contracts entered into with the intention of profiting from anticipated exchange rate fluctuations are recognised immediately in income. The adjustments are calculated by multi-plying the forward contracts' foreign currency amount by the difference between the contracted forward rate and the forward rate available in the market for the contract's remaining maturity.

Forward exchange contracts covering spot positions created by term deposit swap transactions are valued using the spot rate as of the balance sheet date. The forward premiums or discount are amortized evenly to the interest cost of the swaps over the life of the swap transactions.

Gains and losses on forwards designated and effective as hedges of investments in foreign operations are charged or credited directly to retained earnings net of any applicable income taxes as an offset to the gains or losses on these investment positions.

b) Interest rate and currency swaps

Swaps are financial transactions in which two counterparties agree to exchange currencies and/or related interest flows, i.e. fixed rate for float-ing rate or vice versa, on a specified amount of notional principal for a specified period.

When a bank acts only as an agent in a swap, any arrangement fees re-ceived are recognised in "other income" in the year in which the deal is con-summated. Intermediary or guarantee fees received throughout the life of the swap transaction are recorded in "other income" in the year in which they are earned.

When a bank participates for speculative purposes, gains or losses cal-culated by marking the swap transactions to market are reflected in "other income".

The foreign currency gains or losses that arise on swap transactions used for hedge purposes should affect the gains or losses of the underlying instruments being hedged. Similarly, any interest rate adjustments that stem from hedged swap transactions should be recorded as interest income or expense.

The principal amounts involved in swap transactions are not exchanged and remain on the original party's balance sheet. The principal amount of swap transactions arranged or entered into by a bank is not required as note disclosure in Canada.

c) Financial futures

Financial futures represent future commitments to purchase or deliver securities or money market instruments on a specified future date at a speci-fied price. They are used to protect the banks against the risk of adverse interest rate fluctuations and may also be part of trading activities.

The principal amounts outstanding under financial futures represent future commitments and are not included in the balance sheet.

Gains and losses on any of these instruments designated as hedges of assets and liabilities are deferred and recognised in income over the remaining life of the hedged item. Where these instruments are used in trading activities, any gains or losses are recognised in income as they accrue.

d) Forward rate agreements (FRAs)

A forward rate agreement is a contract that calls for cash settlement at a future date for the difference between a contracted rate of interest and the current market rate, on a notional principal amount, for a predetermined period.

A FRA does not require an exchange of principal. The principal is only a notional amount used for calculating the interest differential to be paid or received and does not constitute an asset or liability. The principal amount is therefore not reflected in the balance sheet.

Forward rate agreements entered into for hedging purposes are marked to market and any gain or loss is deferred to be matched against the recognition of the gain or loss on the item being hedged. Similarly, forward rate agreement for speculative purposes are carried at market; however, any gain or loss is recognised immediately.

e) Options

An option is a contract conveying the right, but not the obligation, to buy (call option) or sell (put option) a specified financial instrument at a fixed price before or at a certain future date.

For purchased options, the premiums paid are accounted for as a deferred expense on the balance sheet with adjustments made for subsequent gains or losses accrued until the option is exercised or has lapsed. If it is a hedge, gains or losses are accrued and used to offset the gains or losses arising from the hedged instruments. Gains or losses on options designated as hedges of firm commitments or anticipated transactions may be deferred and included in the measurement of the transaction that results, except to the extent that this adjustment could cause the carrying amount of the hedged item to exceed its fair market value.

Accounting for written options is similar to the treatment of purchased options and futures contracts; the premium received is treated as deferred revenue adjusted by gains or losses accrued after marking the option to market on a daily basis.

The gain on an option written or the loss on an option purchased is limited to the value of the option premium for accounting purposes.

f) Caps, floors and collars

These are treated like interest rate options.

FRANCE

THE WORK OF THE CONSEIL NATIONAL DE LA COMPTABILITE
ON THE ACCOUNTING TREATMENT OF NEW FINANCIAL INSTRUMENTS

by
Jean-Paul Milot
Assistant Secretary-General, Conseil national de la comptabilité
(France)

The increasing use of new financial techniques and the very nature of these techniques require close scrutiny of certain accounting procedures.

The new financial instruments permit the easy international performance of transactions which hitherto had been the preserve of specialists operating on restricted and compartmentalised markets.

This development has affected both the conditions under which the markets operate and the standardization of transactions.

The resulting upheaval has been so great that it raises the question of whether certain economic concepts need to be redefined and whether accounting practices should not be modified as a result.

Before examining the likely course of future events, let us look back at how we tackled these issues when they first surfaced.

I. Early work on the new financial instruments

It should first be noted that in France, as in certain other countries, accounting by banks is to some extent autonomous. As a result, a gap has opened up between the views of bank accounting specialists and general accountancy experts. The major changes referred to above first took place in significant measure in the banking sector, where consideration of the funda-mental problems posed by this type of instrument had already been under way for some time and had also naturally benefitted from the study of practices adopted abroad, particularly in the United States.

Appropriate conclusions were reached, but their conversion into accounting regulations and standards required, and to a large extent still requires, considerable work.

Our approach was pragmatic, attempting to resolve issues as they were raised by users.

In 1986, the Conseil national de la comptabilité (CNC) was asked by the Chambre de compensation des instruments financiers de Paris to draw up accounting standards for transactions on the futures market (MATIF). A work-ing group was set up to examine this issue, and its rapid progress enabled the CNC to issue a standard on 9th July 1986.

1. Transactions on the futures market (MATIF)

This standard makes a distinction between the general case, where transactions are analysed straightforwardly, and that of hedging, where the purchase or sale of the futures contract is linked to one or several other transactions. In both cases, the first concern was economic and financial reality; in the general case, the standard recommends that rises or falls in the market value of the contracts be recognised in the profit-and-loss account by reference to the organisation and operating conditions of the market, since settlement and daily posting of margins can be equated to a sale followed by an immediate repurchase of the future in the case of a buying position, and to the reverse in the case of a selling position. This analysis also justifies from the legal standpoint the daily entry of gains and losses in the profit-and-loss account, since they are effectively realised by this mechanism.

Defining the concept of "hedging" proved more difficult. It was not possible to take over for accounting purposes the practices described as "hedging" by dealers, since that would have resulted in too vague a concept and, above all, would have involved reporting difficulties, as some hedging strategies conducted over several years involve discounting and produce an aggregate result which does not clearly show its links with each accounting period. A specific accounting concept had, therefore, to be devised to reflect the realities of hedges.

With the particular concerns of bank accounting in mind, emphasis was placed on the concept of exposure to global interest rate mismatches, an essential concept for banks, although the risk is hard to measure and one whose precise effect on the non-financial sector is not easy to assess. Once the existence of a global risk has been established, the item to be hedged must be identified: it must be closely correlated with the global risk in order for an explicit link to be established between the hedging transaction and a specific item. This item may be an asset, a liability, an existing commitment or an expected transaction that can be precisely defined and is reasonably likely to be realised. Accounting treatment must identify hedging transactions from the outset and then record their profits and losses in a cash position account or a suspense account, matching the related income and expense.

This definition is intentionally restrictive and is certainly not easy to apply. However, it does not appear possible at the present stage to amend it significantly without introducing factors that would be impossible to check.

2. The general problem

This first standard served as a frame of reference for later work. At the same time, however, the situation became rather more complicated. As more instruments were devised, it became clear that (1) problems could not be resolved in isolation; (2) certain basic principles would have to be reviewed; and (3) the distinction between bank accounting and traditional accounting was becoming blurred by a gradual harmonization of the two approaches.

To this end, a specialist committee was established within the CNC, chaired by a member of the Commission bancaire, with a view to ensuring the closest possible harmonization with banking practices. Before substantive issues could be tackled, however, a pragmatic approach to gather the necessary experience in these new fields was clearly called for. The committee therefore first examined a specific issue, the accounting treatment of interest rate options, even before the official market opened in Paris.

This approach had two advantages: it followed on from previous work since these options concerned futures quoted on the MATIF, and it dealt with the second major category of futures instruments -- options. Thus, although only two specific instruments were dealt with, standards were established covering two fundamental elements underpinning many of today's complex operations, and general principles could thus be extrapolated more easily.

The standard on interest rate options was adopted on 10th June 1987. In content it resembles that on futures transactions. After defining options as assets or liabilities whose value can be measured in terms of the premium, this standard likewise distinguishes between hedging transactions and the general case. In the latter, changes in premium value are recognised in income according to the same economic and financial criteria applied to transactions on the futures market. Here, however, legal justification is more problematic, since for interest rate options, settlement and daily posting of margins are not required in all cases as on the futures market.

Since purchasers of options can only lose their initial premium, the market organisers took the view that a system providing for the posting of margins for purchasers was not necessary, since it would not increase purchasers' security. Furthermore, in the interests of security it was decided that in calculating the amount of the guarantee deposit which sellers must adjust daily, reference should be made not to the change observed in the premium but to an assessment of the maximum risk likely to be incurred during the next day's trading. The accounting treatment of changes in values as expense and income cannot be so firmly based on an analysis of the instant purchase-resale or sale-repurchase type, all the more so as entering premiums in the balance sheet emphasizes the conventional character of this interpretation. The definition and treatment of hedging transactions were simply adapted from the earlier standard.

II. Current work and difficulties still to be overcome

Having established these two frames of reference, the committee was in a position to expand the range of its activities, while mindful of the legal issues that would arise. The new subjects on its agenda -- accounting for sales of redeemable bonds, negotiable credit bonds and warrants, whether or not linked to bonds -- in fact raise these difficulties to a greater or lesser extent as soon as a degree of consistency is sought in the overall approach taken.

1. Repercussions of the October 1987 crash

Work on these subjects is currently under way, but since the October 1987 stock-market crash the context has changed slightly. In France as in other countries, the new financial instruments were called into question, as regards both the consequences of their very existence for the operation of the various markets (knock-on effects, increased opportunities for speculation through high leverage, etc.) and the way they work (monitoring of markets, dealers, information supplied to the various parties involved and accounting treatment).

Although only the accounting side concerns us here, the work of several special committees has shown that it may be preferable to deal with a number of these issues at the same time. It is still important to distinguish between categories of transaction and to dispel any illusion that accounting procedures can resolve all the difficulties or that, on the contrary, the inadequacy of existing accounting regulations can account for and perhaps even excuse inadequate monitoring and supervision of transactions, both internally within enterprises and by the authorities. Nor can the lack of competence of certain dealers be blamed on the weaknesses of the accounting regulations.

This said, work on these matters has highlighted the need to redefine certain basic concepts and adapt the accounting system to cope with all these problems.

On a proposal from the Commission des opérations de Bourse, a working group was set up within a review committee on the new financial instruments and futures markets which had been established by the Minister of State at the Ministry of Economic Affairs, Finance and Privatisation, and was chaired by Mr. Deguen. The working group considered the monitoring, accounting and taxation aspects of these instruments and their use by enterprises.

We shall examine here only the accounting issues summed up in the group's conclusions:

-- Profit or loss should be recognised as realised when it results from changes in the value of an instrument held at the balance sheet date but that can be negotiated at any time on an organised market whose suitability for quotation, liquidity and viability can be certified by the authorities;

-- The current value of assets and liabilities negotiable on such a market should be entered;

-- The regulations for entering and evaluating financial instruments should be, if not identical, at least sufficiently similar, irrespective of the type of enterprise concerned, to prevent any possibility of juggling with profit-and-loss account figures and to ensure the accuracy of the information supplied.

In the light of these considerations and the overall conclusions of the Deguen Committee, the Minister of State asked Mr. Dupont, Chairman of the CNC, to:

-- Complete the work needed to supplement the accounting provisions for new financial instruments; and

-- Inform him of the changes likely to be needed in the regulations currently applied.

174

2. Emphasis of current work

The Committee on New Financial Instruments made an immediate start, but as its work has not yet been completed and the CNC has therefore not yet reached any decisions, the outcome is hard to foresee. However, two main points are being considered: refining the definition of realised profit and attempting to define a concept of "a set of interlinked transactions".

On the first point, consideration cannot be confined to futures instruments, whether firm or conditional. It may seem shocking and dangerous to treat the consequences of fluctuations in rates differently when markets are comparable in terms of liquidity and security. So it is the concept of immediate negotiability that must be studied in depth and defined without ambiguity to ensure that all instruments and bonds constituting a liquidity reserve immediately available at the rate of the day can be treated in the same way.

On the second point, the technical difficulties involved are much greater, going beyond the context of hedging pure and simple and leading to a consideration of the concept of a unitary accounting item which may combine several individual transactions. Implementing this concept would have significant implications both for the evaluation methods employed, which would clearly have to be the same for any given item, and for the presentation of the profit-and-loss account, which could likewise show only a single result per item.

As has already been suggested in connection with hedging, this concept would not in itself be sufficient to prevent any divergence between the calculations made by dealers devising these multiple transactions and the reflection of those calculations in the accounts. But the concept does have the advantage of encouraging greater integration of off-balance-sheet transactions into the overall accounting framework, by singling out those which are part of such combined operations and which would thus be linked to balance sheet items for their evaluation.

It would also allow a simplification of the profit-and-loss account in certain cases, making it easier to understand by outlining in summary form the income from complex transactions organised with the specific aim of achieving a certain result without the volume of income and expense necessarily being substantial.

These ideas, which of course in no way prejudge the outcome of the work now under way, largely call into play concepts which as yet have not been fully developed.

Although the general introduction of these new ideas would not overturn existing theories, it would require a profound change in the habits and thinking of the accounting profession in France. Some will object that this shift towards more systematic attention to economic and financial realities moves rather too far away from careful observance of the principle of prudence. That may be true, but, apart from the fact that excessive prudence is not always the best answer, it is impossible to simply sit back and ignore the challenging financial developments of today. A narrow interpretation of realised profit leaves scope for modulation of the profit-and-loss account that can but grow with the increase in the security and liquidity of markets. It would be paradoxical and dangerous for the future of accounting if the real progress in the organisation of financial activities resulted in the information set out under accounting rules becoming less and less meaningful because those rules had failed to keep up with that progress.

UNITED KINGDOM

FINANCIAL ENGINEERING, FINANCIAL INSTRUMENTS AND OFF-BALANCE-SHEET FINANCE -- DEVELOPMENTS IN THE UNITED KINGDOM

by
Michael Renshall
Chairman of the Accounting Standards Committee
for the United Kingdom and Ireland
(United Kingdom)

London has been among the most active of the major financial centres in the creation of so-called new financial instruments.

However, when we analyse the elements that comprise these instruments we commonly find that the basic ingredients are not new or original in themselves. Essentially, they involve contracts conferring the right to receive money's-worth from other parties. What is innovative is the creative assembly in different sequences, variations or permutations of the traditional ingredients of commercial transactions -- the transfer, exchange and mediation of rights and obligations, risks and rewards. In the United Kingdom the term financial engineering is increasingly used as a generic description of these arrangements. That they flourish and grow bears witness to the fact that they serve important commercial purposes. No criticism of financial instruments, new or old, should be inferred from our discussion of them, since they are essential elements of business and finance. Our concern is simply to ensure that the financial transactions they give expression to are fairly reported in annual accounts so that the reasonably instructed reader can appreciate their impact on the reporting entity's position.

Financial engineering is a global phenomenon. It has been stimulated by the increasing volatility of interest and exchange rates over the past decade and a half, and by the need of major industrial and exporting companies to safeguard themselves against the effects of financial storms. Around the world major industrial companies have long realised that shrewd financial management could not only protect and improve their operating results -- it could in some instances exceed them. A well-known instance is the use of "Zaiteku" (financial technology) by leading Japanese companies, which in recent times has contributed half, or even more, of pre-tax profits for some major industrial companies. Manufacturers such as major users of commodities or exporters who want to safeguard income receivable in foreign currency have long used financial instruments such as hedges and forward contracts to protect themselves. Sometimes the financial engineering becomes audacious, is viewed as a means of profit-generation in itself, and misfires. We need to ask ourselves whether present financial practices always adequately account for and report these complex transactions, the risks, and the outcome. The new financial instruments we are discussing today are certainly the products of financial engineering.

I link the problem of off-balance-sheet finance with the problem of accounting for new financial instruments generally because although they are by no means identical spheres of discussion we frequently find the question arises whether the effects of a particular form of financial instrument should or should not be included in the balance sheet. Thus our approach to off-balance-sheet finance can offer illuminations and insights which will help in our discussions of financial instruments, and I make no apology for concentrating on the off-balance-sheet finance dimension in my discussion of the UK and Irish position.

Just as the range of financial instruments available to meet special needs is constantly expanding, so the associated problems of how and when to recognise them in financial statements grow in parallel. In the United Kingdom, the Accounting Standards Committee (ASC) has chosen to attack first the conceptual problem of off-balance-sheet finance.

The UK analysis of the problem of off-balance-sheet finance classified the transactions at issue into three main groups:

1. Items considered to be entirely outside the scope of the enterprise's financial statements, not affecting its financial position and not requiring reference or disclosure (for example, possibilities of increment or detriment judged too remote, uncertain and improbable to recognise);

2. Items insufficiently certain to warrant inclusion in the accounts but of sufficient significance to require footnote disclosure (for example, various types of contingency); and

3. Items whose legal form was such that by convention or accepted practice they were omitted from the balance sheet, although they represented real elements in the capital and financing of the enterprise (for example, certain types of lease which I discuss below). There was a growing tendency to devise transactions of the last-mentioned class, and exploit to legal form to create arrangements which enabled material assets or liabilities to be omitted from the balance sheet, whether or not they were disclosed in footnotes.

An example of financing arrangements which were argued either to require no disclosure or at most footnote disclosure is the provision of major project finance for a group through the medium of a controlled non-subsidiary. The latter represents perhaps one of the most extreme examples of off-balance-sheet finance. A group creates a special purpose vehicle -- a legal entry -- which it controls but which is not by law a subsidiary company, and does not therefore have to be consolidated: indeed it is argued by some that under British law it would be illegal to consolidate such a vehicle. By this means a major financing operation involving substantial assets and borrowing may be legitimately kept off the consolidated balance sheet, with consequent improvement to reported borrowings, gearing and return on capital. Of course, the borrowings are typically guaranteed by the parent, but in at least one recent notable reported case lending banks were dismayed when they learned at their expense that the consolidated net assets of a group which were reported to be in the order of £40 million were actually negative when the off-balance-sheet obligations were called. The use of such vehicles -- controlled non-subsidiaries -- was not new, but was now adopted on a more organised and extensive scale than before. The ASC's response to these and similar problems is contained in ED42, "Accounting for Special Purpose Transactions", issued in March 1988.

An example of the adaptation of a long-established financial instrument for contemporary purposes was the enormous growth in equipment leasing in the United Kingdom in the 1970s and 1980s. Leasing is one of the oldest and most widely used forms of financial instrument -- and also of off-balance-sheet financing. Its use in the United Kingdom may be cited as illustrative of the adoption of financial engineering techniques to distribute economic benefit.

The combination of high inflation, low profitability, and high tax allowances for plant and equipment in the United Kingdom made leasing attractive to UK industry in the 1970s, and this form of financing grew accordingly. Leasing made it possible for banks and financial institutions, which were generally more profitable and had higher taxable capacity than industrial companies, to buy plant and machinery, on which they obtained high tax allowances, and then lease them to individual companies which at that time generally had insufficient taxable profits to take full advantage of the tax reliefs available. Thus leasing helped disseminate to industry with low tax capacity the benefits of tax allowances which could more effectively be utilised by financial institutions with higher tax capacity. However, the terms of the leases were often such as to transfer to the lessees all or most of the risks and rewards of owning the assets. They were in effect the owners. Accounting convention in the United Kingdom at the time did not require leased assets of this type to be capitalised. The effect was that balance sheets did not fully reflect the assets controlled and used by lessee companies, nor the associated liabilities. This was corrected by the introduction of SSAP 21, requiring finance leases to be capitalised in the balance sheet.

Nevertheless, it must be admitted that this innovation offended some legal purists, who argued that the inclusion of assets in the balance sheet must depend on legal ownership.

The key to ED42 is its definition of "special purpose transaction", defined as a transaction "which combines or divides up the benefits and obligations flowing from it in such a way that they fall to be accounted for differently or in different periods depending on whether the elements are taken step by step or whether the transaction is viewed as a whole". The paper is based on the proposition that "the need to account for a transaction in accordance with its substance is central to the concept of 'true and fair'." Thus, the paper argues that assets and liabilities of "controlled non-subsidiaries" (i.e. where there is control in substance though not in appearance) should be consolidated in the financial statements of the controlling company, just as earlier in SSAP 21 it was argued that leases which were in substance financing arrangements by which ownership was effectively transferred to the lessee, regardless of the legal form, should be presented in the balance sheet as assets and liabilities of the lessee company.

In essence, ED42 takes a conceptual approach to the problems of off-balance-sheet finance, which is equally valid in principle as an approach to many types of financial instruments. Its key elements may be defined as follows:

1. It affirms the primacy of the core financial statements of balance sheet, profit-and-loss account and funds statement as the essential means of fair presentation of financial position, results and changes in financial position. Footnote disclosure alone cannot rectify a defective primary financial statement;

2. Transactions should be accounted for in accordance with their commercial substance or effect;

3. In determining the substance of a transaction, a key step is to identify whether the transaction has increased or decreased an enterprise's assets or liabilities;

4. To assist in making this judgment, the characteristics of assets and liabilities are analysed. Broadly, assets are described as probable future economic benefits controlled by and accruing to an enterprise as a result of past transactions or events. Liabilities are described as present obligations of a particular enterprise entailing probable future sacrifices of economic benefits by transferring assets or providing services to other entities in the future;

5. Illustrations of the application of the principles outlined are given by reference to transactions such as factoring, forward or future contracts, sale and leaseback, consignment goods, securitised receivables, sub-participations and executory contracts;

6. The proposals are reconciled with the provisions of the UK Companies Act 1985 and the EEC Fourth Directive.

ASC is also considering how best to develop further guidance on accounting for new financial engineering products. An option being actively explored with the British Bankers Association is for the latter to develop a banking industry statement of recommended practice on how banks should account for securities and investments including financial instruments in varieties such as warrants, options, futures and contracts based on interest and exchange rate differences. But as such instruments are commonly used by non-banking organisations, ASC is also exploring the best way to develop general guidance on the subject.

I must stress that the ASC has no authority or desire to interfere with the financing arrangements of companies. Its sole concern is with the fair financial reporting of transactions which affect the real wealth of companies.

When we talk about off-balance-sheet finance, and about many of the financial instruments which have been created in the last decade and which have enriched the facilities available to the banking and corporate sectors, we are really talking about new ways of arranging and managing risk. A noted economist has written that "profits are not due to risk, but to superior skill in taking risk". Those are the bankers' skills. The Bank of England's recent guidelines, the Accounting Standards Committee's work on special purpose financing arrangements, and the United States FASB's pioneering work on disclosures about financial instruments are all concerned with finding appropriate ways of recognising, measuring and reporting risk. The problem of developing standards of fair financial reporting for the new wave of financial instruments is not confined to the banking industry, but pervades the wider corporate field and is international in scale. It is important for fair and meaningful financial reporting that clear solutions be developed which will have general acceptance in the international business community.

UNITED STATES

THE FINANCIAL INSTRUMENTS PROJECT OF THE US FINANCIAL ACCOUNTING STANDARDS BOARD

by
David Mosso
Assistant Director of Research and Technical Activities,
Financial Accounting Standards Board (FASB)
(United States)

In May of 1986, the Financial Accounting Standards Board added a project to its agenda to address the accounting for financial instruments and off-balance-sheet financing arrangements. The environment that nurtured the project was inflation. The inflation of the 1970s in the United States and many other countries produced very high interest rates and extraordinary volatility in both interest and exchange rates. That led to a search for escape mechanisms. Consumers, investors and business firms sharpened their understanding of money management and searched for ways to cope with volatile rates and erosion of capital. The resulting pressures broke down many long-standing regulatory barriers. Freer financial markets and more astute market participants led to innovations in financial instruments, instruments designed to facilitate the transfer of interest and exchange risk and to provide, simultaneously, higher investment yields to investors and lower financing cost to borrowers.

These developments were amplified by new technology and buttressed by old instincts: the technology of computers and telecommunications and the instincts to dress up financial statements and to structure transactions to get one answer for tax reporting and another for investor reporting.

More directly, the FASB had found that an issue-by-issue approach to financial instrument problems was not working. The Board had attempted to deal separately with foreign exchange, sale of receivables with recourse, defeasance of debt, interest rate futures, securitised assets, and various other financial instrument issues. It found that some of the standards failed to achieve their intended goals and others were working at cross purposes. The Securities and Exchange Commission and the FASB's Emerging Issues Task Force were being swamped with financial instrument issues for which accounting standards and accounting literature provided very little guidance. The US

Congress was concerned about a series of financial institution failures resulting at least in part from questionable financial instrument transactions.

The FASB's project is somewhat broader than the new financial instruments that are the focus of this OECD Symposium. The FASB project covers old financial instruments too. That is because:

1. Old financial instruments are involved in many of the innovative accounting strategies designed to achieve off-balance-sheet financing;

2. New financial instruments turn out to be essentially combinations of, split-off pieces of, or variations on old instruments;

3. Old and new instruments interact through risk management strategies and accounting strategies to the point that they seem indistinguishable.

The FASB project is transaction-oriented. It deals not just with financial institutions, but with accounting for transactions involving financial instruments by whoever enters into them.

The FASB was reluctant to add this project to its agenda and did not do so for some time after the need for it was apparent, because it seemed that a project encompassing all the known financial instrument issues would be so far-reaching it would be unmanageable. As someone jokingly said, the scope of such a project could be described as "accounting for debits and credits". It held all the promise of a bottomless pit.

When the project was finally added to the agenda, it had been broken into six parts, based on common threads among the dozens of issues. The parts are interrelated but distinctive enough to offer some hope of dealing with them somewhat separately. The different parts are intended to:

1. Improve disclosures in the notes to financial statements about financial instruments and transactions, both (a) about items now recognised in the balance sheet (for example, market prices of items carried at other than market), and (b) about obligations, commitments, and guarantees not now recognised as assets and liabilities (for example, the nature, amounts, and risks of those items). Some disclosures of that nature are now required either under US GAAP or SEC rules for registrants, so part of the disclosure effort will be devoted to making existing disclosures more comparable rather than reporting data not presently disclosed;

2. Consider whether financial assets should be deemed sold if there is recourse or other continuing involvement with them, whether financial liabilities should be considered settled when assets are dedicated to settle them, and other questions of de-recognition, non-recognition, or offsetting of related financial assets and liabilities;

3. Consider how financial instruments and transactions that seek to transfer market risks, credit risks, or both (for example, futures and forward contracts, swaps, options, commitments, non-recourse

arrangements, and guarantees) should be accounted for, as well as how to account for the underlying assets or liabilities to which the risk-transferring items are related or even attached;

4. Consider how financial instruments should be measured -- for example, at market value (or a surrogate for it), at original cost, or at the lower of cost or market;

5. Consider how issuers should account for securities with both debt and equity characteristics;

6. Consider what effect separate legal entities -- such as special purpose subsidiaries, joint ventures, and trusts -- should have on recognition of financial instruments and transactions.

The part of the project dealing with disclosures was undertaken immediately after the agenda decision. Some thought, mistakenly as seen in retrospect, that the disclosure part of the project could be accomplished fairly quickly. The intent was to provide some basic information to help users make some sense out of the array of balance sheet and off-balance-sheet financial items while the more difficult recognition and measurement issues were being deliberated. We are now two years into the disclosure part of the project and the hope of completing it by the end of this year is tenuous.

Except for the first part on disclosure, the focus of the project is essentially on recognition and measurement in financial statements. The second and third parts involve, in part, a study of relationships. Determining whether various contractual or purported relationships between assets, liabilities, and transactions -- for example, collateral pledges, non-recourse arrangements, hedges and guarantees -- affect the application of the definitions and criteria of the FASB's conceptual framework will be an important step in reaching consistent solutions to financial instrument issues.

The third part -- accounting for instruments that seek to transfer risk -- has significant interaction with the fourth item -- measurement -- because solutions to either one would narrow the choices on the other. For example, some rather complex "hedge accounting" techniques that defer recognition of realised gains or losses on futures contracts and other risk-transferring instruments have arisen in the United States. Consistent use of either market value or original cost to measure both the hedging and hedged instruments would reduce or eliminate the motive for hedge accounting.

Work on the six parts of the project was originally intended to progress more or less simultaneously rather than sequentially, although the disclosure effort was given top priority. Staffing availability, however, did not permit that.

Disclosures about financial instruments

With the help of an advisory group of outside experts, the FASB developed a proposed set of financial instruments disclosures and issued an Exposure Draft for public comment in November 1987.

The Exposure Draft would require disclosures for all financial instruments. That term would be defined (see Table 1) in a broad way because an item-by-item or listing approach could not possibly keep pace with changes in the types of financial instruments. The definition includes both recognised items (for example, marketable equity securities and loans) and unrecognised, or off-balance-sheet, items (for example, many swaps and guarantees).

Table 1

PROPOSED DEFINITIONS

Financial instrument:	Any contract that is both a (recognised or unrecognised) financial asset of one entity and a (recognised or unrecognised) financial liability or equity instrument of another entity.
Financial asset:	Any asset that is a) cash; b) a contractual right to receive cash or another financial asset from another entity; c) a contractual right to exchange other financial instruments on potentially favourable terms with another entity; or d) an equity instrument of another entity.
Financial liability:	Any liability that is a contractual obligation a) to deliver cash or another financial asset to another entity; or b) to exchange financial instruments on potentially unfavourable terms with another entity.
Equity instrument:	Any evidence of an ownership interest in an entity.

The proposed disclosures (see Table 2) are of four kinds: credit risk, future cash receipts and payments, interest rates, and market values. They are intended to meet objectives of a) describing both recognised and unrecognised items; b) providing useful measures of unrecognised items and other relevant measures of recognised items; and c) providing information to help investors and creditors assess downside risks and upside potentials of both recognised and unrecognised items. Disclosures about future cash receipts and payments and interest rates would not be required for financial assets and liabilities represented to be held for sale or settlement before maturity for which market value is reported -- for example, trading accounts of banks and broker-dealers.

In addition to the required disclosures, the proposed Statement encourages other disclosures, including information about collateral or other security supporting financial instruments, and disclosure of expected cash receipts and payments and repricing or maturity dates if they differ from contractual amounts or dates (for example, because of prepayment options).

An appendix to the Exposure Draft provides examples of application of the requirements showing how the disclosures could be made in a variety of ways -- parenthetically on the face of the financial statements or in the notes, in tabular or narrative forms.

Table 2

SUMMARY OF PROPOSED DISCLOSURE REQUIREMENTS

Disclosure Area	Requirements
Credit risk	Disclose maximum credit risk, reasonably possible and probable credit losses, and concentrations in individual counterparties or groups of counterparties engaged in similar activities or activities in the same region.
Future cash receipts and payments	Disclose amounts to be received or paid within one year, after one year through five years, and after five years, and amounts denominated in foreign currencies if significant.
Interest rates	Disclose amounts of interest-bearing financial instruments contracted to reprice or mature within one year, after one year through five years, and after five years; their effective interest rates; and amounts denominated in foreign currencies if significant.
Market values	Disclose market value determined by quoted market prices or estimated, unless the entity is unable to determine or estimate the market value.

The area of greatest change will likely be that of unrecognised financial instruments. Unrecognised instruments include interest rate and currency swaps, options, and various commitments and guarantees, about which some entities currently provide little information and others provide none. The Exposure Draft includes examples showing ways to disclose, for example, the interest rate, credit, and cash flow risks that interest rate swaps may cause.

For many financial instruments, little or no disclosure beyond that already provided would be required. For example, the amounts of credit risk of accounts receivable are generally already disclosed, although information about concentrations of credit risk is often not reported now. Since accounts receivable are generally due within one year, further information about future cash receipts and payments is generally unnecessary. Accounts receivable and other financial instruments classified as current in the balance sheet are presumed to be non-interest-bearing unless otherwise stated. The carrying amount of accounts receivable often approximates their market value, making only a statement of that fact necessary.

Long-term debt obligations are another common financial instrument for which little additional information would be required. FASB Statement No. 47,

Disclosure of Long-Term Obligations, now requires certain information, and companies commonly provide additional information about interest rates, including how long they remain fixed. The requirements of the proposed Statement would, for the most part, be met by the existing note about long-term obligations in most entities' financial statements. Long-term debt obligations involve no credit risk to the issuer, but the requirement for information about the market value of obligations would be new.

Unlike long-term obligations, little has typically been disclosed in the United States about most long-term receivables, although the symmetry between the two suggests that such disclosure is appropriate. The proposed Statement calls for disclosure about the amounts of credit risk (generally already disclosed) and any concentrations of credit risk. In addition, future cash flow and interest rate information, similar to that provided for long-term obligations, would be required. The proposed requirements also call for disclosure of the market value of those receivables.

Recognition and Measurement

Although some work was done on the recognition and measurement parts of the project while the disclosure Exposure Draft was being developed, primary attention to those parts did not begin until early 1988. The initial efforts have been directed to sharpening the focus of a work plan so that Board decisions could be made in a systematic way, given the many interrelated issues in the five recognition and measurement parts of the project.

The approach is still evolving but tentatively the plan is developing around what has been described as a "fundamental financial instrument" approach. The approach is based on the premise that all financial instruments are composed of a few basic types of contractual promise. For example, a convertible debenture includes both a debt contract and an option contract. The idea is to examine each type of fundamental instrument in its stand-alone form and then proceed to examine instruments that are compounds of two or more of the fundamental instruments. Beyond that we will look at more complex non-contractual relationships among independent financial instruments, such as hedging relationships.

At this point we have identified six fundamental instruments based on the nature of the contractual promise involved. At one extreme is a simple debt instrument, a receivable to one entity, a payable to another. It embodies an unconditional promise to pay cash (or other assets) to settle an existing debt. A US Treasury bill is a good example -- a promise to pay a fixed amount on a fixed date with no options, no collateral, no guarantees, no frills.

At the other extreme is an equity instrument, such as common stock, in which a promise to pay comes into play only if and when those in control of an entity choose to pay.

Between the extremes, we have identified four other types of instruments: forward contracts and three varieties of contingency contract -- option contracts, guarantee contracts and, for want of a better term, conditional payment contracts or conditional receivables-payables.

Forward contracts carry a pair of promises. Like debt contracts the promises are unconditional but the promises are to exchange financial instruments in the future rather than to settle a pre-existing debt from a past exchange. Each of the counterparties has both a right and an obligation to exchange, the right representing a potentially favourable exchange and the obligation a potentially unfavourable exchange. A futures contract on a US Treasury bond is an example.

The three contingency-type contracts are alike in that the promise to pay or exchange in each case is conditional upon a specified uncertain future event. They could perhaps best be viewed as variations on a single fundamental type; however, their distinctive characteristics may be sufficient to treat them separately.

Option contracts are like forwards in that they carry a promise to exchange financial instruments. Execution of the exchange, however, is conditional on demand by the option holder. Assuming rational behaviour, the option-holder has only a right to a potentially favourable exchange; the option-writer has only an obligation to make a potentially unfavourable exchange.

Guarantee contracts are those in which one party becomes a standby obligor to a second party by guaranteeing the performance of a third party, the primary obligor. A credit guarantee contract in which the conditional event is default by a primary obligor is an example. The guarantor pays the debt and receives from the guarantee-holder the subrogated right to collect the debt from the primary obligor. Thus there is an exchange of financial instruments, with the guarantor acquiring the receivable, usually impaired, from the guarantee-holder.

Conditional payment contracts also provide protection against the potentially unfavourable effect of specified events but do not carry subrogation rights to financial instruments. A pledge of financial instrument collateral is one kind that is particularly relevant to the financial instruments project.

There is no magic to the fundamental instrument approach. We do not expect to be able to use it to shake the "issues tree" and have answers fall out. It is just an analytical tool to help understand complicated instruments and to throw light on the accounting issues. We hope it will help us to develop generic answers to financial instrument accounting questions so that we are not forced to deal one by one with the plethora of new financial instruments that continue to pour into the financial marketplace.

It is too early to tell where the recognition and measurement issues will lead. Work has begun on two sets of issues -- analysing the questions involved in 1) accounting for receivables and payables, including differentiating sales of financial instruments from collateralised borrowings; and 2) accounting for option contracts. We have classified most of the issues we have heard about in terms of a particular fundamental instrument, a compound of several fundamental instruments, or a relationship between separate financial instruments. We have not yet determined what kind of discussion documents will be necessary or whether we can proceed directly to exposure drafts of proposed standards in some cases. In any event, it is likely that several documents will be issued at different times as the project progresses.

2. HARMONIZATION OF ACCOUNTING AND REPORTING PRACTICES RELATING TO NEW FINANCIAL INSTRUMENTS IN THE EC

THE ACCOUNTING TREATMENT OF NEW FINANCIAL INSTRUMENTS IN ACCORDANCE WITH EEC DIRECTIVES

by
Hermann Niessen
Head of Division,
Commission of the European Communities

In preparation for the completion of the internal market by the end of 1992, the European Community is bringing the legislation of its Member States closer together in many areas by means of directives adopted by the Community authorities and incorporated in national law.

The process of harmonization concerns, in particular, the presentation and auditing of accounts and disclosure of the information contained therein. The most important Directives in this respect are: the Fourth Directive of 25th July 1978 on annual accounts (1), the Seventh Directive of 13th June 1983 on consolidated accounts (2) and the Directive of 8th December 1986 on the accounts of banks (3). The scope of the last Directive is quite specific, but the other two are of general purport and at first sight do not seem to cover new financial instruments. Admittedly, the legislator always lags behind actual practice, which poses a problem with which all jurists are familiar. But it is my view that new financial instruments can and should be treated, for accounting purposes, in accordance with the principles laid down by the above-mentioned Directives.

As regards the layout of accounts, the Directives did not restrict their prescriptions to the minimum amount of information that accounts should contain. They also prescribed the layouts applicable to balance sheets (4) and to profit-and-loss accounts (5), and the information to be given in the notes to the accounts (6). Furthermore, it is in the notes to the accounts that off-balance-sheet commitments, if not shown at the foot of the balance sheet, must appear, broken down by category and with commitments existing in respect of affiliated undertakings shown separately (7). But these commitments are recorded off the balance sheet because there is no obligation to record them in the balance sheet under liabilities. But are there circumstances in which such an obligation exists? On this matter, the balance sheet layouts prescribed by the Community Directives offer some useful guidelines.

The Community Directives require debts to be shown on the liabilities side of the balance sheet, with amounts due classified according to their residual maturity, together with the date of final payment. But it would be incorrect to conclude from this that any financial commitment that does not satisfy the criteria for what constitutes a debt automatically falls into the category of off-balance-sheet commitments. On the contrary, in the balance sheet layouts prescribed by the Community Directives, provisions for liabilities and charges are shown under liabilities -- between capital and reserves, and creditors. According to the express definition thereof (8), these provisions are intended to cover losses or debts whose natures are clearly defined and which are either likely to be incurred, or certain to be incurred but uncertain as to the amount or as to the date on which they will arise.

To interpret correctly the provisions in the Community Directives concerning information on the commitments that an enterprise must show in its accounts, it is essential to draw a clear distinction between debts, provisions and off-balance-sheet commitments. The distinction between provisions and off-balance-sheet commitments also serves as the dividing line between those items that should be included in the year's trading results and those that should not.

The above principles apply not only to industrial and commercial enterprises, in whose activities new financial instruments do not perhaps play as important a role, but also to banks, whose use of such instruments is increasing day by day. The layouts that the Community prescribes for bank balance sheets do differ from those applicable to enterprises in general, but as regards the breakdown of commitments into three categories, they are identical.

A brief word should be said about valuation rules. The Directives have established a set of general rules concerning valuation, in particular the principle that valuation must be made on a prudential basis -- i.e. that only profits that have actually been made at the balance sheet date may be booked; the principle that account must be taken of all the foreseeable liabilities and potential losses; and the principle that income and charges must be allocated to the financial year concerned, irrespective of the date of receipt or payment. However, departures from these general principles are permitted in exceptional cases, provided that they are indicated in the notes to the accounts, together with the reasons for them (9). Also, assets shall be valued on the basis of their acquisition cost or production cost (10). However, Member States may permit enterprises to draw up their accounts on a current cost basis, but only on the condition that increases in value are allocated to a reserve that may not be distributed to members (the prudential principle) and that historical costs are also shown so as to ensure comparability of accounts (11). Also, Member States may permit banks to book transferable securities at their market value without the obligation to constitute a revaluation reserve (12).

NOTES AND REFERENCES

1. Official Journal L 222 of 14th August 1978, p. 11.

2. Official Journal L 193 of 18th July 1983, p. 11.

3. Official Journal L 372 of 31st December 1986, p. 1.

4. Fourth Directive -- Articles 9 and 18; Seventh Directive -- Article 17 (1); Directive on "banks" -- Article 4.

5. Fourth Directive -- Articles 22 to 27; Seventh Directive -- Article 17 (1); Directive on "banks" -- Articles 26 to 28.

6. Fourth Directive -- Article 43; Seventh Directive -- Article 34; Directive on "banks" -- Articles 40 and 41.

7. Fourth Directive -- Articles 14 and 43 No. 7; Seventh Directive -- Article 34 No. 7; Directive on "banks" -- Articles 4, 24, 25, 40 (5) and 41 (2h).

8. Fourth Directive -- Article 20 (1); Seventh Directive -- Article 17 (1); Directive on "banks" -- Article 1 (1).

9. Fourth Directive -- Article 31; Seventh Directive -- Article 29 (1); Directive on "banks" -- Article 1 (1).

10. Fourth Directive -- Article 32; Seventh Directive -- Article 29 (1); Directive on "banks" -- Article 1 (1).

11. Fourth Directive -- Article 33; Seventh Directive -- Article 29 (1); Directive on "banks" -- Article 1 (1).

12. Directive on "banks" -- Article 36 (2).

ACCOUNTING AND FINANCIAL REPORTING FOR NEW FINANCIAL INSTRUMENTS IN EUROPE
-- CURRENT SITUATION AND FUTURE PERSPECTIVES

by the Fédération des experts-comptables européens (FEE)

I. INTRODUCTION

Financial reporting harmonization in the EC is based on the Fourth EC Directive (on annual accounts) and the Seventh EC Directive (on consolidated accounts). These two texts relate only to certain types of non-bank undertakings. A specific EC Directive on the annual accounts and consolidated accounts of banks and other financial institutions was adopted on 8th December 1986, the implications of which are being examined by FEE's EC Committee.

Part II of this paper, entitled "Current Situation", includes a description of current practices in accounting and reporting for new financial instruments in the context of annual accounts (1). It reflects the results of a study currently being conducted by FEE's EC Committee on the subject. The Committee has deliberately extended its enquiry beyond the EC Member States and has so far collected information relating to the following countries: Austria; Belgium; Denmark; France; Germany; Greece; Italy; Luxembourg; the Netherlands; the United Kingdom; and Sweden.

Part III of the paper, entitled "Future Perspectives", raises some theoretical and practical issues that are currently being considered by FEE. Its purpose is not to list all potential problems related to new financial instruments, but rather to focus on some aspects that have so far been identified as being of particular significance.

The first two parts described above focus mainly on banks. Part IV is a discussion on accounting for new financial instruments in industrial and commercial undertakings. Part V mentions some side aspects of the problems involved, mainly off-balance-sheet financing.

II. CURRENT SITUATION

1. Note issuing facilities (NIFs)

The results of the survey to date suggest that NIFs have widespread use only in the United Kingdom. In Germany, Denmark and the Netherlands, they are used by major banks. The principal constraints on their use are requirements in certain countries (e.g. Germany and the United Kingdom) for capital backing. Marketing, where appropriate, is through the international markets and Euro-markets.

In the United Kingdom, where the use of NIFs is most widespread, there are no accounting policies specifically laid down for this instrument, other than the general principle that contingent losses should be provided for in the balance sheet if a loss is probable, and referred to in the notes if it is not. However, in Denmark, such instruments are included in the balance sheet above the line and, in Germany and the Netherlands, they are included below the line (if the bank is committed to providing these facilities). Practice varies whether the information is given separately or aggregated with other similar commitments.

Where disclosure is made, or amounts are included in the accounts, the amount included is normally the amount for which the bank is committed to provide backing.

2. Currency swaps

Currency swaps exist in all countries and are widespread in Belgium, Denmark, France, Germany, Italy, Luxembourg, the Netherlands and the United Kingdom.

There are two main categories of restraints on the use of the instrument:

a) Currency control (Italy, Sweden, Greece).

b) Capital requirements (Germany, the United Kingdom).

Marketing is international.

Accounting policies

a) According to our study, there is no disclosure of these transactions with the exception of Italy and sometimes Greece;

b) On 8th December 1986 an EC Directive on the annual accounts and consolidated accounts of banks and other financial institutions was adopted. It must be implemented in Member States by the end of 1990. Provisions on currency swaps include the following:

Article 39:

"2. Uncompleted forward and spot exchange transactions shall be translated at the spot rate of exchange ruling on the balance sheet date.

The Member States may, however, require forward transactions to be translated at the forward rate ruling on the balance sheet date.

3. Without prejudice to Article 29 (3), the differences between the book values of the assets, liabilities and forward transactions and the amounts produced by translation in accordance with paragraphs 1 and 2 shall be shown in the profit and loss account. The Member States may, however, require or permit differences produced by translation in accordance with paragraphs 1 and 2 to be included, in whole or in part, in reserves not available for distribution, where they arise on assets held as financial fixed assets, on tangible and intangible assets and on any transactions undertaken to cover those assets.

4.   The Member States may provide that positive translation differences arising out of forward transactions, assets or liabilities
not covered or not specifically covered by other forward transactions, or by assets or liabilities shall not be shown in the
profit and loss accounts.

5.   If a method specified in Article 59 of Directive 78/660/EC is
used, the Member States may provide that any translation differences
shall be transferred, in whole or in part, directly to reserves.
Positive and negative translation differences transferred to reserves shall be shown separately in the balance sheet or in the
notes on the accounts."

Article 41, paragraph 2:

"(h) a statement of the types of unmatured forward transactions
      outstanding at the balance sheet date indicating, in parti-
      cular, for each type of transaction, whether they are made to
      a material extent for the purpose of hedging the effects of
      fluctuations in interest rates, exchange rates and market
      prices, and whether they are made to a material extent for the
      purposes of hedging the effects of fluctuations in interest
      rates, exchange rates and market prices, and whether they are
      made to a material extent for dealing purposes. These types
      of transaction shall include all those in connection with
      which the income or expenditure is to be included in
      Article 27, item 6, Article 28, items A 3 or B 4 or
      Article 29 (3), for example, foreign currencies, precious
      metals, transferable securities, certificates of deposit and
      other assets."

In some countries, in case of hedging instruments, these are accounted
for in the same way as the items hedged. Speculative transactions are
"marked to market" and the resulting profits or losses taken into income (the United Kingdom and partly France).

c) US practice refers to FAS 52 accounting rules, under which the
   treatment differs depending on whether the position is a hedge or a
   position taken in expectation of changes in exchange rates. The
   accounting treatment for forward contracts identified as hedges depends on the nature of the commitment that is hedged. The accounting treatment required for open positions (non-hedges) is to include
   all gains and losses due to price changes in current income.

3. Interest rate swaps

Interest rate swaps are fairly widespread (Denmark, France, the United
Kingdom, the Netherlands) but less so than currency swaps.

Marketing is international, and the restraints on use are similar to
those relating to currency swaps.

Accounting policies

a) The results of our study reveal policies similar to those for currency swaps. The EC Directive does not deal with interest rate swaps at all;

b) US practice refers to FAS 80 on accounting for futures contracts, although this statement has stricter criteria for considering a contract as a hedge than does current practice for swaps accounting.

4. Futures

Futures are widespread in Denmark, France (interest rate futures) and the United Kingdom, and are commonly used by major banks in the Netherlands. In the other countries surveyed, so far their use is insignificant. Legal and regulatory constraints are similar to those relating to swaps. Marketing is international.

Accounting policies

As for swaps, in some countries a distinction is made between hedging and speculative instruments (the United Kingdom, France):

-- Gains or losses on speculative operations immediately impact the income statement;

-- Gains or losses on trading operations are taken in the income statement over the lifetime of the hedged item.

There is no disclosure requirement.

5. Forward rate agreements (FRAs)

FRAs are widespread in Denmark, France and the United Kingdom. In the Netherlands, Luxembourg and Belgium they are commonly used by major banks. Legal and regulatory constraints are similar to those relating to swaps. Marketing is international.

Accounting policies

There is no disclosure requirement. The accounting treatment is close to the one described under "Futures" as FRAs are similar to rate futures.

6. Options

Options are widespread in Denmark, France and the United Kingdom. They are commonly used in Germany, the Netherlands, and to a lesser extent in Italy and Belgium.

Legal and regulatory constraints are similar to those relating to swaps. Marketing is international.

Accounting policies

There is no disclosure requirement for these transactions, with the exception of Italy.

As for futures, in some countries a distinction is made between hedging and speculative instruments. In the case of speculative instruments or when no distinction is made the instruments are, when practicable, marked to market. In the case of hedging transactions, the premiums are taken to income symmetrically with the hedged item.

7. Capital raising instruments

These instruments include the following:

-- A deep discount bond is one issued at a large discount to ultimate redemption value on maturity and consequently bears a low coupon rate of interest;

-- Stepped interest bonds generally bear a low rate of interest in early years with the rate of interest periodically increasing during the bond's life;

-- A convertible bond allows the investor to convert the bond at a point in future time into fixed-rate bonds or equity at a predetermined price;

-- A warrant gives the holder the right to subscribe for future fixed-rate bonds or equity issues at a predetermined price;

-- A capped FRN is one where an upper limit is set on the interest rate payable to a borrower. A floor sets a lower limit. A collar involves both a cap and a floor, i.e. the interest rate payable will vary only within pre-defined limits.

Accounting policies

Deep discount bonds: The discount is normally amortized over the term of the bond, either on a straight line or constant yield basis. The bond is disclosed as a liability at its full redemption amount and any unamortized discount is disclosed separately as a sundry asset.

Stepped bonds: Where the interest rate is known to rise over the term of a bond, the average rate of interest over the term as a whole is accrued in each period.

Convertibles and warrants: Where a favourable rate of interest or a premium is obtained on an issue as a result of offering the right to convert or subscribe for future issues, the gain is usually calculated by reference to the terms on which it is anticipated that the issue would have been made without such benefits. If material, any such gain is deferred and released to income over the term of the second bond, or included as share premium if it relates to equity.

Caps, floor and collars: Where an issuer pays a premium for a cap or received a premium for a floor the premium or discount is normally amortized over the term of the bond.

III. FUTURE PERSPECTIVES

1. Increased off-balance-sheet disclosure

A principal purpose of the annual accounts of a bank or other financial institution is to give the reader a reasonable understanding of the nature and extent of the risks to which the institution is exposed. The main risks of banking business include credit risk (the risk that a debtor will be unable to meet his commitments), interest risk (the risk that changing interest rates will cause the bank to earn an insufficient margin between the interest that it receives and the interest that it pays), exchange risk [the risk that changing exchange rates will cause the value of the bank's foreign currency assets to rise (or fall) by less (or more) than the value of its foreign currency liabilities], and finance and liquidity risk (the risk that a bank will be called upon to provide funds at a time when it cannot easily do so).

These risks exist not only in respect of business that is reflected in the bank's balance sheet (for example, loans and foreign currency balances). They exist also in respect of off-balance-sheet business (for example, existing commitments to make future loans, which entail credit risk, or interest rate swaps, which entail interest risk). At present, these instruments are frequently shown "below the line" in the balance sheet or in the notes, or not at all. When disclosed, the quality of disclosure is often much less than for assets and liabilities in the balance sheet.

Given that both on-balance-sheet and off-balance-sheet assets and liabilities are often interrelated and have a similar potential for creating risk, we believe that there should be a greater degree of disclosure of off-balance-sheet items. We are reinforced in that opinion by the fact that it is the general practice of the regulatory bodies when assessing the capital requirements of the banks under their supervision (itself a measure of risk exposure) to follow the same practice of treating on-balance-sheet and off-balance-sheet exposure alike.

The FASB Exposure Draft "Disclosures about Financial Instruments" published in November 1987 can be considered as a benchmark, as it requires full disclosure on risk, future cash receipts and payments, interest rate and market value.

Although a more extensive disclosure is desirable, it could be argued that disclosure on the scale envisaged by the FASB is unlikely to be achieved easily in Europe as current practice shows:

a) Significant differences among countries as regards the amount, the nature and the analysis of information provided;

b) The absence of similarly extensive disclosure requirements for traditional financial instruments (e.g. loans).

2. Disclosure to shareholders and/or regulatory bodies

In considering the extent of disclosure which may be appropriate for new financial instruments, this paper deals only with the requirements of a bank's annual accounts prepared for submission to shareholders, and not with the information requirements of the regulatory bodies by which that bank is supervised, even when these requirements are very similar. However, it will be worthwhile to consider briefly the main differences between them.

The principal purpose of the annual accounts is to give a true and fair view of the bank's state of affairs as at the balance sheet date and of its profit or loss for the year then ended. It is not a purpose of these accounts to show whether the bank has been prudently or efficiently managed, although they may contain information relevant to that question. Nor is it expected that the accounts will deal extensively with items that are immaterial in the context of the accounts as a whole. Financial information presented to a regulatory body is similarly expected to give a true and fair view of a state of affairs and profit or loss, but the regulatory body has a far wider range of concerns than are those of the shareholders -- for example, protection of the depositors, adherence to economic policies laid down by government, the ability of the bank to continue operations, and the health of the banking sector as a whole. Typically, also, a regulatory body will be interested in certain items that are too small to be of interest to the shareholders.

It follows that, while there will be a broad similarity between many of the disclosures made to shareholders and to the regulatory bodies, there is no need for those disclosures to be identical. Equally, it is no argument for withholding information from shareholders that the information supplied has been separately supplied to the regulatory body, which can be relied upon to protect the shareholders' interests. Shareholders and regulatory bodies have separate information needs: each should be met without regard to what is supplied to the other.

3. Hedging and trading transactions

The accounting treatment of new financial instruments commonly depends on whether the contract can be viewed as a trading or hedging transaction.

There is, to some extent, agreement on the fact that trading positions and portfolios should be marked to market, that is, valued at the market liquidation value. However, inclusion of unrealised gains on speculative operations in income is often questioned and is not permitted in some countries. It is argued in those countries that the method adopted for valuing both on-balance-sheet and off-balance-sheet assets and liabilities should be the lower of cost and market.

Hedging instruments are typically treated symmetrically with the hedged operation.

The main problem now faced is not so much the best accounting treatment for hedging or trading transactions as the ways to distinguish between them.

This raises both a conceptual and a practical problem. The practical problem relates to the enormous amount of transactions involved. The conceptual problem is threefold.

a) Overall matching or direct matching

The question is to determine whether it is possible to match any individual position taken by the bank with the corresponding hedging transaction designed to cover it (direct matching), or whether the situation of the bank should be examined on an overall basis in order to ascertain the ultimate global position (overall matching). By "global position" is meant the overall position in any given currency. A bank will therefore have as many "global positions" as the number of currencies in which it operates.

The former approach brings an obvious distinction between hedging and matching transactions. However, some banks claim that such an approach does not reflect economic reality.

It could be argued that the latter approach is more realistic from an economic point of view, as it considers the overall uncovered risk borne by the bank as a result of all on-balance-sheet and off-balance-sheet positions. However, if the overall position is not perfectly covered (perfect coverage is seldom met in practice), it is extremely difficult to determine which are the individual operations that must be considered as trading and accounted for accordingly.

A theoretical answer to this problem is to value all on-balance-sheet and off-balance-sheet transactions at market value. The trading operations are then marked to market, this method having no effect on the net financial position or the net income arising from hedging transactions, but "revaluation" of on-balance-sheet positions at market value when such value is higher than historical cost would be regarded in many countries as being in conflict with general accounting concepts. This leads to a general discussion on the validity of the historical cost concept applied to banks. For those banks that are engaged in multi-currency business it is difficult (sometimes impossible) to identify a single functional currency, and therefore a single historical cost basis. However, that does not enter within the scope of this paper.

b) Perfect matching or partial matching

If a hedging transaction can be defined as the use of an instrument in order to eliminate a risk in the business, the nature of a transaction that merely reduces the risk (without eliminating it fully) remains unclear.

c) Identified matching or non-identified matching

The question is to find out whether only transactions designed and identified as hedging should be treated as such, or whether this treatment should be extended to transactions not specifically designed as hedging but that nevertheless happen to eliminate (or contribute to eliminate) a risk borne by the bank.

4. Valuation of trading instruments in the absence of a liquid market

As explained above, trading positions are often marked to market. However, it sometimes happens that there is no liquid market one can refer to, especially in the case of "tailor-made" instruments such as interest rate swaps.

Two approaches might be adopted in order to solve the problem, provided that it is possible to calculate or estimate a future maturity value:

a) Valuation by discounting future cash flows (with an obvious problem in fixing the discount rate);

b) Spreading the predetermined premium or discount to maturity evenly over the lifetime of the instrument.

Method b) would tend to result in lesser fluctuations than method a) or a true mark-to-market valuation.

IV. ACCOUNTING AND REPORTING FOR NEW FINANCIAL INSTRUMENTS IN UNDERTAKINGS OTHER THAN BANKS

While new financial instruments are commonly used between banks, a significant proportion of transactions take place between bank and non-bank undertakings as industrial and commercial companies increasingly use new financial instruments.

We believe that, as a matter of principle, the accounting treatment of financial instruments (including disclosure requirements) as applicable to banks should also apply to other types of companies.

However, this statement must be tempered by the following considerations:

1. As already pointed out, the accounting treatment of financial instruments usually depends on whether the transaction can be viewed as a hedging or a speculative operation. However, industrial and commercial companies do not as a general rule take speculative positions (with the exception of those companies whose activity generates significant available funds). Consequently, differences in accounting treatments met in practice should be reduced;

2. Accounting principles and related presentation followed by industrial and commercial undertakings are extensively regulated, and though these regulations do not address the treatment of all new financial instruments, the general accounting principles might be perceived as conflicting with the treatments suggested for banks.

Furthermore, such treatments can possibly be inconsistent with the accounting for traditional financial instruments.

For these reasons, differences arise in practice when undertakings account for financial instruments among and within European countries. Future efforts should be devoted to reducing these differences, with a view to promoting common principles applicable to both bank and non-bank undertakings.

At a European level, the principles laid down by the Fourth EC Directive are applicable to all aspects of financial reporting, including those related to new financial instruments, in so far as they are relevant. Current research within FEE's EC Committee includes consideration of the practical implications of such principles as regards all financial instruments. In that respect, Articles 31 (Valuation Rules) and 43 (Contents of the Notes to the Accounts, and especially paragraph 1.7 on financial commitments) are particularly significant.

V. OFF-BALANCE-SHEET FINANCING

The EC Committee of FEE is actively considering these accounting issues as well as presentation and disclosure problems which are related to various off-balance-sheet financing activities. There are indications that groups are increasingly interested in the possibilities of "hiving off" certain activities which are considered "high risk" through the creation of so-called "dependent non-subsidiary companies" and then carrying out such activities through these companies. The EC Committee's prime consideration in this respect has been to consider whether the current rules embodied in the Seventh Directive would preclude the creation of such "subsidiaries" and, if so, how. Furthermore, some enquiries have also been made in order to ascertain the extent of the use of such "subsidiaries" within the EEC.

1. The Seventh EC Directive

A. Article 1:

"1. A Member State shall require any undertaking governed by its national law to draw up consolidated accounts and a consolidated annual report if that undertaking (a parent undertaking):

(a)   has a majority of the shareholders' or members' voting rights in another undertaking (a subsidiary undertaking); or

(b)   has the right to appoint or remove a majority of the members of the administrative, management or supervisory body of another undertaking (a subsidiary undertaking) and is at the same time a shareholder in or member of that undertaking; or

(c)   has the right to exercise a dominant influence over an undertaking (subsidiary undertaking) of which it is a shareholder or member, pursuant to a contract entered into with that undertaking or to a provision in its memorandum or articles of association, where the law

199

governing that subsidiary undertaking permits its being subject to such contracts or provisions. A Member State need not prescribe that a parent undertaking must be a shareholder in or member of its subsidiary undertaking. Those Member States the laws of which do not provide for such contracts or clauses shall not be required to apply this provision; or

(d)   is a shareholder in or member of an undertaking, and:

(aa) a majority of the members of the administrative, management or supervisory bodies of that undertaking (a subsidiary undertaking) who have held office during the financial year and up to the time when the consolidated accounts are drawn up, have been appointed solely as a result of the exercise of its voting rights; or

(bb) controls alone, pursuant to an agreement with other shareholders in or members of that undertaking (subsidiary undertaking), a majority of shareholders' or members' voting rights in that undertaking. The Member States may introduce more detailed provisions concerning the form and contents of such agreements.

The Member States shall prescribe at least the arrangements referred to in (bb) above.

They may make the application of (aa) above dependent upon the holding's representing 20 per cent or more of the shareholders' or members' voting rights.

However (aa) above shall not apply where another undertaking has the rights referred to in subparagraph (a), (b) or (c) above with regard to that subsidiary undertaking.

2. Apart from the cases mentioned in paragraph 1 above and pending subsequent coordination, the Member States may require any undertaking governed by their national law to draw up consolidated accounts and a consolidated annual report if that undertaking (a parent undertaking) holds a participating interest as defined in Article 17 of Directive 78/660/EEC in another undertaking (subsidiary undertaking), and:

(a) it actually exercises a dominant influence over it; or

(b) it and the subsidiary undertaking are managed on a unified basis by the parent undertaking."

B. Article 16:

"1. Consolidated accounts shall comprise the consolidated balance sheet, the consolidated profit-and-loss account and the notes on the accounts. These documents shall constitute a composite whole.

2. Consolidated accounts shall be drawn up clearly and in accordance with this Directive.

3. Consolidated accounts shall give a true and fair view of the assets, liabilities, financial position and profit or loss of the undertakings included therein taken as a whole.

4. Where the application of the provisions of this Directive would not be sufficient to give a true and fair view within the meaning of paragraph 3 above, additional information must be given.

5. Where, in exceptional cases, the application of a provision of Articles 17 to 35 and 39 is incompatible with the obligation imposed in paragraph 3 above, that provision must be departed from in order to give true and fair view within the meaning of paragraph 3. Any such departure must be disclosed in the notes on the accounts together with an explanation of the reasons for it and a statement of its effect on the assets, liabilities, financial position and profit or loss. The Member States may define the exceptional cases in question and lay down the relevant special rules.

6. A Member State may require or permit the disclosure in the consolidated accounts of other information as well as that which must be disclosed in accordance with this Directive."

2. The definition of control under the Seventh Directive

Article 1, paragraph 1, implicitly defines control by reference to four legal situations.

Article 1, paragraph 2 a) accords recognition to the concept of de facto control, but only in the case where a participating interest is held by the parent.

Consequently, the definition of control under the Seventh Directive is sufficiently restrictive to permit groups to design arrangements under which it is possible to exclude a "dependent" company from the scope of the consolidated accounts, unless Member States chose to exercise the option stated in the Seventh Directive, Article 1, paragraph 1 c), i.e. exercising of dominant influence without at the same time being a shareholder in or a member of the subsidiary undertaking.

It should be noted that IASC's E30 provides a solution to this specific problem by giving a broader definition of control based on the concept of economic entity. Control is defined in Article 30, paragraph 5 as:

"The power to govern the financial and operating policies of the management of the enterprise so as to obtain benefits from the activities of the enterprise."

Furthermore:

"A subsidiary is an enterprise that is controlled by another enterprise (known as the parent)."

3. The scope of Article 16

a) Article 16 raises the following question: Can the scope of consolidated accounts as defined in Article 1 be modified by the application of Article 16, or in other words, can the provisions of Article 16 be used to consolidate "dependent" companies not covered by Article 1?

b) As paragraph 4 of Article 16 is applicable to all articles of the Directive, and paragraph 5 only to Articles 17 to 35 and 39, the answer to this question is doubtless: it is not possible to consolidate "dependent" non-subsidiary companies on the grounds of the true and fair view principle; however, compliance with this principle can only be achieved by appropriate disclosure in the notes of the relevant information relating to such companies.

4. Practical considerations

There are three types of reasons for groups wishing to exclude dependent companies:

a) Improve financial ratios based on accounting figures (e.g. debt/equity or current-assets/turnover rations);

b) Non-disclosure of significant risks;

c) Improve the picture of the overall financial position (e.g. maximise profits or equity).

In order to achieve these objectives, groups may concentrate debts, idle assets, risks or losses in companies that do not fall under the definition of control within the existing regulations.

If it is assumed that the provisions of the Seventh EC Directive are correctly interpreted above, in order to exclude a company from the scope of the consolidation, the group will need to:

a) Avoid any participating interest; and

b) Exercise a dominant influence.

The first condition can easily be met by asking an independent third party (e.g. a merchant bank) to hold the shares of the company.

The second condition can be met in two manners:

-- By creating a legal link. For example, the group might hold options, whose exercise would allow it to become the major shareholder;

-- By creating an economic link. For example, the group can provide through "arm's-length" contracts substantially all the personnel, the equipment and the financial resources (through loans) the undertaking requires.

Furthermore, the Member States within the EC must not have chosen to exercise the option stated in Article 1, paragraph 1(c), as the exercising of this option (no participating interest) will result in a requirement to consolidate solely on the basis of dominant influence, although it is not clear whether a legally binding written agreement or contract between the legal entity exercising the dominant influence and the _de jure_ shareholder in the "subsidiary" would be required in order to consolidate under this option.

5. Some current trends

At present, such a dependent company would not necessarily be consolidated in France and Germany, the only two EC countries having implemented the Seventh Directive so far. The situation in EC Member States that have not yet implemented the Seventh Directive is uncertain. However, in the Netherlands, current draft legislation explicitly introduces the concept of a group of companies as an economic entity, as a basis for the determination of the entities that have to be included in the consolidation. In the United Kingdom, the Accounting Standards Committee (ASC) has recently suggested, through a proposed statement of standard accounting practice entitled "Accounting for Special Purpose Transactions", that the existence of a controlled non-subsidiary creates special circumstances requiring it to be treated in the same way as a legally defined subsidiary.

The IASC apparently proposes to require consolidation according to Exposure Draft E30 on the basis of the exercising of a dominant influence alone.

NOTES AND REFERENCES

1. Concerning the definition of the instruments and the risks associated to them, reference is made to the background document prepared by the OECD Secretariat and the Study by the Bank for International Settlements, _Recent Innovations in International Banking_ (April 1986).

3. PERSPECTIVES FOR INTERNATIONAL ACCOUNTING STANDARDS

by
Herman Marseille
Board Member, International Accounting Standards Committee (IASC)

The development of new instruments is in full swing. The volatility of interest rates and currency exchange rates, growing international markets and increasing competition are factors which will no doubt stimulate further innovation of financial instruments.

Different countries are in the process of considering the new phenomenon and studying the possible implications for accounting treatment, with a view to eventually issuing guidelines dealing with recognition, measurement and disclosure. Some countries have already issued guidelines; some are in the process of preparing them; others have yet to address the subject.

In standard-setting, due regard should be given to the function of the parties to the contract. The question of whether a contracting party is acting in an intermediary capacity -- as might be the case with banks -- or in some other capacity might have a bearing on the recognition and measurement criteria, even on the disclosure requirements.

The use of new financial instruments may lead to changes in exposures -- e.g. in foreign currencies, interest charges or revenues -- and therefore may constitute either an effective hedge or a speculative transaction. Criteria should be developed for identifying a new financial instrument as an effective hedge, because that classification has consequences for the accounting treatment of either the financial instrument itself or the transaction or position hedged by it.

Accounting treatment should not view the new financial instruments as an isolated phenomenon; this could lead to all kinds of special requirements. Instead, this new phenomenon should be seen as only part of the broader issue of business risks. A conceptual rather than an ad hoc approach is needed. The real issue, then, is how to account for business risks generally. Emphasis should be laid on the coherence of information; disclosure should go for the whole story rather than the pieces making up the story, in order to be understandable by users.

In striving for global harmonization, the IASC should take action as soon as possible in order to avoid a position that an international standard on financial instruments can only be developed on the basis of the common denominator of national practices or national standards, which would inevitably lead to a number of options. I am aware of the call for action that has been addressed to the IASC; I am certain that this call will be answered.

The IASC has already issued an Exposure Draft E29, dealing with disclosures in the Financial Statements of Banks, which requires disclosure of various off-balance-sheet commitments and contingencies (these include many financial instruments). The IASC invited the bank regulators (the Basle Committee of Banking Supervisors) to assist it in updating a standard based on E29. The work of the IASC on banks will continue with proposals for the

204

recognition and measurement of items in the financial statements. This will also involve the supervisors and the bankers.

Financial instruments also affect enterprises other than banks -- hence the decision of the Board of the IASC to set up a new project on financial instruments. Work on this new project has to be co-ordinated with that on banks and will also involve people outside the accountancy profession.

The IASC, throughout its work, will keep in touch with the standard-setting activities in different countries and with international organisations like the OECD and the EC.

Complex and broad as the issue might be, the challenge is worth the effort.

4. CO-OPERATION BETWEEN REGULATORY AUTHORITIES

by
Peter Cooke
Associate Director, Bank of England;
Chairman of the Committee on Banking Regulations and Supervisory Practices

I propose in my remarks to avoid detailed accounting issues and to discuss rather relationships and objectives from the perspective of the bank regulator, most particularly of those bank supervisors of the Group of Ten major industrialised countries who meet regularly at the Bank for International Settlements in Switzerland. The views I express, however, are my own and not necessarily theirs.

The paper will be in two parts. First, I will describe briefly the supervisor's response to the rapid development in recent years of the new instruments, and particularly the growth in new off-balance-sheet risks. Secondly, I will discuss the importance to the supervisor of the way in which banks account and report for these instruments and the importance of links between the supervisor and the accountant or auditor.

Faced with the acceleration in the pace of financial innovation in the early 1980s, the supervisors' first steps, in 1984, were to examine the extent to which off-balance-sheet risks were being captured in the existing reporting systems. This survey was not reassuring and it was evident that much, particularly new, off-balance-sheet activity was not being captured. Also, assessment of the risks was rudimentary, not least because there was little if any historic experience of loss.

This first survey was followed by another to examine banks' actual involvement in the major new instruments. This revealed that, in total, these engagements were, already in 1984, of a significant size and in some cases were of a magnitude several times that of a bank's capital resources.

In mid-1985, as a result of these preliminary examinations, the Basle Committee circulated a note to banks drawing attention to the risks involved in this new innovatory off-balance-sheet business and calling on them to strengthen their procedures for training staff and monitoring the new risks they were running.

At about the same time, the Committee established a technical working party to assess more carefully and comprehensively the risks arising from the different off-balance-sheet activities, and to consider whether and to what extent capital requirements would be appropriate against those risks. In starting off serious work on this topic, the Committee saw a rare opportunity to formulate a supervisory regime which would closely follow developments in markets rather than lag too far behind them.

In March 1986, the first results of this work emerged in the form of a fairly substantial document which was circulated to banks and supervisors world-wide. This paper reviewed the prudential risks arising from off-balance-sheet activity in general, and the credit risk on specific instruments, and indicated broad categories of weightings which were applicable to different types of instruments within a risk-based capital ratio.

This comprehensive identification of new instruments provided a common basis for discussions between supervisors in different countries. I hope and believe that, as a basic document, it commanded a broad measure of agreement. It also helped to direct supervisors in their continuing debate with banks at a national level.

Since the paper's publication this work has been carried forward in the wider capital convergence discussions and most of the points are incorporated within the proposals which the Committee published in December 1987, where on the whole much of the original analysis and the risk weightings suggested in the 1986 paper have not been substantially changed.

There are three points to note from this paper which are of continuing relevance. Point one: the paper expresses concern about the significant national differences in the accounting for off-balance-sheet activities. It was noted that items may be recorded on the balance sheet, below the line, as notes to the accounts, or in prudential reports, or within banks' internal reports, or not at all. The view was expressed that many supervisors consider that the information given in banks' published accounts is generally insufficient for shareholders and depositors. The paper expressly said that supervisory authorities would welcome discussions with the accounting profession on the issues raised in the paper. I hope that this invitation has been taken up in all countries -- I know it has been in my own -- and that it is leading to useful changes in management information systems or in published financial accounts.

Point two: the paper emphasized the importance of maintaining adequate management and control systems for off-balance-sheet products. The paper commended banks to develop formal written policies to govern trading activities; to monitor risk exposures on a centrally co-ordinated basis; and to introduce adequate internal reporting systems to control the activities of their traders. Furthermore, in addressing these issues, banks should consult with their auditors in their capacity as professional accounting advisers. At the same time, the supervisors' views would need to be taken into account when preparing authoritative guidance. This underlines the importance of a proper dialogue between supervisors and the accountancy profession. In Basle we have over the years been involved in several projects involving the accounting profession, both in their role as auditor and as the body responsible for promulgating and disseminating sound accounting standards, nationally and internationally. This is a dialogue to which I continue to be committed.

Point three underlines the importance of proper identification and measurement of the risks involved. Supervisors need accurate and complete information from banks, prepared on a consistent and fair basis, so that capital and risk can be measured and assessed in a similar way.

This leads me to my second subject -- the importance to the supervisor of the accounting and reporting arrangements for new instruments and techniques.

There are a number of different points at issue here. First, supervisors need to be clear how and when so-called off-balance-sheet transactions affect the balance sheet.

Second, because retained profits will be part of a bank's core capital under convergence, supervisors need to be able to satisfy themselves that banks are properly accounting for income and expenditure arising from the new financial instruments and that the recognition of profit is being undertaken on a consistent basis. There is presently a lot of inconsistency between national systems.

The third issue to note is that supervisors rely on the development of consistent accounting standards in order to determine whether, and if so to what extent, management are able to control successfully the risks arising from new instruments. Common high standards in effect enforce a discipline on the way in which banks account and report for these instruments.

So there is an interdependence between the harmonization of supervisory rules internationally and the harmonization of accounting standards. How do they come together? There are two basic possibilities:

-- The supervisor can set his own rules solely for regulatory purposes regardless of the rules drawn up by the accounting profession;

-- The supervisor accepts for his purposes the accounting rules laid down by statute and by the accountancy profession for external financial reporting purposes.

Fortunately, the choice is not necessarily as stark as this. It is to be hoped that, in practice, supervisors and accountants will discuss the issues in a co-operative manner and will as far as possible arrive at final solutions which are mutually acceptable. There may be occasions when they diverge but hopefully not very many.

A co-operative process raises a number of questions. What is the proper body to set these rules and to what extent should the supervisors involve themselves and thereby influence their development and finalisation? Should each country's supervisors do this in bilateral discussion with that country's profession or should the whole process be conducted on an international scale? If the latter, which body of supervisors should do this and to which accountancy body or bodies should the supervisors address their concerns?

We are not very far down this road as yet. However, one thing that has become clear in recent years is that banking is an international business, and the needs of an international business have to be tackled on an international basis. Accounting issues are no exception. If supervisors are serious in their intent to move towards closer convergence of supervisory rules and practices for international banking business -- and I believe they are -- then they cannot afford to wait indefinitely for a greater degree of harmonization of accounting standards at the international level.

This is not to suggest that the accountancy profession is deliberately dragging its feet in this matter. The issues are indeed very complex and it is quite legitimate for different views on accounting treatment to be held. It is important though that efforts persist to try to reconcile these divergent views sooner rather than later. In this connection the recently published International Accounting Standards Committee's Exposure Draft on a "Framework for the Preparation and Presentation of Financial Statements" has been a particularly useful step forward.

The work of the International Accounting Standards Committee can only be strengthened if supervisors join together to press for international harmonization in accounting rules and, importantly, are prepared to contribute to their development by the international accountancy standard bodies. More particularly, supervisors should give the profession every encouragement in its efforts to produce authoritative guidance on best practice in accounting and reporting for new financial instruments. It is not surprising that regulators are likely to be influenced by their respective national accounting, tax and legal systems and may not, therefore, be able easily to arrive at a consensus view. But, in my view, continuing efforts will be required to narrow gaps.

Having had contacts with the International Accounting Standards Committee almost since its inception, I do believe it seems to be developing some greater momentum and hopefully will increase in authority. Its work in this area is to be commended, particularly as it is being taken forward in a truly international framework of negotiation. However, progress is also possible -- as the EC Bank Accounts Directive demonstrates -- at a regional level; hopefully this progress will be consistent with a wider international approach.

So, to conclude, there are a number of developments in the pipeline -- for example, the International Accounting Standards Committee's Exposure Draft "Disclosure in the Financial Statements of Banks" and any further work they may decide to pursue following its publication, and the implementation of the EC Bank Accounts Directive. This gives some reassurance that the harmonization of accounting standards will remain a top priority for the accountancy profession in the coming years -- in particular as it affects the banking industry. This work is especially important in the area of new financial instruments.

It poses great challenges to accountants and supervisors alike and I would repeat that further progress in producing consistent regulatory standards in this area will in large part depend on further harmonization of accounting treatment. I hope supervisors and accountants will continue to be exhorted to co-operate further to this end.

Chapter V

NEW FINANCIAL INSTRUMENTS: MAIN ISSUES OF ACCOUNTING AND REPORTING

PANEL 1: RISK ASSESSMENT AND DISCLOSURE

DISCUSSION SUMMARY

by
Dana Cook
Special Assistant to the Comptroller,
Office of the Comptroller of the Currency
(United States)

Our Panel, which was formed to handle risk evaluation and disclosure, came up with three or four problem areas on which we need to reflect further. First of all the time element is vital, the market is speeding ahead of both the accounting profession and the regulators. The regulators and supervisors are trying to adjust quickly to the changing market and perhaps have the ability to do so. A witness to that is the Cooke Committee, and the new rules on risk-based capital and international convergence it has elaborated. Regulators are bound to consider disclosure items related to new financial instruments, regardless of whether they end up being on or off the balance sheet. The accounting profession needs to move faster.

The second problem relates to risk measurement. We need to devise new methods and new underpinnings of risk assessment comparable with the new financial, economic and mathematical techniques that are being developed. We talked earlier of the possibility to use some work from the Cooke Committee for financial statements. If accounting rules are not developed, regulators and supervisors will be forced to go it alone. At the international level the opportunity to do something in this area before country differences become so entrenched is an opportunity we should not miss -- but we must remember that in doing so, local legal considerations have to be taken into account.

We also discussed the concern of the central banks as a lender of last resort that financial instruments, whether they are really new or not, do not abolish the risk but just redistribute it.

In the area of disclosure we discussed several issues. One is that in addition to regulators, the marketplace needs to be able to evaluate the internal control systems of an enterprise. Unless harmonization of disclosure is achieved, there is a risk of distortion and then the markets themselves will have to find a solution. In discussing disclosure I will try to summarise the issues we talked about by putting forth four questions.

The first one is: what needs to be disclosed? International convergence will not be achieved unless country differences are resolved. The second question is: who is the audience, what is their education and what are their needs? The third question is: what is the purpose of the information? Should we, for instance, indicate total exposure on some of these new instruments or a quantitative amount of the risk involved? Perhaps as important is the question when to disclose? What good is information that is three months old when a bank or another enterprise is working in a current environment?

Finally, we talked about who should be setting the standards: the accountants, regulators or the industry. I personally believe there is a role for all and I think we all should be working together in a consultative environment to solve this question. Finally, I would like to sum up what was said in one simple statement. The accounting profession and the regulators cannot ride a bicycle to reach their conclusions while the market is driving a Porsche.

RISK ASSESSMENT AND DISCLOSURE: COMMENTS

by
Arthur J. McHugh
Senior Director, Corporate Law,
National Companies and Securities Commission
(Australia)

I would like to develop a few propositions about the nature and assessment of risk.

It is necessary to define what is meant by risk. I think of it as the probability of the occurrence or non-occurrence of a particular event. For example, interest rate risk may be represented by the probability that at some future point of time t_1, the present rate will be $i = i_1$, as opposed to the present rate i_0 at t_0. Without developing this concept in depth, it would follow that any assessment of risk should be based on statistical concepts. In particular the notions of joint, marginal and conditional probability measures will be relevant. Conceivably their distributions will exist in more than a single variable and may be quite complex and non-stationary.

Some of the risk measures proposed by the Financial Accounting Standards Board in the Exposure Draft on Disclosures about Financial Instruments represent, at a theoretical level, well-known concepts such as the end-point(s), confidence limits, etc. of a distribution, which in turn are functions of the first and higher moments of the (frequently unknown) distribution.

If there is a time element involved in the assessment of risk, it suggests that actuarial principles, including sampling, establishing population parameters and especially discounting, will be useful concepts to employ. However, in dealing with the assessment of extreme cases where the probability of occurrence is very low but the outcome is large in financial terms if the event in question occurs, the methodology of model-building and sensitivity analysis may be an alternative way of conceptualising the possibilities.

That brings us back to how successful methods in pure accounting have been to date in measuring and reporting on risk. I think the level of achievement is not great, perhaps partly because it has not previously been seen as a high priority for general purpose financial statements. We have in every Member State fairly similar approaches to the assessment and disclosure of provisions such as bad and doubtful debts, contingent liabilities and solvency. The last, often described as the "going concern" basis of accounting, is an initial assessment of whether insolvency is seriously at issue. If it is not, one proceeds to ignore the various fine gradations in the financial reports. It is a solvent-or-not decision at least as a practical matter, although the auditor may make comments or issue a qualified opinion to indicate particular assumptions. These aspects are a matter of routine and mandatory disclosure to investors and other users. If assessed by the external auditors as inadequate in a material respect, the internal control system would also be mentioned in the report.

All this is useful as far as it goes, but the question that is raised in this Symposium is whether it is appropriate for accountants to give greater attention to the measurement of risk of individual assets of the company or of the entity as a whole. Leaving aside the special case of banks for one moment, and the needs of management, let us examine the information needs of an investor who, we must presume, will act rationally. Finance theory would have us believe that that investor will be "fully" diversified in the composition of his or her portfolio and will not be compensated in terms of returns for diversifiable risk. Thus, provided the market is given sufficient information to price the securities in the market portfolio properly, the investor should only be concerned with systematic risk and the choice of the degree of risk, which can be manipulated by means of appropriate weightings of risk-free assets (i.e. sovereign debt) and the market portfolio. While this scheme is familiar and to an extent abstract, the paradigm should not be lightly dismissed. This suggests that we should take care not to over-emphasize the magnitude of the problem for general purpose reporting.

Considering the two kinds of risk -- namely asset class risk and entity risk -- now assessed by accountants, it is my belief that it is proper or at least only within the accountant's present competence to deal with the risk assessment of assets in detail. Beyond the broad assessment of the "going concern", I would advocate no general purpose external reporting on the nuances and degree of solvency of the entity.

Turning to the particular problems of banks, it is clear that not only banking supervisors are concerned with the riskiness of banks. For example, a current issue in Australia concerns the acceptability of bank-endorsed bills as good delivery in certain professional short-term money markets. Bank X bills are "acceptable" whereas Bank Y bills normally attract a different discount rate. Thus the professional market perceives differences in quality, albeit measured in a small fraction of a per cent, between banks in a single country. Banking supervisors would, one assumes, be equally interested in the extent and causes of these differences without necessarily wishing to expunge the differences. Once a given level of prudential adequacy of capital or other measure is met, there seems to be a willingness to let the market make refined and informed judgments regarding differences. I agree with this approach.

Finally, I offer some brief observations on why we are currently concerned with financial instruments and risks. It is of course because of the volatility of the financial markets, which react to the actions of government fiscal and monetary policies and to exogenous shocks such as the imposition of tariffs or trade barriers, war, natural disasters, etc. The presence of risk leads to attempts to contain it within acceptable limits, and this has a cost. A broad macro-economic consideration of the issue would need to address whether the underlying volatility can be reduced in the context of national and international economic management.

RISK ASSESSMENT AND DISCLOSURE: COMMENTS

by
Zane D. Blackburn
Director, Division of Bank Accounting,
Office of the Comptroller of the Currency
(United States)

With over two hundred bank failures last year and a similar number expected during 1988, one may question the ability of banks and regulators to adequately assess risk, whether it be that of a traditional or of a new financial instrument. In fact, the analysis of these failures yields an interesting statistic. The majority of failures were the result of that age-old problem -- poor management. Very few failures resulted from investments or creations of new financial instruments, although there were some.

Yet the explosive development of new financial instruments does cause concern and requires that we not only understand the potential risks of a particular instrument, but also have a mechanism to monitor the risk.

This paper discusses some approaches to new financial instruments created by banks, attempts to achieve some discipline in the use of those instruments purchased by banks and, finally, presents views on disclosure.

An initial approach in reviewing bank-created new financial instruments is to determine their balance sheet status. Although numerous institutions have excellent systems for monitoring and assessing risk for off-balance-sheet items, our experience indicates that items on the balance sheet still receive the greater amount of attention -- both from the banks and from regulatory authorities.

In determining whether an item should be on or off the balance sheet, our primary focus as a US bank regulator is the risk to the bank and the traditional classification of similar instruments. For example, letters of credit, commitments and other guarantee-type instruments involve risk, but have traditionally been off the balance sheet. Loans and other receivables of course contain risk and are on the balance sheet.

Whereas a number of years ago a bank's objective may have been to have the largest balance sheet footings possible, the opposite is true today. Under our current capital requirements, less capital is needed for smaller balance sheets and there are no specific capital requirements for off-balance-sheet items. For this reason and other valid business purposes, banks now create new financial instruments that allow existing assets to be sold and removed from the balance sheet. For example, banks have pooled a number of homogeneous loans (i.e. automobile, mortgage and credit card loans) and then sold interests in the pool.

We have also encountered other types of sales involving individual commercial loans. These generally involve a single commercial loan having a stated short-term maturity (generally ninety days) to the investor, but are effectively medium-term loans to the borrower (typically five years). They are referred to as "loan strips".

Following United States generally accepted accounting principles (GAAP), these latter transactions may qualify as a sale even though the bank may remain at risk for losses the investor incurs. However, the US bank regulatory agencies have not accepted this method of accounting for regulatory reporting purposes.

Although we endeavour to follow US GAAP, there are instances in which our supervisory concerns cause us to require different accounting and reporting principles. In the area of loan sales, we rely upon the premise that if the bank retains any potential loss (or recourse) on loans sold, the transaction cannot be reported as a sale with the loans remaining on the bank's balance sheet.

This particular requirement has itself created a new financial instrument. As indicated earlier, banks have sold consumer loan pools which involve different interest rates for the individual borrower and investor. In order to meet our regulatory requirements for sale treatment, the difference in the interest rates (or spread) is placed in an escrow account which is used to absorb any losses the investor incurs, but only up to the amount of the account. If at the end of the contract period the escrow account has a balance, the bank receives the remainder as additional income.

Hence the bank is protected from losses and has the potential for more income if loss experiences are good. And since the escrow account is usually much larger than expected losses, the investor is similarly protected while receiving a market rate of interest.

Loan strips, selling a medium-term loan in short-term strips, is another illustration of how we approach new financial instruments. As indicated earlier, following US GAAP, these transactions are accounted for as a sale. However, we analysed the transaction to determine if the bank is effectively at risk. In this instance, we conclude that because the bank is committed to a borrower over a longer period, a sale of the borrower's obligation with a shorter effective maturity is simply a collateralised borrowing.

The question of on balance/off balance also arises regarding issues of agent versus principal. As one bank found a number of years ago, the lack of a clear distinction can be very costly. Again, when analysing these transactions we focus primarily on risk to the bank. If the investor is effectively looking to the bank to absorb potential losses, we generally conclude that the bank is acting as principal and therefore the transaction must be an "on"-balance-sheet item.

An interest rate swap contract, on the other hand, is an example of an off-balance-sheet item, on which we are just beginning to focus. These contracts can be very effective hedge and portfolio management tools -- and as a result, the number of these contracts and the amounts involved are expanding greatly. Recently, the US banking regulatory agencies became concerned about these contracts and particularly how some banks trading in the instruments were reporting the transactions. The concern involved income recognition, but the proposed response also involved a mechanism for risk measurement. We concluded that traders in these instruments should limit income recognition to that which is earned over the contract period and any subsequent changes in the market values of the contracts. In this instance, because of the ongoing risks associated with these contracts, we determined that the practice of immediately recognising the anticipated income from the contract is inappropriate. And, to obtain market discipline, we will be requiring the banks to recognise any changes in the contracts' market value.

Hence in this area, we have considered some aspects of an off-balance-sheet item as having balance sheet status and insisted upon conservative accounting treatment.

As we have in the United States a highly regulated banking system in comparison with other countries, we employ other vehicles which attempt to control risk in many new financial instruments. Some of these vehicles include outright prohibitions for certain types and size limits for others.

As recently as April of 1988, the agencies advised banks of certain securities which are viewed as unsuitable in an investment portfolio. Some of these included when-issued, pair-off, interest-only, principle-only and residual interest securities. Our message to bankers was that only the more knowledgeable banks should be trading in these instruments and bankers should be aware of their volatility.

This mechanism was an attempt to educate our bankers, who are the ultimate risk assessors. In the actual examination system, we assess risk by utilising an individual review process similar to a loan review. Significant volume changes in off-balance-sheet categories trigger an in-depth review of the bank's involvement with these instruments, and part of this process is distinguishing between trading account and investment account classification. The belief here is that since many new instruments are not permissible investment account securities, requiring the securities to be reported in the trading account imposes significant discipline. The mark-to-market requirements for trading account securities and resulting disclosure ensure this discipline when examiners are not there.

A second risk assessment vehicle is just beginning to take hold. Risk-based capital will attempt to establish a capital discipline for both the on- and off-balance-sheet risk that a bank takes. Although this system will be imperfect at first, it offers the possibility of assessing capital requirements on the risk a bank cares to take instead of imposing regulatory prohibitions.

Hence, as this system develops and improves, we will probably be less concerned about balance sheet status and better prepared to ensure that a bank has adequate capital associated with the new financial instruments and other risks.

Turning to the subject of disclosure -- both in general and with respect to the new financial instruments -- the view of the US banking regulatory agencies has changed dramatically over the last decade and a half.

When the US Securities and Exchange Commission first began to require significantly expanded disclosure for bank holding companies, the banking agencies were very concerned that the public might lose confidence.

Obviously this did not happen, and bank holding company reports today probably contain more disclosure than any other industry in the United States.

Over the past fifteen years, the banking agencies have moved from gradually making more bank financial information available from the agencies to a point where the individual banks (some 15 000) are now required to make certain information available to the public.

This change is based upon the belief that marketplace discipline is an excellent tool for achieving a sound banking system.

Disclosure does have its occasional pitfalls; indeed, certain new financial instruments render meaningful disclosure very difficult. The sometimes frightening magnitude of many larger banks' off-balance-sheet commitments can easily be taken out of context. Yet disclosure can bring attention to these activities and achieve a certain amount of discipline. If the Financial Accounting Standards Board achieves its objective regarding all financial instruments, better disclosure and improved market discipline will result.

In short, the US bank regulatory agencies view many new financial instruments cautiously. Although the magnitude and variety continue to grow, we believe that our current and developing systems are adequate to ensure the continuation of a sound banking system.

PANEL 2: EVALUATION OF ASSETS AND LIABILITIES AND INCOME RECOGNITION

DISCUSSION SUMMARY

by
Guy Gelders
Chairman of the Accounting Standards Commission;
Director of the Banking Commission
(Belgium)

The aim of this Symposium was to allow speakers and participants to make general comments on the accounting treatment of new financial instruments, on the way in which they should be valued in financial statements, and on their impact on the presentation of results and assets. In particular, it was useful to examine to what extent the accounting rules for new financial instruments are consistent with existing general standards and with certain fundamental accounting concepts.

It is difficult to summarise in a few lines the views that have been exchanged, for there is always the danger of misrepresenting them, if only by missing something out. The following comments should thus be regarded as a few annotations to the foregoing discussions -- some I make in my capacity as bank supervisor; the rest are delivered from the point of view of someone jointly responsible for drawing up the accounting standards that apply to some 100 000 enterprises in Belgium and to some 3 million enterprises in the European Community.

First of all, however, mention should be made of the imagination and capacity to innovate and adjust that the financial sector has shown in meeting the challenges and risks that the present monetary and financial environment poses. The new financial instruments that have been introduced, and the scale of their development, attest to the financial sector's ability to respond flexibly to requirements.

But at the same time, does not their expansion indicate a relative incapacity on the part of governments to ensure the necessary harmonization of national monetary and economic policies that they are pursuing? Do not the tasks and responsibilities of the OECD lie primarily with this type of harmonization?

The point of view of a bank supervisor

In my capacity as a bank supervisor, I should first like to say that the new financial instruments developed in recent years undoubtedly constitute a positive and considerable advance. Their importance has been sufficiently underlined in the preceding papers, and their rapid growth is evidence of how useful they are. But at the same time it is difficult to suppress entirely a certain amount of disquiet and a feeling that caution is required in dealing with these new instruments -- for the following reasons:

-- We all know that these instruments, which were initially devised to eliminate, cover or reduce the risks attaching to exchange and interest rates, can themselves give rise to risks and speculation, and hence to losses;

-- As they involve no initial cash movements or capital outlay, such transactions can involve enormous, indeed virtually unlimited, risks. They do not have the automatic control devices that are generally built into movements of funds. Everyone still recalls how some of the largest credit institutions in many countries got into serious foreign exchange difficulties in 1974-1975 as a result of the exponential growth in forward exchange transactions following the demise of the Bretton Woods system;

-- Such fears are particularly well founded in the case of new financial instruments on account of their sophisticated and esoteric nature, which can render them incomprehensible to the general managers of credit institutions and difficult to grasp by internal controllers;

-- Credit institutions' traditional sources of profit are dwindling, while at the same time competition is intensifying and obliging them to trim their margins. It may be feared that they will take increasing risks by adopting speculative positions;

-- Lastly, when the new financial instruments are abused they can cause havoc, as recent experience has shown.

Before looking at the provision of external information (i.e. to shareholders, public authorities, etc.), high priority should be given to internal information for management, the organisation of front and back offices, the manner in which transactions are booked, the setting of appropriate accounting standards, and internal control and auditing.

The point of view of someone who is jointly responsible for drawing up accounting standards

Bearing in mind the enterprises for whom these standards are intended, the increasingly sophisticated direction in which accounting law is moving and the calling into question of fundamental concepts are a cause for concern.

It is important to ensure that accounting law does not become an esoteric body of rules requiring highly specialised training beyond the reach of most managers from the administrative and accounting standpoint. It is important that accounting principles be clear and that they help managers, controllers and auditors to resolve the many specific problems that arise in markets.

It is striking to what extent the discussions at this Symposium have called into question many fundamental concepts. It is no longer clear what a balance sheet is or what should be recorded in it, what an asset or a commitment is, what constitutes income, profit or a hedge, what the matching principle or current value mean, or what a risk is.

But at the same time the discussions have highlighted the role and importance of general principles and the need to frame and define them clearly, particularly as regards the way they relate to, or conflict with one another (for example, the contradiction between the principle of prudence and the mark-to-market rule).

These remarks would seem to indicate the direction in which the future work of the OECD Working Group on Accounting Standards should move. We are faced, in our respective countries, with our own institutional and legal framework and with the traditions and ways of thinking that underpin them. In my view, the greatest scope for cross-border harmonization at the present time lies in the field of fundamental concepts.

EVALUATION OF ASSETS AND LIABILITIES AND INCOME RECOGNITION: COMMENTS

by
James L. Goodfellow
Partner, Touche Ross;
Former Chairman, Canadian Institute of Chartered Accountants
(Canada)

I. INTRODUCTION

The purpose of this paper is to explore some of the accounting issues involved in the evaluation of assets, liabilities and income recognition policies which relate to new financial instruments. This paper is based on three premises:

1. Many new financial instruments are presently accounted for as "off-balance-sheet" items and not presented as assets and liabilities in the balance sheets of the parties to the instrument or the financial institution that is involved;

2. A meaningful evaluation of assets and liabilities of an enterprise should take into account an evaluation of the risks and rewards relating to all financing activities, including off-balance-sheet financing activities; and

3. To perform a meaningful evaluation of financing activities, including off-balance-sheet financing activities, the reader needs both qualitative and quantitative information that is often not presented.

Many of the financial instruments discussed in this publication have been described in various papers, articles and speeches as the foundation of the "invisible banking system", which encompasses both the financial institution and its customers. The term "invisible banking system" is appropriate because the assets and liabilities created, modified or changed as a result of these new financial instruments often do not appear on the formal balance sheets of the parties to the arrangement or the financial institution that facilitated it.

In simple terms, the challenge facing the accounting profession is to make the invisible banking system visible! The purpose of this presentation is to put forward some ideas of how that could be achieved and what information is necessary for the evaluation of assets, liabilities and income recognition policies.

II. SOME STRUCTURAL AND FUNDAMENTAL PROBLEMS OF ACCOUNTING

It is clear that accountants and the accounting profession are having difficulty in coping with new financial instruments. There are three fundamental problems inherent in our accounting system that are creating difficulties in accounting for, and evaluating the effect of, these instruments. These three problems are:

a) The problem of historical cost;

b) The problem of a transaction-based system; and

c) The problem of presenting uncertainty.

1. The problem of historical cost

The foundation of our accounting system as we know it today is historical cost. Even the double-digit inflation of the early 1980s failed to dislodge our commitment to historical cost. Yet, most of the new financial instruments are market-related, and designed to protect, minimise or exploit changes in market prices -- be they securities prices, interest rates or currency rates. This raises the first problem -- how to account for (within the framework of historical cost) a new financing instrument that is designed to protect the market price of an asset that is carried on the financial statements not at market values but at its historical cost.

Many financial institution entities are now moving away from historical cost in their accounting for certain items, as we can see through the increasing use of "marking to market". One example is that when a forward contract is considered speculative in nature it is often "marked to market", while it may be carried at historical cost if it is considered a hedge.

However, this piecemeal abandonment of historical cost is creating new problems. For example, in accounting for hedges we now have to develop separate standards and make different assessments for:

a) The hedge of an existing item carried at historical cost;

b) The hedge of an existing item carried at fair value;

c) The hedge of an existing item carried at the lower of cost or market (which permits the recognition of losses but not gains before realisation).

A related problem is encountered in making assessments on the adequacy of capital. Regulators of financial institutions and others are now proposing new requirements and formulae based on both cost and market values for on- and off-balance-sheet items. Clearly, this shows some significant limitations in our traditional accounting methods and the usefulness of the balance sheet as it is now presented.

However, when we attempt to assess the adequacy of capital by using off-balance-sheet information -- together with assets measured at market values -- without adjusting our traditional historical cost capital maintenance concepts, we may have some new problems. For example, "marking to market" automatically produces unrealised gains and losses and raises the question of whether these are income or capital. The basis of asset measurement cannot be selected in isolation from the capital maintenance concepts, which in turn determine how income is to be measured.

2. The problem of a transaction-based system

Accounting was designed originally to record and reflect transactions between parties which had an economic effect. Much of our accounting literature and standards deal with the point in time when transactions should be recorded, how they should be measured and how incomplete transactions should be allocated between accounting periods. The measuring and recording of other "accountable events" has been more difficult, and the accounting for treasury products seems to have brought us to our knees.

Consider the accounting for swaps by a financial institution. Legally a swap is neither a deposit nor a loan nor a security, and the swap market is unregulated. The fee income earned on a swap is clearly a transaction for both those who pay it and those who receive it, but what about the swap itself? Is it a transaction, an economic event or an arrangement? When is the income earned? What is the income earned? What about other arrangements like note issuance facilities, revolving underwriting facilities?

This raises the second problem -- how do we fit an accounting for arrangements and facilities into a system designed to capture, measure, record and present transactions?

3. The problem of presenting uncertainty

Traditional accounting poses another problem: it does not deal very well with the uncertainty inherent in measuring many assets and liabilities. As an example, consider the IASC accounting standard for contingencies.

"27. The amount of a contingent loss should be accrued by a charge in the income statement if:

a. it is probable that future events will confirm that, after taking into account any related probable recovery, an asset has been impaired or a liability incurred at the balance sheet date, and

b. a reasonable estimate of the amount of the resulting loss can be made.

28. The existence of a contingent loss should be disclosed in the financial statements if either of the conditions in paragraph 27 is not met, unless the possibility of a loss is remote.

29. Contingent gains should not be accrued in financial statements. The existence of contingent gains should be disclosed if it is probable that the gain will be realized." (Paragraphs 27-29, IAS 10)

The above quotation demonstrates that we have three options: put an item on the balance sheet (with or without supplementary disclosure), leave it off the balance sheet but disclose it in the notes to the financial statements, or leave it out of the financial statements altogether. Accounting also requires all events and transactions to be measured and presented as single amounts. Ranges of possible outcomes are not permitted on the balance sheet, otherwise the books will not balance.

Information on uncertainty involved in the measurement process may be important in the evaluation of assets and liabilities. For example, suppose one company can measure its warranty liability within a range of the estimate plus 5 per cent and the estimate minus 5 per cent, and a competitor can only make the same estimate with a precision of plus and minus 25 per cent (assuming both companies use the same confidence levels in making the estimates). Clearly, any evaluation or comparison of net income should include an assessment of the measurement uncertainty involved in making these estimates. Unfortunately, information on measurement uncertainty and the related probabilities is not presented in the financial statements.

Within the balance sheet the only way to communicate uncertainty is to change the classification of the item and provide supplementary disclosure. The more certain we are about the payment of a potential obligation, the higher the obligation gets on the balance sheet and the disclosure is minimised.

This simple framework has served us well in the past, but it is now showing its age with the result that the readers of financial statements may not be getting the information they need with respect to uncertainty involved in measuring various assets and liabilities. We need better ways of presenting uncertainty than the present approach of balance sheet classification and disclosure.

III. THE ASSESSMENT OF RISKS AND REWARDS

Assessing the transfer of risks and rewards is fundamental to the evaluation of assets and liabilities related to all financial instruments, and to the determination of how transactions and arrangements should be presented in the financial statements.

1. Examples of accounting standards

The following examples illustrate the application of this basic principle in the IASC accounting standards for revenue recognition and lease accounting.

"A key criterion for determining when to recognise revenue from a transaction involving the sale of goods is that the seller has transferred to the buyer the significant risks and rewards of ownership of the asset sold." (Paragraph 6, IAS 18)

"Whether a lease is a finance lease or not depends on the substance of the transaction rather than the form of the contract. A lease is classified as a finance lease if it transfers substantially all the risks and rewards incident to ownership." (Paragraph 5, IAS 17)

2. Problems in assessing risks

While the assessment of risks and rewards in these new financial instruments is fundamental to their evaluation, it is often difficult. Many of these instruments are complex, difficult to understand and can be designed to meet the unique needs of particular financial institutions and their customers. The goal of this new generation of financial instruments is not just to raise capital, but to transfer, share or minimise risk and uncertainty -- or at least that is what they purport to do. But the risks inherent in these new instruments are often not obvious. Like the ingredients of a cake, they seem to lose their identity when the batter is mixed and put in the oven. But should the proportions be wrong, or the environment not be what was expected, then the real exposure that lies beneath the surface becomes all too obvious.

To properly account for and disclose information relating to these new financial instruments, we have to understand the substance of the instrument, risks and rewards inherent in the instrument and how they will change in response to changes in inflation, interest rates, currency rates, other market prices, or the default by one or more parties to the arrangement. Many accountants in industry, financial institutions and public practice may need to improve their knowledge and skills in this area.

Consider the case of assessing the risks involved in a bank actively involved in the swap market. One must ascertain which positions are hedged, the strength of the hedges and the extent of deliberate (or not so deliberate) mismatches and open positions. To assess the extent of the exposure in these open or mismatched positions we need to assess the impact on the bank in the forward position under various interest rate and foreign exchange scenarios. This can be a complex process involving many different permutations and combinations.

To examine the risks involved if one party defaults or terminates early, one must examine the details of the contractual arrangements to see if the exposure is limited to basis points, what lump sum payments may be involved, and whether any other commitments or guarantees are involved. In addition, an assessment of credit risk has to involve an assessment of the solvency of the parties involved in the swap, which implies an assessment of the markets in which these parties operate and the countries in which they do business.

Finally, it is often very difficult to assess how these various kinds of risk overlap with each other within products, how one kind of risk in one product can trigger another kind of risk in a related product, how the risks change under different interest rate or currency rate scenarios, and what the likely outcomes might be. To make matters even worse, by the time we compute our assessment of risks, the market has moved, more transactions have been entered into and our analysis is out of date.

3. Framework for assessing risk

In measuring income, assets and liabilities relating to new financial instruments, we should determine what rewards accrue or are likely to accrue to the shareholder, and what the risks are for the shareholder. The risk profile of the financial instruments as measured from the perspective of the shareholder is fundamental to the determination of income, the use of deferral accounting methods, and the evaluation of assets and liabilities.

It would be useful for both the evaluation of liabilities and the development of accounting standards if the risks involved in new financial instruments were grouped into the following categories:

a) Credit risk: the risk that the other party fails to honour its commitment at the maturity date;

b) Market risk: the risk that interest rates and/or currency rates move in an unfavourable direction;

c) Liquidity risk: the risk that the entity cannot meet the obligation when it is required to do so;

d) Management risk: the risk that management does not establish reasonable controls and procedures to safeguard its assets and the interests of the shareholders.

These risks can be assessed at the transaction level, the portfolio level, the business unit level, or at the entity level. It is worth noting that FAS 80 requires that for a futures contract to be accounted for as a hedge, it must not only reduce the volatility of a particular transaction or position (referred to above as market risk), but it must also reduce the risk of the enterprise. This notion of enterprise risk further complicates the already complex process of assessing risks.

IV. ACCOUNTING FOR UNCERTAINTY AND RISK

In spite of the difficulties in measuring risks and rewards involved in new financial instruments, an analysis of these risks and rewards is fundamental to the evaluation of assets and liabilities, and determining the proper accounting methods for income recognition. The following accounting framework might be useful as a starting point in developing general principles for new financial instruments:

1. When financial instruments are speculative in nature, the entity bears all risks and rewards, and the instruments should be accounted for in the financial statements on a market value basis, with adjustments to market being reflected in income;

2. When a financial instrument transfers from one entity to another all of the benefits and risks (relating to an underlying asset, liability or cash flow), then the accounting for the instrument should be the same as if the transaction involved the underlying asset, liability or cash flow directly. For example, if an instrument transfers all of an entity's receivables to another party without recourse, and the other party assumes all of the risks formerly borne by the entity, then a sale should be recorded;

3. When a financial instrument transfers some but not all of the benefits and risks relating to an underlying asset, liability or cash flow, then the remaining risks should be appropriately accounted for and presented in the financial statements of the entity. For example, suppose an entity purchases a forward contract to preserve the value of a foreign-denominated receivable, thereby protecting itself against currency risk, but remains exposed to credit risk. The receivable should be recorded on the balance sheet at the exchange rate provided in the contract (reflecting the elimination of the currency risk, but the retention of the credit risk);

4. Deferral accounting methods for premiums, gains and losses involved in hedge accounting, swaps and the like are appropriate if the financial instrument effectively transfers the market risks to another party and decreases the overall risk profile of the shareholder. However, the need for deferral accounting methods and other smoothing practices is eliminated if all components of the transaction are "marked to market".

1. The need for enhanced disclosure

It is all too obvious that the risks inherent in many of these new financial instruments cannot be measured with absolute certainty, as they often depend and vary with future events or market conditions. As a result, there is a significant need for enhanced disclosure about the financing activities of an enterprise. However, disclosure by itself can only be a temporary strategy, and cannot overcome the basic problems of accounting identified earlier.

Understanding the risks involved in particular financial instruments is difficult enough; communicating them effectively to a third party reader is even harder. One must ask, what is the information needed by readers of financial statements? I suggest that the mythical "prudent investor" and "reasonable person" would want to:

1. Assess the reasonableness of the accounting policies used by the entity for recognising income and providing for losses;

2. Understand the nature and extent of both on-balance-sheet and off-balance-sheet financing activities entered into by the entity, including assets and liabilities that have been "immunised" through various mixing and matching arrangements;

3. Assess the possible risks and exposures to the entity as a whole as a result of entering into these types of financial instruments, and the constraints on the entity's future operations which have been imposed or agreed to;

4. Assess how the risks and future rewards to the shareholder have been increased or decreased (or under what conditions will they be increased or decreased) as a result of entering into these new financial instruments;

5. Understand management's objectives in participating in these new financial instruments and whether management is controlling the risks and exposure relating to new financial instruments and off-balance-sheet activities.

Clearly, the organisation and presentation of this information is a major challenge that requires experimentation and judgment. Many attempts have been made in recent years to improve the disclosure of financial instruments, such as:

1. Various papers issued by the Bank of England on the measurement of capital and measuring risk;

2. Schedule RC-L: Commitments and Contingencies, issued by the Federal Reserve Board in the United States in 1983;

3. The proposals made by the Bank for International Settlements (BIS) for a common way to account for these off-balance-sheet items which will require capital to be reserved against them; and

4. The Exposure Draft issued by the FASB proposing additional disclosures about financial instruments.

Of these proposals, only those of the FASB are intended to serve a general purpose objective and to be used by financial institutions and non-financial institutions alike. All of these proposals suggest that the solution to the challenges of innovative financial instruments can be met through additional disclosures. While this solution does not solve the inherent problems in our present accounting system identified earlier, they at least bring more relevant information to the readers of the financial statements, and serve as a good interim step.

To help readers evaluate assets, liabilities and overall risk, I suggest accounting standard-setters consider a separate statement, a sort of off-balance-sheet balance sheet, which would present the various classes of financial instruments (e.g. swaps, options, forward contracts, securitised assets, etc.) and explain what potential risks exist for the entity and the shareholder in these items. The information that might be disclosed in such a statement is based on the proposals put forward by the FASB, and is suggested as follows:

1. Accounting policies: a description of the accounting policies used for income recognition and measuring any assets and liabilities that have been recorded on the balance sheet;

2. Nature and volume: the classes or types of financial instruments or arrangements entered into by the entity, including information on the volume of activity for each class of financial instrument;

3. Maximum exposure: for each class of financial instrument, the maximum exposure due to credit, interest rate, currency or other risk, together with the conditions under which this maximum exposure is likely to occur;

4. Concentration of risk: the concentration of risk with any counterparty or groups of counterparties which creates a significant economic dependency or exposure to either the entity as a whole or the shareholders;

5. Provisions: the amount of any provisions or accruals made in the financial statements for probable losses on financial instruments, or, if the amount of probable losses cannot be estimated, disclosure of this fact together with other appropriate information;

6. Market values: information on the market values, such as the market value of instruments that are held for resale, or the market value of assets, liabilities or cash flows that the instrument is designed to hedge or protect;

7. Interest rate sensitivity information: information about the effective interest rates inherent in the various classes of financial instruments, their contractual or repricing maturity dates, and the sensitivity of the entity's earnings to changes in interest rates; and

8. Future cash flows: information on amounts and timing of receipts and disbursements that are specified by these financial instruments.

The challenge will be to determine what information is essential for the decisions readers are likely to make, and how it can be summarised and presented in a way that does not further contribute to disclosure overload. In my view standard-setters need to articulate general principles and provide an overall framework for such disclosures, and leave preparers and their advisers room to exercise their professional judgment in presenting the information. I suggest we need to gain experience in this type of disclosure before we can proclaim specific rules and practices.

2. Management control of off-balance-sheet risk

Both traditional and off-balance-sheet financing activities are extremely volatile, complex and -- in the case of a financial institution -- changing day by day. As a result, it may be just as important for a reader of financial statements to understand the objectives of the directors and/or management, and whether they are effectively controlling the risks and exposures related to these financing activities, as it is to have a summary of financial information at a specific point in time.

Such a representation by the directors and/or management might be made in the management report, a practice that is becoming more common in North America, or perhaps in the notes to the financial statements. This representation by management might include:

1. A statement of the objectives that the directors and/or management have established for both their balance sheet and off-balance-sheet financing activities, and the extent to which these goals and objectives have been realised;

2. Representations by management as to whether appropriate policies and control procedures have been implemented to provide reasonable assurance that the assets involved in these financing activities have been safeguarded;

3. Representations by management as to whether significant risks and exposures relating to financing activities are identified, carefully monitored and managed; and

4. Representations by management as to whether their management control systems have been appropriately changed in response to new products, and changes in markets, interest rates, currency fluctuations, etc.

Having the directors and/or management make a formal representation on how they control the risks and exposures in this area is a new approach that expands the disclosure in the financial statements beyond the numerical figures. In my view, making a formal representation of this nature is likely to have a significant and positive impact on the attitudes of management, the accountability of a particular entity and the financial system as a whole.

If readers of financial statements are to make a meaningful evaluation of the assets and liabilities related to new financial instruments, we need new accounting concepts and information that is presently not available. As we have seen, much of the work that is now being done in this area is being performed by regulatory bodies and is closely linked to a reassessment of the capital adequacy requirements for financial institutions. This activity demonstrates how the off-balance-sheet activity is really linked to on-balance-sheet capital, and shows the imperfections of our present accounting methods. If we do not act promptly in this area, the accounting standards for these new financial instruments may be set by regulators to meet their regulatory objectives, and not the needs of readers of general purpose financial statements.

In responding to this challenge, standard-setters have a significant decision to make. They can choose to develop general principles and an overall framework and rely on the professional judgment of management and auditors to determine how these general principles should be applied to particular financial instruments; or they can try and develop specific measurement and disclosure standards for each type of instrument. While there are pros and cons to both approaches, I share the view put forward by Robert Sprouse, a former member of the Financial Accounting Standards Board, in the September 1987 issue of Accounting Horizons:

"Financial services is a burgeoning field of economic endeavor. Investment bankers and their legal and accounting advisors have proved to

228

be remarkably creative in devising new financial arrangements that often appear to have been designed, with one eye on the existing authoritative literature, to avoid recognition and measurement in the financial statements. Establishing accounting standards for each new financial transaction or instrument is woefully ineffective."

There is one final point that I would like to make, which is the importance of international harmonization of accounting standards in this area. These new financial instruments and off-balance-sheet activities are a direct consequence of the globalisation of the world's capital and currency markets. How accountants measure the present information on off-balance-sheet activities of financial institutions will likely impact the decisions made by regulators on capital adequacy and decisions made by credit rating agencies, as well as decisions made by investors and creditors. These decisions will impact how financial institutions in various countries are structured, how they compete with each other in world markets, the products that they offer, and how these products are priced. Without harmonization of accounting standards in this area, there is a real danger that competitive advantage will be won or lost not on the basis of economic performance but on the basis of differences in accounting standards and regulatory requirements.

EVALUATION OF ASSETS AND LIABILITIES AND INCOME RECOGNITION: COMMENTS

by
Jean-Paul Milot
Assistant Secretary-General, Conseil national de la comptabilité
(France)

Current accounting standards distinguish two broad uses of "new financial instruments": market transactions and hedges. Two questions may be raised in respect of this distinction:

-- Does the accounting concept of hedges reflect traders' actual practice?

-- What is the essential characteristic of market transactions?

To answer the first question, a thorough knowledge and detailed analysis of traders' strategies would be required, both of which are outside the present speaker's competence. It is nonetheless possible to make a few general remarks. The main aim with these strategies is to put together packages of interrelated transactions in such a way as to attain certain precise objectives. These packages do not comprise only hedges; they may include arbitrage and other more complex transactions. However, my aim here is not to classify the various types of transactions but to describe their accounting implications. At first sight, the ideal solution would seem to be to book transactions at their market value; since instruments are combined with a view to achieving symmetrical results, it would be logical to book them in a symmetrical fashion.

However, combinations of instruments are not necessarily limited to attaining a result within one accounting period, but may be spread over very long periods. In the latter case, the trader usually calculates an overall result by revaluing flows at present worth.

The accountant is thus faced with a tricky problem: how should results be booked to accounting periods? Is an overall result sufficient? If so, to which accounting period should it be assigned? Is it permissible to revalue results at present worth given that, by definition, they will never have a direct counterpart in cash flow terms? In fact, it seems that two approaches are involved, each of which emphasizes different elements. The first seeks to calculate results by individual transaction, whereas the second emphasizes the overall result of the transactions during a given period.

However, in practice the difference in approach will be all the less significant to the extent that transactions are systematically booked at market values.

To answer the second question, it is necessary to define some of the basic features of these new financial instruments. Two especially concern us. New instruments are created for a specific or general purpose. When the purpose is of a sufficiently general nature, the instruments are traded in markets of unprecedented size and liquidity.

The combination of these two factors -- increased size and liquidity -- leads to innovations in market transactions that accounting practice cannot ignore for fear of losing touch permanently with economic and financial realities.

If a transaction is not directly linked with other transactions, the nature of the market in which it takes place needs to be considered. The development of markets is as much a novelty as the appearance of new instruments; in many cases there is so much liquidity that the only realistic and prudent way of assessing results is to book them at market value. Although this may seem excessive to accountants who remain firmly attached to the principle of prudence, it is not in conflict with fundamental accounting principles. It needs to be considered that in these markets exits and entry are possible at any time, that maintaining a position is a management decision taken in the light of the manager's expectations, and that it is just as "real" as the decision to liquidate a position. The accounting implications should therefore be identical: if a position is liquidated, the resulting gain or loss must be recognised; likewise, if a position is maintained, the resulting gain or a loss must also be recognised. Only the prices from the day's or previous day's trading should be taken into consideration. An accounting method that did not recognise gains would oblige managers who wanted to show them in their accounts to sell the instruments and then to buy them back again immediately. By virtue of the very definition of liquidity this is always possible, but it is a costly operation and one that puts artificial pressure on prices. In particular, it makes it possible to adjust results since it is also possible not to show gains. Such a method is thus neither realistic nor prudent in this specific context.

It might be objected that this state of affairs has always existed insofar as a liquid securities market has always existed. This objection prompts two remarks: first, the issue today is the scale of the phenomenon and its financial implications; second, while it may have been possible in the past to ignore the situation because it did not have any major consequences (which is perhaps too optimistic a view of the matter), this can no longer be done without running a major risk. But it is also true that this reasoning should be taken to its logical conclusion and that if the novelty, at this level, lies not so much in the instrument as in the features of the actual markets, then all transactions (whether "new" or "old") in sufficiently liquid markets should be treated in the same way, failing which the adverse effects will reappear.

CONCLUDING REMARKS

by
Jean Dupont
Chairman of the Symposium;
Chairman of the OECD Working Group on Accounting Standards;
Chairman of the Conseil national de la comptabilité
(France)

Our purpose was to increase awareness of the issues involved, and this aim has certainly been achieved.

The speeches, panel sessions and discussions have brought to light:

-- Technical difficulties stemming from the complexity of the subject;

-- Conceptual difficulties which may involve the rethinking of fundamental principles;

-- Legal difficulties, insofar as the question arises whether standards covering the new financial instruments can in all cases be drawn up under existing provisions.

Our debate has, however, also underlined the importance of these issues and the urgent need for harmonization, without which capital movements may be generated simply by divergences in national accounting and disclosure practices.

Despite the undoubted importance of international harmonization of accounting standards, it would nevertheless be an absurd overstatement to claim that all such problems can be resolved by establishing relevant standards.

The authorisation to carry out high-risk financial transactions, the competence of the dealers involved and the relevant monitoring and supervisory procedures are also clearly of great importance.

A whole range of issues has in fact been raised, and accounting matters form only a part of them.

Despite this call for modesty on our part, we should nevertheless not forget the important role which accounting standards can play.

Their harmonization may not be a sufficient condition for warding off all dangers, but it is certainly a necessary condition.

I welcome the announcement by Mr. Barthès de Ruyter, Chairman of the IASC Board, that his organisation intends to speed up its work on the new financial instruments.

May I repeat, both to him and to all national standard-setting bodies, that time is pressing.

Without being alarmist, may I sound a warning note: act fast, or the market could leave you behind.

I therefore appeal to each participant, according to his responsibilities and resources, to establish -- for what is essentially an international phenomenon -- standards that could be recognised throughout the world.

The OECD Working Group on Accounting Standards will, for its part, make an immediate start on following up the work of this meeting, in accordance with the Secretary-General's request.

I hope that our exchange of views has been enriching for all, will stay fresh in the mind in the coming months and may thus bear fruit in the form of further development of international harmonization.

WHERE TO OBTAIN OECD PUBLICATIONS
OÙ OBTENIR LES PUBLICATIONS DE L'OCDE

ARGENTINA - ARGENTINE
Carlos Hirsch S.R.L.,
Florida 165, 4º Piso,
(Galeria Guemes) 1333 Buenos Aires
Tel. 33.1787.2391 y 30.7122

AUSTRALIA - AUSTRALIE
D.A. Book (Aust.) Pty. Ltd.
11-13 Station Street (P.O. Box 163)
Mitcham, Vic. 3132   Tel. (03) 873 4411

AUSTRIA - AUTRICHE
OECD Publications and Information Centre,
4 Simrockstrasse,
5300 Bonn (Germany)   Tel. (0228) 21.60.45
Gerold & Co., Graben 31, Wien 1 Tel. 52.22.35

BELGIUM - BELGIQUE
Jean de Lannoy,
Avenue du Roi 202
B-1060 Bruxelles   Tel. (02) 538.51.69

CANADA
Renouf Publishing Company Ltd/
Éditions Renouf Ltée,
1294 Algoma Road, Ottawa, Ont. K1B 3W8
Tel: (613) 741-4333
Toll Free/Sans Frais:
Ontario, Quebec, Maritimes:
1-800-267-1805
Western Canada, Newfoundland:
1-800-267-1826
Stores/Magasins:
61 rue Sparks St., Ottawa, Ont. K1P 5A6
Tel: (613) 238-8985
211 rue Yonge St., Toronto, Ont. M5B 1M4
Tel: (416) 363-3171
Federal Publications Inc.,
301-303 King St. W.,
Toronto, Ont. M5V 1J5
Tel. (416)581-1552
Les Éditions la Liberté inc.,
3020 Chemin Sainte-Foy,
Sainte-Foy, P.Q. G1X 3V6,
Tel. (418)658-3763

DENMARK - DANEMARK
Munksgaard Export and Subscription Service
35, Nørre Søgade, DK-1370 København K
Tel. +45.1.12.85.70

FINLAND - FINLANDE
Akateeminen Kirjakauppa,
Keskuskatu 1, 00100 Helsinki 10   Tel. 0.12141

FRANCE
OCDE/OECD
Mail Orders/Commandes par correspondance :
2, rue André-Pascal,
75775 Paris Cedex 16
Tel. (1) 45.24.82.00
Bookshop/Librairie : 33, rue Octave-Feuillet
75016 Paris
Tel. (1) 45.24.81.67 or/ou (1) 45.24.81.81
Librairie de l'Université,
12a, rue Nazareth,
13602 Aix-en-Provence   Tel. 42.26.18.08

GERMANY - ALLEMAGNE
OECD Publications and Information Centre,
4 Simrockstrasse,
5300 Bonn   Tel. (0228) 21.60.45

GREECE - GRÈCE
Librairie Kauffmann,
28, rue du Stade, 105 64 Athens Tel. 322.21.60

HONG KONG
Government Information Services,
Publications (Sales) Office,
Information Services Department
No. 1, Battery Path, Central

ICELAND - ISLANDE
Snæbjörn Jónsson & Co., h.f.,
Hafnarstræti 4 & 9,
P.O.B. 1131 - Reykjavik
Tel. 13133/14281/11936

INDIA - INDE
Oxford Book and Stationery Co.,
Scindia House, New Delhi 110001
Tel. 331.5896/5308
17 Park St., Calcutta 700016   Tel. 240832

INDONESIA - INDONÉSIE
Pdii-Lipi, P.O. Box 3065/JKT.Jakarta
Tel. 583467

IRELAND - IRLANDE
TDC Publishers - Library Suppliers,
12 North Frederick Street, Dublin 1
Tel. 744835-749677

ITALY - ITALIE
Libreria Commissionaria Sansoni,
Via Lamarmora 45, 50121 Firenze
Tel. 579751/584468
Via Bartolini 29, 20155 Milano   Tel. 365083
La diffusione delle pubblicazioni OCSE viene
assicurata dalle principali librerie ed anche da :
Editrice e Libreria Herder,
Piazza Montecitorio 120, 00186 Roma
Tel. 6794628
Libreria Hœpli,
Via Hœpli 5, 20121 Milano   Tel. 865446
Libreria Scientifica
Dott. Lucio de Biasio "Aeiou"
Via Meravigli 16, 20123 Milano   Tel. 807679

JAPAN - JAPON
OECD Publications and Information Centre,
Landic Akasaka Bldg., 2-3-4 Akasaka,
Minato-ku, Tokyo 107   Tel. 586.2016

KOREA - CORÉE
Kyobo Book Centre Co. Ltd.
P.O.Box: Kwang Hwa Moon 1658,
Seoul   Tel. (REP) 730.78.91

LEBANON - LIBAN
Documenta Scientifica/Redico,
Edison Building, Bliss St.,
P.O.B. 5641, Beirut   Tel. 354429-344425

MALAYSIA/SINGAPORE -
MALAISIE/SINGAPOUR
University of Malaya Co-operative Bookshop
Ltd.,
7 Lrg 51A/227A, Petaling Jaya
Malaysia   Tel. 7565000/7565425
Information Publications Pte Ltd
Pei-Fu Industrial Building,
24 New Industrial Road No. 02-06
Singapore 1953   Tel. 2831786, 2831798

NETHERLANDS - PAYS-BAS
SDU Uitgeverij
Christoffel Plantijnstraat 2
Postbus 20014
2500 EA's-Gravenhage   Tel. 070-789911
Voor bestellingen: Tel. 070-789880

NEW ZEALAND - NOUVELLE-ZÉLANDE
Government Printing Office Bookshops:
Auckland: Retail Bookshop, 25 Rutland Stseet,
Mail Orders, 85 Beach Road
Private Bag C.P.O.
Hamilton: Retail: Ward Street,
Mail Orders, P.O. Box 857
Wellington: Retail, Mulgrave Street, (Head
Office)
Cubacade World Trade Centre,
Mail Orders, Private Bag
Christchurch: Retail, 159 Hereford Street,
Mail Orders, Private Bag
Dunedin: Retail, Princes Street,
Mail Orders, P.O. Box 1104

NORWAY - NORVÈGE
Narvesen Info Center – NIC,
Bertrand Narvesens vei 2,
P.O.B. 6125 Etterstad, 0602 Oslo 6
Tel. (02) 67.83.10, (02) 68.40.20

PAKISTAN
Mirza Book Agency
65 Shahrah Quaid-E-Azam, Lahore 3 Tel. 66839

PHILIPPINES
I.J. Sagun Enterprises, Inc.
P.O. Box 4322 CPO Manila
Tel. 695-1946, 922-9495

PORTUGAL
Livraria Portugal,
Rua do Carmo 70-74,
1117 Lisboa Codex   Tel. 360582/3

SINGAPORE/MALAYSIA -
SINGAPOUR/MALAISIE
See "Malaysia/Singapor". Voir
« Malaisie/Singapour»

SPAIN - ESPAGNE
Mundi-Prensa Libros, S.A.,
Castelló 37, Apartado 1223, Madrid-28001
Tel. 431.33.99
Libreria Bosch, Ronda Universidad 11,
Barcelona 7   Tel. 317.53.08/317.53.58

SWEDEN - SUÈDE
AB CE Fritzes Kungl. Hovbokhandel,
Box 16356, S 103 27 STH,
Regeringsgatan 12,
DS Stockholm   Tel. (08) 23.89.00
Subscription Agency/Abonnements:
Wennergren-Williams AB,
Box 30004, S104 25 Stockholm Tel. (08)54.12.00

SWITZERLAND - SUISSE
OECD Publications and Information Centre,
4 Simrockstrasse,
5300 Bonn (Germany)   Tel. (0228) 21.60.45
Librairie Payot,
6 rue Grenus, 1211 Genève 11
Tel. (022) 31.89.50
United Nations Bookshop/Librairie des Nations-
Unies
Palais des Nations,
1211 – Geneva 10
Tel. 022-34-60-11 (ext. 48 72)

TAIWAN - FORMOSE
Good Faith Worldwide Int'l Co., Ltd.
9th floor, No. 118, Sec.2
Chung Hsiao E. Road
Taipei   Tel. 391.7396/391.7397

THAILAND - THAILANDE
Suksit Siam Co., Ltd., 1715 Rama IV Rd.,
Samyam Bangkok 5   Tel. 2511630
INDEX Book Promotion & Service Ltd.
59/6 Soi Lang Suan, Ploenchit Road
Patjumamwan, Bangkok 10500
Tel. 250-1919, 252-1066

TURKEY - TURQUIE
Kültur Yayinlari Is-Türk Ltd. Sti.
Atatürk Bulvari No: 191/Kat. 21
Kavaklidere/Ankara   Tel. 25.07.60
Dolmabahce Cad. No: 29
Besiktas/Istanbul   Tel. 160.71.88

UNITED KINGDOM - ROYAUME-UNI
H.M. Stationery Office,
Postal orders only: (01)211-5656
P.O.B. 276, London SW8 5DT
Telephone orders: (01) 622.3316, or
Personal callers:
49 High Holborn, London WC1V 6HB
Branches at: Belfast, Birmingham,
Bristol, Edinburgh, Manchester

UNITED STATES - ÉTATS-UNIS
OECD Publications and Information Centre,
2001 L Street, N.W., Suite 700,
Washington, D.C. 20036 - 4095
Tel. (202) 785.6323

VENEZUELA
Libreria del Este,
Avda F. Miranda 52, Aptdo. 60337,
Edificio Galipan, Caracas 106
Tel. 951.17.05/951.23.07/951.12.97

YUGOSLAVIA - YOUGOSLAVIE
Jugoslovenska Knjiga, Knez Mihajlova 2,
P.O.B. 36, Beograd   Tel. 621.992

Orders and inquiries from countries where
Distributors have not yet been appointed should be
sent to:
OECD, Publications Service, 2, rue André-Pascal,
75775 PARIS CEDEX 16.

Les commandes provenant de pays où l'OCDE n'a
pas encore désigné de distributeur doivent être
adressées à :
OCDE, Service des Publications. 2, rue André-
Pascal, 75775 PARIS CEDEX 16.

71784-07-1988

OECD PUBLICATIONS, 2, rue André-Pascal, 75775 PARIS CEDEX 16 - No. 44509 1988
PRINTED IN FRANCE
(21 88 06 1) ISBN 92-64-13159-0